SCIENCE, PSEUDO-SCIENCE, AND UTOPIANISM IN EARLY MODERN THOUGHT

SCIENCE, PSEUDO-SCIENCE, AND UTOPIANISM IN EARLY MODERN THOUGHT

EDITED BY
STEPHEN A. MCKNIGHT

UNIVERSITY OF MISSOURI PRESS
COLUMBIA AND LONDON

Copyright © 1992 by
The Curators of the University of Missouri
University of Missouri Press, Columbia, Missouri 65201
Printed and bound in the United States of America
All rights reserved
5 4 3 2 1   96 95 94 93 92

Library of Congress Cataloging-in-Publication Data

Science, pseudo-science, and utopianism in early modern thought /
edited by Stephen A. McKnight.
    p.   cm.
Includes bibliographical references and index.
ISBN 0-8262-0835-5 (alk. paper)
1. Science—History. 2. Occultism and science—History.
I. McKnight, Stephen A., 1944-
Q125.S43463   1992
509—dc20   92-6275
                                                              CIP

∞™ This paper meets the minimum requirements of
the American National Standard for Permanence of Paper
for Printed Library Materials, Z39.48, 1984.

Designer: Rhonda Miller
Typesetter: Connell-Zeko Type & Graphics
Printer: Thomson-Shore, Inc.
Binder: Thomson-Shore, Inc.
Typeface: Trump Mediaeval

CONTENTS

PREFACE

Significant changes are occurring in the understanding of the relation of magic, alchemy, and other esoteric traditions to the development of science in the early modern period. A similar reconsideration is under way regarding connections between utopian myths derived from alchemy and magic and sixteenth- and seventeenth-century notions of historical progress and social perfection. The purpose of this collection of essays is to provide an interdisciplinary perspective on the impact these developments are having on the history of science, intellectual history, and political theory.

An illustration of the fundamental nature of these reevaluations can be found in the contrasting terms used to describe magic, alchemy, and other occult philosophies. There is a long-standing practice of referring to them as *pseudo-science*—a term that carries obvious, negative connotations. Pseudo-science is by definition an ersatz attempt to achieve an understanding and mastery of nature that only science can attain. While *pseudo-science* is a term in wide usage in contemporary scholarship, it was not used in the early modern period, and its pejorative connotations do not characterize the views of many of the most important figures of the fifteenth, sixteenth, and seventeenth centuries. Ficino, the founder of the Platonic Academy; Bruno, the religious reformer and defender of Copernicanism; and even Newton, the great patriarch of science, regarded the magical and alchemical traditions as components of a rediscovered and revitalized ancient revelation of the workings of nature and of man's exalted role in God's creation. A term that Ficino and others frequently used to denote this tradition was *prisca theologia*, or "pristine theology," a term with profoundly different connotations than the derogatory term *pseudo-science*.

This contrast between the interpretive term *pseudo-science* and the recently introduced term *prisca theologia* illustrates how fundamentally this work on the Ancient Wisdom tradition challenges long-standing interpretive models in the history of science and in intellectual and cultural history. The term *pseudo-science* was introduced into the history of science by George Sarton and the other founders of the discipline, and it reflects their positivistic conviction that the history of science is a narrative of the progressive victory of the physical, mathematical sciences over religious, metaphysical, and occult views of nature. This model is, of course, not Sarton's creation and it is not unique to the history of science. It is drawn from the progressivist civilizational histories that dominated the nineteenth century and are epitomized in Auguste Comte's famous three-stage pattern developed in *Cours de philosophie positive* (1830–1842). In Comte's account, the decisive epochal break separating the dark ages of religion and metaphysics from the Age of Reason and Enlightenment is the result of the Scientific Revolution and the consequent utilization of science by the intellectual and political elite to master nature and perfect society.

Recent scholarship showing the persistence of ancient traditions of esoteric religion and occult philosophy well into the modern epoch poses a fundamental challenge to these historiographical models—particularly when primary sources show that Bacon, Newton, and other founders of the modern age had a deep reverence for the truths hidden in the myths and symbols of the *prisca theologia*. It not only brings the adequacy and accuracy of the interpretive models into question, but also challenges the basic assumption of an epochal leap from religion and philosophy into an age of reason and science. By drawing on primary sources that reveal the complex interrelation of science, the Ancient Wisdom tradition, and utopianism, the essays in this collection examine fundamental changes in approach and theme in the history of science and in intellectual and cultural history. Before explaining the organization and thematic focus of the essays, however, it will be useful to explain more fully the early phases of the *prisca theologia*'s entry into the mainstreams of early modern thought, because the essays assume and build upon this background.

Recent Renaissance scholarship has demonstrated that the *prisca theologia* was introduced into the main lines of philosophy and theology by Ficino and other Neoplatonists as part of the recovery of ancient learning. As the term suggests, the *prisca theologia* was believed to be a record of God's revelations to non-Christian wisemen (magi) of the ancient Near East and Mediterranean. As such, it was prized as a source for synthesizing Christian and non-Christian revelation and resolving conflicts between Christian theology and Greco-Roman philosophy and science. This view spread from Italy throughout Europe, so that the *prisca theologia* was widely regarded as a source of insight into man's true nature and his role in the natural order during the fifteenth, sixteenth, and seventeenth centuries.

Though the term *prisca theologia* implies a uniform or single theology, it was actually a wide-ranging, diverse collection of magic, alchemy, and other forms of esoteric religion and occult philosophy. Fifteenth- and sixteenth-century philosophers and theologians, therefore, held different views of its most important elements and were frequently drawn to those that seemed to speak most poignantly to their own existential longings or to the critical needs of their time. Ficino, for example, studied the Hermetic cosmology in great detail but was not concerned with the workings of nature *per se*. He was, instead, fascinated by the Hermetic description of man as a magus and "terrestrial god" able to "overcome fate" through the manipulation of the world spirit (*spiritus mundi*). Ficino's pupil, Pico della Mirandola, incorporated the Hermetic view of man into his famous *Oration on Human Dignity* and proudly announced that he had mastered the Ancient Wisdom and developed a system of knowledge that could answer every important metaphysical question.

In the sixteenth and seventeenth centuries, interest in the *prisca theologia* shifted from Ficino's and Pico's interest in self-divinization to the broader concerns with political order and religious revitalization. Tommaso Campanella, for example, drew from the Hermetic writings the utopian vision of a perfectly ordered society governed and protected by a magician-priest-king. Campanella's utopia was not regarded as idle fantasy or as a dream of an unrealizable ideal. It was Campanella's blueprint for the necessary and realizable reforms in religion and politics that would restore order to Europe, and it received favorable (if short-lived) reception from the pope and from the kings of Spain and France. Frances Yates's well-known study of Bruno and the Hermetic tradition has shown that Bruno, a vociferous defender of Copernicanism, had similar religious and political interests, and his purpose in journeying to France and England was evidently to persuade the monarchial courts that the Egyptian religion could eradicate the ignorance and error of Christianity and produce religious harmony and political order. More recent work has developed the ties between the *prisca theologia* and major scientific figures and movements. B. J. T. Dobbs, a contributor to this collection, has shown, for example, that Newton, the most revered figure in the Scientific Revolution, had strong interests in alchemy and in prophecy.

What is more, her work makes it clear that these subjects were not marginal to his scientific endeavors. Alchemy played an important role in his scientific theories, and his scientific interests were closely tied to his religious speculations on the restoration of nature and man.

As already noted, the implications of these studies extend beyond a challenge to the positivistic narratives in the history of science. They pose fundamental questions regarding the forces shaping early modern concepts of historical progress and social perfection and raise equally important issues concerning the origins of the distinctly modern equation of knowledge with the power to control nature and transform society. A single collection cannot, of course, deal exhaustively with the range of complex issues opened by the reassessment that is under way. It can, however, highlight fundamental theoretical issues, provide documentary evidence to support new theories and approaches, and demonstrate interconnections between recent research in the history of science, intellectual history, and political theory. In developing these themes, the essays move from a discussion of changing perspectives in the history of science to an analysis of the pervasiveness of alchemical myths and symbols at the time of Newton to an analysis of the relation of the myths and symbols of the *prisca theologia* to the yearning for religious revitalization and political stabilization in the seventeenth and eighteenth centuries.

The first two essays are contributed by Allen G. Debus, Morris Fishbein Professor of History of Science and Medicine at the University of Chicago. The first, "Science and History: The Birth of a New Field," offers a description of developments in the history of science from Debus's days as a graduate student to the present. This account provides a concise discussion of the positivist orientation of Sarton and other shapers of the discipline and demonstrates how these historiographical assumptions shaped the way the history of science was written. In doing so, it helps explain why the differentiation of science and pseudo-science was such a basic part of the conceptual and interpretive framework in the history of science for nearly fifty years. Debus then offers a concise account of the developments which led to a reevaluation of the importance of alchemy as part of the Scientific Revolution. Debus's second essay, "The Scientific Revolution: A Chemist's Reappraisal," moves from the historiographical considerations of the first essay to an analysis of primary sources which demonstrates how prominently alchemy, or the "chemical philosophy," figured in scientific debates and curricular controversies throughout Europe.

The third essay, "Alchemical Death and Resurrection: The Significance of Alchemy in the Age of Newton," is contributed by B. J. T. Dobbs, Professor of History at the University of California-Davis. As its title suggests, this essay shows that interest or belief in alchemy was not confined to a small intellectual minority. Alchemical themes and imagery were an integral part of the public myths and religious symbols of birth and rebirth, death and resurrection. Professor Dobbs's essay is important to the aims of the collection as a whole because it demonstrates the widespread familiarity with alchemical symbols and documents their incorporation into speculations about God, man, world, and society. By doing so, it sets the context for the next three essays' examinations of the relation of the *prisca theologia* to the yearning for political stability and religious reformation that permeates the early modern period.

My own contribution, "Science, the *Prisca Theologia*, and Modern Epochal Consciousness," relates the Hermetic myths and symbols revived by Ficino and the Neoplatonists to the distinctly modern emphasis on progress and perfectibility through the mastery of nature. This examination includes a comparison of the Hermetic and the humanist conceptions of rebirth and an investigation of the relation of this imagery to Bacon's concept of a great instauration.

Klaus Vondung, Professor of German Literature, Universität Gesamthochschule, Siegen, Germany, demonstrates that the Hermetic views of human nature and of utopian perfection persisted as part of European culture well into the eighteenth century. His essay, "Millenarianism, Hermeticism, and the Search for a Universal Science," shows that religious and political turmoil of the early modern period created the yearning for a universal science—that is, a comprehensive understanding of nature and human nature that overcomes man's alienation and restores his God-given role as the master of nature. Vondung connects this conception to Hermetic myths and symbols and points to their influence on such major figures as Oetinger, Herder, Schelling, and Hegel.

David Walsh, Professor of Political Science at Catholic University, examines the influence of the *prisca theologia*'s myths and symbols on the themes of historical progress and social perfection. Walsh's provocative thesis is that the progressivist, utopian visions of Comte, Marx, and other revolutionary "social scientists" of the nineteenth century stayed closer to the magic and alchemy of pseudo-science than to the principles of modern experimental science.

The last essay is by Wilbur Applebaum, Professor of History of Science at Illinois Institute of Technology. Its purpose is to provide a description and analysis of the shifts in perspective and emphasis in historical scholarship on the relation of science to early modern intellectual and cultural history. Applebaum's analysis complements the opening historiographical essay by Allen Debus. Debus describes the emergence of the history of science and the internal developments that shaped its perspective and approach. Applebaum examines the recent historiographical developments stemming from external factors, namely, intellectual and cultural developments that contributed to the Scientific Revolution and to the elevated role of science in society. His analysis covers the current debate on the "revolutionary" nature of the Scientific Revolution, the reassessment of the relation of early modern science to humanism, the relation of the development and institutionalization of science to the ideals and the practical interests of the new entrepreneurial commercial class, and the reassessment of the complex interrelation of science and religion. Applebaum's essay also complements the other essays by placing the scholarly reexamination of the connections of science and pseudo-science in the context of the current reassessment of the interrelationship of science to social and political ideals, values, and needs.

The Topical Bibliography is also intended to complement the essays by providing a concise, selective list of primary and secondary sources treating the following themes: recent developments in the historiography of science, the history of science and pseudo-science, the revival of the *prisca theologia* in the early modern period, millenarian and utopian themes in the age of science, and thematic studies of modernism.

Before concluding these prefatory remarks, I have the pleasant obligation and opportunity to thank the distinguished historians of science and intellectual historians who have contributed to this project. I am grateful not only for their essays, but for the spirit of interdisciplinary collaboration that lies behind them. I also wish to make the following acknowledgments. The University of Coimbra in Portugal gave permission to modify and reprint lectures Allen Debus gave there. The university's press printed a limited-circulation edition of the lectures as *Science and History*.

Professor Dobbs's essay was originally published for limited distribution by the Smithsonian Institution Libraries and has been incorporated into her Cambridge University Press book, *The Janus Faces of Genius.*

I want to thank the following libraries for providing the illustrations used in Professor Dobbs's essay. The Library of Congress Rare Book and Special Collections Division supplied figure 1. Figure 2 is reproduced from an image in a book from the collections of the Department of Rare Books and Special Collections, Memorial Library, University of Wisconsin-Madison. Figures 3–7 are reproduced by permission of the Huntington Library, San Marino, California.

I would like to express a personal debt of gratitude to Patti Fabré for typing the several versions of this manuscript, and to Jay Malone for his excellent work on the notes and bibliography. Finally, I wish to thank the Earhart Foundation for a 1989 summer fellowship which allowed me to complete my essay for this collection.

SCIENCE,
PSEUDO-SCIENCE,
AND UTOPIANISM IN
EARLY MODERN THOUGHT

SCIENCE AND HISTORY
The Birth of a New Field
Allen G. Debus

When I was an undergraduate student at Northwestern University thirty-five years ago, the history of science did not exist as a field of study. My major field was chemistry, and while it is true that a short course of lectures on the history was offered through that department, few students knew of it and fewer still attended these lectures. At the time I had a minor field in history, but as far as the members of that department were concerned, the subject was one to be avoided. To be sure, it was acknowledged that there had been a Scientific Revolution, but what its meaning might have been for world history was never told to us. Nor was reference made to the science or technology of the past hundred years. The standard teaching fare continued to emphasize politics, society, and religion. Even the few lectures we heard on intellectual history seemed to ignore the sciences. The student of history was left with the impression that world history had been untouched by the rise of the sciences and medicine, while for the student majoring in any of the sciences, the subject was to be ignored for fear of cluttering the mind with obsolete theories and facts.

Of course, I see now that my impressions as a student were wrong. The study of the history of science and medicine is important. Furthermore, although I did not know it then, I know now that the writing of the history of science and medicine has a long history. This is true even for the ancient period. The short histories of geometry and medicine written by Proclus and Celsus are well known. Nor did this tradition expire in the Middle Ages. Gui de Chauliac prefaced his famous *Surgery* (1343) with a historical survey of the field.[1] True, there are not many of these early histo-

---

1. Morris R. Cohen and I. E. Drabkin, eds., *A Source Book in Greek Science* (Cambridge: Harvard University Press, 1958), 33–38 (Proclus), 468–73 (Celsus). Gui de Chauliac's history of surgery is conveniently available in *The Portable Medieval Reader*, ed. James Bruce Ross and Mary Martin McLaughlin (New York: Viking, 1973), 640–49.

ries, but there are enough of them to indicate that it was considered important to know not only the subject matter of one's field, but its historical development as well.

It would be a matter of considerable interest to discuss the writing of the history of science and medicine in detail, but there is hardly enough time to do this in the short space that I have. Here I will range over nearly four hundred years, from the late sixteenth through the mid-twentieth centuries, but I will do so only to make a few points. I would like to show that there is a difference in the types of scientific histories written before and after the great scientific watershed of the mid-seventeenth century. Indeed, the scientific beliefs of the authors affected their historical outlooks. I would like to touch further on the scientific histories of the Enlightenment and the early nineteenth centuries to indicate their influence, which extended into the present century.

Scientific History in the Renaissance: The Paracelsians and Antiquity

Let me turn first to the Scientific Revolution. It was during the sixteenth and seventeenth centuries that we see for the first time a growing number of historical writings in the sciences. These show us one of the most characteristic features of historical writing in all periods, that the historian writes with a purpose in mind. Indeed, the historian is often a propagandist even when he may not be aware of it himself. In the late 1960s we witnessed the birth of a new school of radical historians whose work fit the temper of the times. In the sixteenth and seventeenth centuries, we see a similar situation. The move for reform in religion and science was then reflected in the writings of contemporary historians. Thus, the medical and chemical reforms of Paracelsus (1493–1541) were to be seen in the works of his followers.[2] These reforms were both theoretical and practical in nature. On the one hand they sought a new understanding of the world based on a mystical view of the cosmos, which they interpreted through man the microcosm and the all-encompassing macrocosm. Everything in the small world of man was to be found in the great world of the macrocosm. And man, as a true natural magician, was to learn of his Creator through

---

2. My views on the Paracelsian tradition are elaborated in *The Chemical Philosophy: Paracelsian Science and Medicine in the Sixteenth and Seventeenth Centuries*, 2 vols. (New York: Science History Publications, 1977).

the study of God's created nature. Chemistry was to be the key to this new knowledge since both nature and man were best understood through chemical processes and analogies. Therefore, if the Paracelsians argued for a new theoretical basis of knowledge, they also saw a need for practical reform because human physiology was described in chemical or alchemical terminology. New chemically prepared medicines were used to combat what were thought to be chemical disorders in the body. These were considered to be far more useful than the traditional Galenical herbal mixtures. In short, the Paracelsian medicine and science of the sixteenth century was anti-Galenic and anti-Aristotelian. It called for fresh observations, and it was argued that these could be interpreted properly only by chemists for the benefit of physicians.

This message was elaborated on by a number of authors who used history to support their convictions. Let me illustrate this through the works of two sixteenth-century authors. The first of these was interested primarily in the theoretical aspects of the Paracelsian philosophy, while the second confined himself primarily to the practical aspects of the introduction of the new chemically prepared medicines. The title of the first work is long and typically descriptive for the period: *The difference betwene the auncient Phisicke, first taught by the godly forefathers, consisting in vnitie peace and concord: and the latter Phisicke proceeding from Idolaters, Ethnickes, and Heathen: as Gallen, and such other consisting in duality, discorde, and contrarietie* (1585). The author, R. Bostocke, Esquire, attacked the false natural philosophy and medicine being taught at the universities. Although the new chemical medicine could be proven to be valid by experience, how were students to know this?

> In the scholes nothing may be receiued nor allowed that sauoreth not of *Aristotle, Gallen, Aluicen,* and other Ethnickes, whereby the yong beginners are either not acquainted with this doctrine, or els it is brought into hatred with them. And abrode likewise the Galenists be so armed and defended by the protection, priuiledges and authoritie of Princes, that nothing can be allowed that they disalowe and nothing may be receiued that agreeth not with their pleasures and doctrine.[3]

With Bostocke as with other writers of this period religion was a major factor. Aristotle and Galen were heathens. Their false phi-

---

3. R. Bostocke, Esq., *The difference betwene the auncient Physicke . . . and the latter Physicke* (London: Robert Walley, 1585), sig. Fii.

losophy and medicine had been perpetuated by lecturers who read and commented on their texts without any search for confirmation. Rather than the books of the ancients, the seeker of truth should learn from God. "The Almighty Creatour of the Heauens and the Earth (Christian Reader), hath set before our eyes two most principall Bookes: the one of Nature, the other of his written Word."[4]

Here was a different approach to nature, calling for the destruction of the philosophy of the ancients and its replacement by a new science based upon Holy Scripture, observation, and experiment. This would be a Christian philosophy.

For Bostocke history was an important tool, and he devoted nearly one half of his treatise to the history of chemistry and medicine.[5] Believing that the pristine knowledge granted to Adam could be recovered from the Old Testament and the *Corpus Hermeticum*, which was thought to be almost as old, he argued that these truths had been partially preserved in the writings of the pre-Socratics and Plato. But Aristotle had attacked his teacher, while Galen, who had adopted the philosophy of Aristotle, had compounded his sins by persecuting Christians. In the succeeding centuries only a dedicated few—for the most part Byzantine and Islamic alchemists—had preserved the most ancient truths, which they passed on from master to pupil. Thus, Paracelsus was not an innovator. Rather, his reforms in medicine were properly to be compared with the reforms of Copernicus, who had rediscovered the true ancient astronomy, and the reforms of Luther, Melanchthon, Zwingli, and Calvin, who had rediscovered the theological truths of antiquity.[6]

It was to be expected that such accounts would be attacked by those who considered the work of Aristotle and Galen the glory of the learned world. Such an author was Thomas Erastus (1524–1583), who pictured Paracelsus as an ignorant charlatan who preferred magic and the devil to the classical authorities. More interesting, however, is the reaction of those who sought compromise. Johann Albertus Wimpenaeus (1569) saw value in the work of Paracelsus, but he did not reject the ancients, since wisdom was to

4. Thomas Tymme, *A Dialogue Philosophicall* (London: T. S. Nodham for C. Knight, 1612), sig. A3.
5. Bostocke's history is reprinted with an introduction and annotations by Allen G. Debus in "An Elizabethan History of Medical Chemistry," *Annals of Science* 18 (1962; published 1964): 1–29.
6. See Debus, *Chemical Philosophy* 1:131–34.

be found in both. Guinter of Andernach (ca. 1505–1574) is even more interesting as a man who was perhaps the most famous of the Renaissance medical humanists.[7] As a young scholar he prepared translations of much of Galen as well as Paul of Aegina, Oribasius, and Alexander of Tralles. As Professor of Medicine in Paris, he taught Andreas Vesalius and Michael Servetus, both of whom served as his assistants.

In many respects Guinter represents the quintessential scholar, for he never ceased to study or to learn. Thus, we find that as he grew older he carefully read the new Paracelsian medical works. But how were these to be assessed by a learned Galenist? Guinter's answer is to be found in his massive *De medicina veteri et nova*, published in 1571. Here it may be seen that he had formed a high opinion of the chemical medicines that were to be essential to Paracelsian authors. Indeed, he wrote that the "medicines of the chemists are more than divine."[8] Still, this humanist insisted that the theoretical basis of medicine must remain grounded on Galenism. Paracelsian thought was offensively mystical and its proponents were arrogant.

Guinter's problem was to dismiss Paracelsus and his fanatical disciples while retaining the benefits of the chemical medicines. This goal was quite different from the goal of a Paracelsian such as Bostocke, but like Bostocke, Guinter turned to history for his answer.[9] The earliest men, he wrote, were strong and needed only simple and mild remedies for retaining their health. More debilitating diseases arose only later when the accumulated luxuries of centuries resulted in a permanent corruption of mankind. It is then that we see different medicines—resins and aromatic substances—introduced in the texts of the Islamic and Indian authors. It was the destiny of Paracelsus not only to restore to use chemicals known to other authors, but also to enrich them with a treasury of new waters, liquors, salts, and oils—medicines often more efficacious than the traditional ones. Guinter's answer to the current medical debate therefore was compromise. Both medicines were needed. "The ancients on account of time honored authority are to be given first place," but there was much of great value in the work of the more recent chemists. Would that Galen had been more brief and more accurate; would that Theophrastus [Para-

---

7. Ibid., 135–45.
8. J. Guintherius von Andernach, *De medicina veteri et noua tum congnoscenda, tum faciunda commentarij duo*, 2 vols. (Basel: Henricpetrina, 1571), 2:650.
9. Ibid., 26, 28, 621–22.

celsus] had been more open and candid! There are faults and virtues in the work of both factions, and physicians must choose the best from each.[10]

In contrast with Bostocke, Guinter of Andernach did not seek to recover a pristine medicine known to Adam as a means of proving the antiquity of Paracelsian truths. Instead, the ancient art of medicine was once more ascribed to Greek authors. Chemical medicine had been introduced by the Arabic physicians. They were later forgotten and eventually rediscovered by Paracelsus. This had been a notable achievement and he was to be praised for it. But his mystical cosmology could be safely ignored—or else simply shown to be a restatement of concepts known to the ancient Greeks.

Scientific History in the Enlightenment

Had the course of the Scientific Revolution followed the path charted for it by the Paracelsians, the Hermetic history of Bostocke might still be read today. But it did not. The triumph of the mechanists in the seventeenth century placed an emphasis not on chemistry and medicine, but on astronomy and the physics of motion. This change may also be followed in contemporary histories.

Mechanists of the late seventeenth and the eighteenth centuries sought to divorce themselves from the mysticism and the magic of their predecessors no less than their dependence on the Greek philosophers. But when they wrote of the warfare between the "ancients" and the "moderns," they specifically meant the adherents of the Greek philosophers versus the mechanical philosophers. These mechanists found atomism a useful tool as they sought an explanatory model based upon the size, shape, and motion of the small parts of matter. Mathematical abstraction became in their hands a powerful tool for the analysis of natural phenomena, and the *Principia mathematica* (1687) of Isaac Newton was almost to become the bible of the new science.[11]

Because of the importance of Newton for the eighteenth cen-

10. Ibid., 31–32.
11. I. Bernard Cohen's *Franklin and Newton: An Inquiry into Speculative Newtonian Experimental Science and Franklin's Work in Electricity as an Example Thereof* (Philadelphia: American Philosophical Society, 1956) presents the argument that Newton's influence in the eighteenth century derived largely from his widely read *Opticks*, but there seems little doubt that the *Principia mathematica* was the foundation of his fame even if it had a smaller audience.

tury it is of some interest to pause for a moment to look at the work of John Freind (1675–1728). Freind was a disciple of Newton who held the chairs of chemistry and medicine at Oxford. He published both on chemistry and medicine, and his views, as we should expect, were colored by the science he believed in. His chemical work was an open attempt to divorce himself from earlier chemical authors. Indeed, he sought to explain chemical reactions as the interaction of spherical atoms possessed of forces similar to the gravitational forces Newton had postulated for the solar system. This was an attempt to establish a Newtonian chemistry. But it is in Freind's history of medicine, published in 1725 and 1726, that we can compare his views with those of Bostocke and the earlier Paracelsian apologists. For Freind the mystical religious outlook of the Paracelsians could not be tolerated. Friend rejected Paracelsus as an idle systematizer whose whole cosmology and religious-vitalistic outlook toward nature were the very antithesis of the new science. On the other hand, by the opening years of the eighteenth century there seemed to be little doubt of the value of chemically prepared medicine. However, Freind would not permit Paracelsus to be credited with their discovery. Rather, like Guinter, he insisted that the honor of their discovery be given to Arabic chemists and physicians.[12] How very different are the histories of Freind and Bostocke! They are both histories of medicine, but written from two opposing viewpoints separated by the scientific watershed of the mid-seventeenth century.

For the philosophies of the eighteenth century, the example of Newton and the new science signified the birth of a new age. The historian was told to abandon his traditional studies. What moral value was to be found in the story of kings, popes, and wars? Far different was the history of science, since in it we witness the ennobling example of human progress wrought from ignorance by the true heroes of mankind. Late in the century a journalist wrote:

> The incredible discoveries that have multiplied during the last ten years . . . the phenomena of electricity fathomed, the elements transformed, the airs decomposed and understood, the rays of the sun condensed, air traversed by human audacity, a thousand other phenomena

12. Arnold Thackray, *Atoms and Powers: An Essay on Newtonian Matter-Theory and the Development of Chemistry* (Cambridge: Harvard University Press, 1970), 52–73. John Freind, *The History of Physick; From the Time of Galen, to the beginning of the Sixteenth Century* . . . , 4th ed., 2 vols. (London: M. Cooper, 1750), 2:204.

have prodigiously extended the sphere of our knowledge. Who knows how far we can go? What mortal would dare set limits to the human mind?[13]

Not only would science continue to progress, perhaps its history would permit us to forecast the future, as Gelbart has written:

Toward the end of the century this faith in the internal dynamism of science becomes much more explicit and encourages a very optimistic picture of the future. The same force that propelled man to his present state of scientific sophistication and technical prowess still operates, and will spur him on in the future. While progress may not always be steady and even, it will eventually take man to intellectual heights which he cannot even imagine. The scientific past, then, offers valuable clues for the future. The search for truth is not ended. Great as we are, our science and the science of our children will be ever surpassed.[14]

Belief in being able to plan the future was to prove an unfulfilled hope, but a deep-seated belief in the importance of scientific history as evidence of progress was to become a characteristic of eighteenth- and nineteenth-century science. Joseph Priestley's histories of electricity and the gases of the air, J. E. Montucla's history of mathematics, and Jean Sylvain Bailly's various histories of astronomy are serious studies still referred to by scholars. This is a period when scientists began to add histories of their subjects to scientific treatises, as we see in Boerhaave's New Method of Chemistry and Laplace's System of the World.[15]

And yet, in its own way, this was as biased a history as that of the Renaissance Paracelsians. These historians wrote of progress

13. Nina Rattner Gelbart, " 'Science' In Enlightenment Utopias: Power and Purpose in Eighteenth-Century French 'Voyages Imaginaires,' " (Ph.D. diss., University of Chicago, 1973), 155; she cites the Journal de Bruxelles, (29 May 1784), 226–27.
14. Ibid., 158.
15. Joseph Priestley, The History and Present State of Discoveries Relating to Vision, Light and Colours (London: J. Johnson, 1772); The History and Present State of Electricity with Original Experiments (London: J. Dodsley, J. Johnson and B. Davenport, 1767); Jean Étienne Montucla, Histoire de Mathématiques . . . , 2 vols. (Paris, 1758), expanded to 4 vols., completed and edited by J. J. Le Francais de Lalande, (Paris: H. Agasse, 1799–1802); Jean Sylvain Bailly, Histoire de l'Astronomie Ancienne . . . (Paris: Frères Dubure, 1775); Histoire de l'Astronomie Moderne . . . , 3 vols. (Paris: Les Frères de Bure, 1779–1782); Hermann Boerhaave, "Prolegomena, or the History of Chemistry," in A New Method of Chemistry . . . , trans. P. Shaw and E. Chambers (London: J. Osborn and T. Longman, 1727), 1–50. Pierre Simon de Laplace, "Precis de l'Histoire de l'Astronomie," in Exposition du Système du Monde, 3d ed., 2 vols. (Paris: Courcier, 1808), 2:259–415.

in the past leading to the current state of the sciences. The emphasis was invariably placed on the science of Western Europe. The religious aura of the period of the Middle Ages was treated with contempt and blamed for the lack of progress in that period. Little more consideration was given to the accomplishments of the Far East or Islam.

Science and Religion in the Nineteenth Century

The Enlightenment view that science is essentially progressive has left its stamp on the field to our own day and it is only in recent decades that there has been a search for a broader historical context in which to place scientific history. Again let me recall my own graduate training. Then we were told that the first true history of science—that is, a history of science as a whole in contrast to the histories of individual sciences so common in the eighteenth century—was to be found in William Whewell's *History of the Inductive Sciences* (1837). Whewell was one of the great physicists of Victorian England and his title reflects his belief in the ideal of Baconian science, a science that is primarily inductive rather than deductive—one that is based upon observation and experiment. Like Bacon, Whewell sought to avoid a science that was based too heavily on mathematics. Also like Bacon, he felt that the primary goal of the history of science was to furnish the subject matter for the philosophy of science. History for Whewell was subordinate to philosophy, or to put it another way, our goal as historians is to elucidate scientific method.[16]

Whewell's history leaves great areas untouched. He ignored the achievements of the ancient Near East partially because solid information was sketchy when he wrote, but also because he felt that the science of Egypt and Babylonia was devoid of theory. The accomplishments of the Far East and Islam fared little better, and he even wrote harshly of Greek science because of its deductive nature. As for his description of the science during and after the Scientific Revolution, it is easy to recognize his dependence on the viewpoint of the Enlightenment. Separate chapters are devoted

16. William Whewell, *History of the Inductive Sciences: From the Earliest to the Present Time*, 3 ed., 2 vols. (New York: D. Appleton, 1873). For Whewell's approach see his preface and introduction, 1:7–11, 41–51. He states openly that his work is "aimed at being, not merely a narration of the facts in the history of science, but a basis for the Philosophy of Science" (8).

to each of the sciences or current areas of research. It was certainly not an integrated history, and because of Whewell's personal interests, there is little to be found here on the biological or medical sciences.

It is in Whewell's chapters on the Middle Ages that his prejudices are most evident. For him this was "the stationary period" resulting from Christianity which caused a neglect of physical reasoning. The so-called scientists of the period had added nothing new to knowledge. He derided them for their indistinctness, dogmatism, mysticism, and their commentatorial spirit. To be sure, he made a few exceptions (Roger Bacon and the architects of the cathedrals come to mind), but in general he dismissed a millennium of history with distaste and the belief that during that time the physical sciences had become little more than magic. With evident relief he turned his back on this period of dogmatism:

> The causes which produced the inertness and blindness of the stationary period of human knowledge, began at last to yield to the influence of the principles which tended to progression. The indistinctness of thought, which was the original feature in the decline of sound knowledge, was in a measure remedied by the steady cultivation of Pure Mathematics and Astronomy, and by the progress of inventions in the Arts, which call out and fix the distinctness of our conceptions of the relations of natural phenomena. As men's minds become clear, they become less servile: the perception of the nature of truth drew men away from controversies about mere opinion; when they saw distinctly the relations of *things*, they ceased to give their whole attention to what had been *said* concerning them; and thus, as science rose into view, the spirit of commentation lost its way.[17]

Wherever we look among nineteenth-century historians we find views similar to those of Whewell. W. E. H. Lecky wrote of the *History of the Rise and Influence of the Spirit of Rationalism in Europe* (1865), Georges Cuvier titled a survey of recent work at the Parisian Academy of Sciences the *Histoire des progrès des sciences naturelles depuis 1789*, and of course, Auguste Comte's positivism was based upon scientific progress. All those imbued with this essentially Enlightenment attitude were faced with the contrast between medieval and early modern science. As Whewell had noted, the first coincided with a period of the dominance of the Roman Catholic Church. Others were to make much of the fact that the Scientific Revolution occurred during the Reforma-

17. Ibid., 1:255. See 1:185–239 for Whewell's discussion of the Middle Ages.

tion and its aftermath. Both cases forced scholars to look at the relationship of science to religion, and this was to become a subject of debate beginning in the late nineteenth century. This may be well illustrated in the works of many authors, but it is seen with great clarity in the works of three: John William Draper, Andrew D. White, and James Walsh.

John William Draper (1811–1882) was a prominent American chemist and physiologist.[18] He was well known as a student of photography and a participant in the famous Oxford debate of 1860 that pitted T. H. Huxley against Bishop Wilberforce over the truth of Darwinism. Draper was a disciple of Auguste Comte and devoted much of his effort in later years to the study of history. His *A History of the Intellectual Development of Europe* (1863) is an important example of nineteenth-century intellectual history, while his *History of the Conflict Between Religion and Science* (1874) has become one of the most widely read books of the past century. By 1910 it had reached a twenty-fifth edition, and it has been reprinted as recently as 1972. There is probably no other work in the history of science that can match this record.

In both of these works Draper upheld the validity of science over that of religion, but the more moderate tone of the first text was lost in his *History of the Conflict Between Religion and Science*. The reason? Draper's reaction to the Vatican Council of 1869–1870, which declared the supremacy of the Pope and included canons such as the following:

Let him be anathema—
Who shall say that human sciences ought to be pursued in such a spirit of freedom that one may be allowed to hold as true their assertions, even when opposed to revealed doctrine.
Who shall say that it may come to pass, in the progress of science, that the doctrines set forth by the Church must be taken in another sense than that in which the Church has ever received them and yet receives them.[19]

For Draper the aspirations of the papacy threatened to renew the Dark Ages. He believed that the demand for unquestioned belief in things above reason had ended the scientific advance of antiq-

18. The standard study is Donald Fleming, *John William Draper and the Religion of Science* (Philadelphia: University of Pennsylvania Press, 1950; New York: Octagon Books, 1972).
19. John William Draper, *History of the Conflict Between Religion and Science*, 25th ed. (London: Kegan Paul, Trench, Trübner, 1910), 350–51.

uity. A scientist required something far different—a belief that the universe is governed by immutable law. The mind of the scientist must be open to all possibilities in his quest for truth, not tied to blind faith.

Andrew Dickson White (1832–1918) was a prominent American diplomat and educator who served as United States minister to Germany and Russia, as well as head of the United States delegation to the Hague Peace Conference (1899). More important for our story is the fact that White organized Cornell University with Ezra Cornell and then went on to serve as its first president. In contrast to most universities at that time, the institution White sought was a nonsectarian institution that would serve as a refuge for the sciences and humanities. He was both shocked and surprised to find strong opposition to this goal from members of organized religions. White hoped first to convince his adversaries through reason, but eventually he delivered a lecture (1875) on "The Battlefields of Science," in which he took this thesis:

> In all modern history, interference with science in the supposed interest of religion, no matter how conscientious such interference may have been, has resulted in the direst evils both to religion and to science, and invariably; and, on the other hand, all untrammelled scientific investigation, no matter how dangerous to religion some of its stages may have seemed for the time to be, has invariably resulted in the highest good both of religion and of science.[20]

Reaction to his lecture was immediate and encouraging. He was soon invited to speak on the subject at numerous university associations and literary clubs. The lecture was expanded and published as a small book, *The Warfare of Science*, and he continued his work on the subject to contribute "New Chapters in the Warfare on Science" to *The Popular Science Monthly*. In the meantime he had seen Draper's *Conflict Between Science and Religion*. His first thought had been that nothing more need be added to the subject until he realized that Draper "regarded the struggle as one between Science and Religion. I believed then, and am convinced now, that it was a struggle between Science and Dogmatic Theology."[21]

In many ways, White's history (published in final form in 1895)

---

20. Andrew Dickson White, *A History of the Warfare of Science with Theology in Christendom*, 2 vols. (New York: D. Appleton, 1900), 1:viii.
21. Ibid., ix.

is similar to that of Draper's. He deplored the impact of *Genesis* on the history of science, he argued that a belief in the imminent end of the world is useless for the growth of science, and inveighed against a dogmatic reading of Scripture. Draper had aimed his work primarily at the Roman Catholic church. White agreed, but his experience at Cornell had taught him that the Protestant churches were no more liberal in these matters. Above all, he returned again and again to the Enlightenment, which he saw as a period of the conflict of reason and mystery. And if the sciences had managed to progress, he believed that the complete triumph of reason over mystery had not yet occurred.

The case for Roman Catholicism was to be made by James Joseph Walsh (1865–1942), professor at Fordham Medical School and later the director of the Fordham School of Sociology, whose *The Thirteenth, Greatest of Centuries* (1907; fourteenth edition, 1952) and *The Popes and Science* (1908) were directed against White and Draper. Walsh wrote of the importance of the Papacy as a patron of the sciences and education in the medieval period. As a physician, Walsh emphasized the important anatomical work carried out in the Italian universities in the late Middle Ages, and characterized this work as essential background for the work of Vesalius and Harvey. He also pointed to specific work in chemistry and physics, while he attributed the experimental method to thirteenth-century authors, primarily Roger Bacon and Albertus Magnus. It was the Church that had established hospitals and universities, while in contrast, the Reformation "had carried away with it in its course nearly everything precious that men had gained during the four centuries immediately preceding. Art, education, science, liberty, democracy—everything worth while had been ruined for the time."[22]

As for the Enlightenment of the eighteenth century:

> The fact of the matter is that . . . there was a great decadence of interest in scholarship and true education. There is a distinct descent in human culture at this time. Education was at its lowest ebb, hospitals were the worst ever built, art and architecture were neglected, and human liberty was so shackled that the French Revolution was needed to lift the fetters from men's minds as well as bodies.

Walsh had written originally to refute the views of Andrew Dick-

---

22. James J. Walsh, *The Popes and Science: The History of the Papal Relations to Science* . . . (New York: Fordham University Press, 1915), 334.

son White. As for Draper, he dismissed his work as little more than a "comic history" founded on ignorance.[23]

The Draper-White-Walsh debate was more than a dispute over science and religion. More important was the fact that it called for a new assessment of science and medicine in the Middle Ages. Here Walsh was to be vindicated. Nineteenth-century editions of medieval medical texts led the way toward a new appreciation, and by the early years of the new century, there were a host of new works—many of them still useful—penned by Max Neuberger, Julius Pagel, Karl Sudhoff, and others.[24] Indeed, medical history matured in Germany, which remained its center until well after the first World War. At the same time, in the physical sciences, Moritz Cantor was at work on his four volume *Vorlesungen über Geschichte der Mathematik* (1880–1908), while Paul Tannery, Sir Thomas Little Heath, and Johan Ludvig Heiberg prepared their monumental editions of Greek mathematicians and early modern scientists. The great French physicist and philosopher of science, Pierre Duhem, carried out his research, which led to his ten-volume *Le Système du Monde* (10 vols.; first five volumes, 1913–1917) a work which led to a completely altered view of medieval science and a debate over the originality of Galileo that is not yet settled.

George Sarton: The Establishment of a New Academic Field

In short, by the early years of the twentieth century, there was a conscious realization among a small number of scholars that scientific and medical history were not only interesting, they were essential for understanding history as a whole. This was clearly a period of ferment, and it was the time that George Sarton (1884–1956) was a student. A Belgian, he received his B.Sc. in 1906 and his Sc.D. in 1911, both from the University of Ghent. However, most of his career was spent in the United States because he left his homeland during World War I.

Sarton was trained as a mathematician, but his interests em-

23. Ibid., iii, 500–19, 513.
24. A most interesting summary of the late nineteenth- and early twentieth-century pioneers in the field (Moritz Cantor, Paul Tannery, Karl Sudhoff, Johan Ludvig Heiberg, Pierre Duhem, Sir Thomas Little Heath, and Also Mieli) is to be found in George Sarton's "Acta atque Agenda" (1951), conveniently reprinted in *Sarton on the History of Science: Essays by George Sarton*, ed. Dorothy Stimson (Cambridge: Harvard University Press, 1962), 23–49.

braced all of the sciences. He was a dedicated man who believed that his was the most valuable form of history. To this end, he took part in the founding of societies for the history of science throughout the world. He also worked for the establishment of scholarly journals in the field. He was the founding father of the History of Science Society and *Isis*—still the best-known journal in the field—which was first published in 1912. He wrote an enormous number of books, articles, and reviews. Perhaps the best-known of these is his *Introduction to the History of Science*, which began with Homer and eventually reached the fourteenth century in three massive volumes in five parts. This work was published over a twenty-year span and finally given up only when Sarton realized that it would be impossible to continue because of the vast amount of material still to cover. He also planned the publication of the lectures that composed his two-year survey of the field that he gave at Harvard University—only two of the planned eight volumes had been completed by the date of his death. In the short space I have here it would be impossible to list even his major writings. Nor is it necessary to do so for our purposes. However, it is necessary to say a few words about his approach to the field because of his enormous influence.

George Sarton frequently expressed his debt to the writings of Auguste Comte, and there is no doubt that he considered himself a positivist. Writing in 1927, he defined science as "systematized positive knowledge": "Our main object is not simply to record isolated discoveries, but rather to explain the progress of scientific thought, the gradual development of human consciousness, that deliberate tendency to understand and to increase our part in the cosmic evolution."[25]

In the *Introduction* he had little to say about ancient science prior to the Greeks because he felt that oriental science was largely devoid of theory. On the other hand, he felt that his work contained the first real account of medieval science. This is doubtful because as late as 1927 he had made no reference to Duhem's *Système du monde* which was to transform our views of medieval physics in a way that Sarton's never was to do. By the time of the publication of the first volume of his Harvard lectures (1952), he corrected both omissions.

25. George Sarton, *Introduction to the History of Science*, 3 vols. in 5 parts (Baltimore: Williams and Wilkins, for the Carnegie Institution of Washington 1927–1947), 1:3, 6.

Sarton did not retreat on other points. As a positivist, he wished a history of real science—that is, science as we know it today. Subjects outside of science that may have formed part of man's outlook to nature in earlier periods were ignored or branded as "pseudo-sciences." We know now that alchemy and natural magic were important elements in the development of modern science. Sarton was willing to accept the actual chemical reactions and equipment described by the alchemists in his history of science, but nothing else.

> The historian of science can not devote much attention to the study of superstition and magic, that is, of unreason, because this does not help him very much to understand human progress. Magic is essentially unprogressive and conservative; science is essentially progressive; the former goes backward; the latter, forward. We can not possibly deal with both movements at once except to indicate their constant strife, and even that is not very instructive, because that strife has hardly varied throughout the ages. Human folly being at once unprogressive, unchangeable, and unlimited, its study is a hopeless undertaking. There can not be much incentive to encompass that which is indefinite and to investigate the history of something which did not develop.[26]

A second point is that Sarton maintained the division that had developed between the history of science and the history of medicine. As we have seen, the history of medicine had developed independently in the late nineteenth and the early twentieth centuries. Henry Sigerist, a pupil of Sudhoff, left Leipzig late in the 1920s to take over the directorship of the recently founded Institute for the History of Medicine at Johns Hopkins University in Baltimore. There he hoped to continue the German tradition in the United States. But for Sarton the claims of the historians of medicine posed a threat to his fledgling history of science. He believed that there was a hierarchy of the sciences. Mathematics stood at the top, since it was necessary for the mathematical sciences: astronomy, physics, and chemistry. Only eventually as we followed this scheme would we descend to the life sciences. He explained:

> Men understand the world in different ways . . . some men are more abstract-minded, and they naturally think first of unity and of God, of wholeness, of infinity and other such concepts, while the minds of

26. Ibid., 19.

other men are concrete and they cogitate about health and disease, profit and loss. They invent gadgets and remedies; they are less interested in knowing anything than in applying whatever knowledge they may already have to practical problems; they try to make things work and pay, to heal and teach. The first are called dreamers . . . ; the second kind are recognized as practical and useful. History has often proved the shortsightedness of the practical men and vindicated the "lazy" dreamer; it has also proved that the dreamers are often mistaken. The historian of science . . . is not willing to subordinate principles to applications, nor to sacrifice the so-called dreamers to the engineers, the teachers, or the healers.[27]

Sarton surely idolized the dreamers. And, as he believed that the biological sciences stood far below the mathematical sciences, he believed that medicine was lower still. Because he was convinced that medicine was a practical art, he was distressed by those medical historians who claimed that medicine is the real foundation of the other sciences. Indeed, he wrote, "the main misunderstandings concerning the history of science are due to historians of medicine who have the notion that medicine is the center of science."[28] Sarton felt that medical historians had presented a warped version of scientific history because of their insufficient scientific knowledge. We need not be too surprised that societies of medical history seldom meet jointly with societies of the history of science even today, or that for decades the history of science centered on the physical rather than the biological sciences.

I have covered four hundred years of the writing of the history of science and medicine in abstracted form hoping to make a few general points. The first of these is almost obvious, that historians write with a purpose, and it may frequently become propaganda for their own deeply held beliefs. Thus we looked briefly at a few histories written in the sixteenth century. For the followers of Paracelsus, scientific and medical truths were closely allied with their religious convictions, their desire to overturn the educational establishment, and their belief that the truths of the Paracelsian medicine could be connected with divine truths imparted to Adam at the Creation. Their histories were written to establish their medicine and natural philosophy.

The success of the mechanical philosophy in the course of the seventeenth century led to a different historical model, one in

27. George Sarton, *A History of Science: Ancient Science Through the Golden Age of Greece* (Cambridge: Harvard University Press, 1952), xii.
   28. Ibid., xi.

which religion was divorced from scientific progress. Enlightenment philosophies, looking on the science of the Middle Ages as a
barren period of science, erased a millennium of science from
their works, pausing only to refer to Roger Bacon and a few other
authors who seemed to rise above the general intellectual mal-
aise. Indeed, during this period the history of science was consciously divorced from the traditional historical subjects since
science represented human progress while politics, warfare, and
religion did not. This essentially Enlightenment approach to the
sciences dominated the history of science well into this century.
Walsh's reply to the histories of Draper and White stands as one of
the early defenses of religion and medieval science and medicine.
Indeed, it is not until we reach the closing decades of the nineteenth century that we begin to see an important series of texts
and historical analyses that were to reshape our views of medieval
science.

Although there are many works on the history of science and
the history of medicine that were published prior to the World War
I, the field was not yet established academically, and it is for this
reason that George Sarton is such an important figure. This is
surely due more to his efforts than those of any other individual.
He not only established the field at Harvard University, he founded
the journal *Isis* and was the person most responsible for organizing the international History of Science Society. He diligently
sought out others with similar interests and encouraged them to
pursue their work. It is little wonder, with Sarton's worldwide
activities, that by the middle decades of this century the field
reflected his prejudices. In the post-World War II era a few Ph.D.s
were being graduated from the new field at Harvard University
and elsewhere, but the work of these young scholars as well as the
pages of *Isis* still reflected a positivistic approach emphasizing the
development of the physical sciences. This was to change radically in the following years.

The History of Science: Professionalization and Disunity

In the foregoing discussion I have sketched the background to
the establishment of the history of science as an academic discipline, ending with the almost monumental efforts of George Sarton and pointing out that his positivistic approach to the field had
much in common with the work of earlier historians. However, in

contrast with his contemporaries and predecessors, Sarton had founded journals and an international society for scholars in this field. At Harvard University his work had resulted in a program in the history of science both on the graduate and undergraduate levels. And in the 1940s this program was to graduate its first American Ph.D.s in the history of science.

It was not my intention to make this essay autobiographical in nature, but I have found that to a certain extent it has been unavoidable because I am now speaking of a period when I first became interested in the history of science. I wrote a master's thesis on seventeenth-century chemistry at Indiana University in 1949 under John J. Murray, a professor of history who recognized the importance of the history of science. While doing research on that project I first became aware of *Isis* and the work of George Sarton. Then, after further graduate study in chemistry and five years of chemical research in the pharmaceutical industry, my wife and I decided to return to graduate study. In 1956 there were only three graduate programs in the field in the United States: the Harvard Program directed by I. Bernard Cohen, the Cornell University program directed by Henry Guerlac, and the University of Wisconsin Program directed by Marshall Clagett. The first two were students of Sarton while the third had been trained by Lynn Thorndike, Columbia University's great medievalist who is best known for his eight-volume *History of Magic and Experimental Science.*

Our decision was to go to Harvard, where I enrolled in the autumn of 1956. George Sarton had died only a few months earlier. Announcements of his recent death that had been sent to the subscribers of *Isis* were still being used as scratch paper in the Program Office at Widener Library. Not long after, many of his books were sold at library sales for as little as fifty cents each.

There were very few students in this somewhat esoteric field, but we soon found that the subject was being interpreted somewhat differently than we had expected. The most recent writings in the field were critical of Sarton, and the author most frequently referred to as a model was Alexandre Koyré, the Russian philosopher of science who spent most of his later years in Paris. It is understandable that Koyré should have insisted on a close linkage between scientific and philosophical thought; but history was also important to him, for only through it could we be given a sense of the "glorious progress" of the evolution of scientific ideas. Like most other scholars in the field, Koyré centered his research on the development of physics and astronomy in the period from Copernicus to Newton. Galileo was an author of special concern, but he rejected the "Duhem thesis"—that is, that the sources for Galileo's mechanics were to be found in his medieval predecessors. For Koyré, Galileo was an innovator far removed from the medieval critics of Aristotle, and if he had any predecessor at all, one would have to find him in Archimedes. He explained the Scientific Revolution as a fundamental change in worldviews (from Aristotelian to Copernican): "I have endeavored in my *Galilean Studies* to define the structural patterns of the old and the new world-views and to determine the changes brought forth by the revolution of the seventeenth century. They seemed to me to be reducible to two fundamental and closely connected actions that I characterised as the destruction of the cosmos and the geometrization of space."[29]

This revolution was not to be explained by changes in society, a move from contemplation to active research, or even "the replacement of the teleological and organismic pattern of thinking and explanation by the mechanical and causal pattern." In many ways the Scientific Revolution was for Koyré the triumph of Plato over Aristotle in the Renaissance. And yet, if Sarton would have disagreed with Koyré over the importance of Plato for the rise of modern science, both would have agreed that the subject of the history of science was science and that this was the story of progress.[30]

As students we were also introduced to the encyclopedic works that in many ways characterized this "heroic age" of the history of science: Lynn Thorndike's *History of Magic and Experimental Science*, published in eight volumes between 1923 and 1958; Pierre Duhem's *Le Système du Monde*, published in ten volumes between 1913 and 1959; the many works of George Sarton; the first two (and what proved to be the only) volumes of Henry

29. Alexandre Koyré, *Études Galiléennes*, 3 parts (1935–1939), reprinted in 1 vol. (Paris: Hermann, 1966), 11; *From the Closed World to the Infinite Universe* (New York: Harper, 1958), vi. See also Pierre Duhem, *Le Système du Monde*, 10 vols. (Paris: Hermann, 1913–1959).

30. Koyré, *From the Closed World*, v. For Sarton on Plato, see *A History of Science*, 395–430. He discusses Plato's scientific thought in relation to the *Timaios:* "The influence of *Timaios* upon later times was enormous and essentially evil. . . . The scientific perversities of *Timaios* were mistaken for scientific truth. I cannot mention any other work whose influence was more mischievous, except perhaps the Revelation of St. John the Divine. The apocalypse, however, was accepted as a religious book, the *Timaios* as a scientific one; errors and superstititons are never more dangerous than when they are offered to us under the cloak of science."

Sigerist's planned multivolumed history of medicine. It seemed that vast areas of the field were just then being opened to our view. The multiauthored *A History of Technology*, published in five volumes by Oxford, gave us insight into a subject that had been ignored by most historians of science. And in 1961 both the first volume of Joseph Needham's *Science and Civilisation in China*— a work that is still under way and must rank as one of the great achievements of the present century—and the first volume of James Riddick Partington's *A History of Chemistry* (actually volume two) were published.[31] These works represented lifetimes of study by scholars who believed that they could cover entire fields over long chronological periods. It was a young field that had not yet reached the age of the specialized monograph.

However, it was also evident in the fifties that there were gaps in our learning. For those interested in Islamic science there did not seem to be very much to turn to. I had a special interest in the science of the Iberian peninsula, but other than accounts of the great voyages of discovery there was little to be found. A dedicated group of young scholars had already gathered around Otto Neugebauer and as a group they were rediscovering the mathematics and the astronomy of the ancient Near East. However, this group believed in specialization and they made little effort to integrate their research into the main stream of the history of science.[32]

Above all, the nineteenth century seemed to be a wasteland. Writing in 1954, I. Bernard Cohen noted:

> Once we pass the boundary between the eighteenth and nineteenth centuries, we encounter no general surveys written in a way that will serve the historian of ideas. Merz's older work, dull, myopic, and often poorly written, is still the major presentation of the science of the nineteenth century. The fourth volume of Ernst Cassirer's *Erkenntnis-*

---

31. Lynn Thorndike, *A History of Magic and Experimental Science*, 8 vols; (New York: Columbia University Press, 1923–1958). Henry Sigerist, *A History of Medicine*, 2 vols. (New York: Oxford University Press, 1955); Charles Singer, E. J. Holmyard, and A. R. Hall, eds., *A History of Technology*, 5 vols. (New York: Oxford University Press, 1954–1958); Joseph Needham, *Science and Civilisation in China*, Vol. 1, *Introductory Orientations* (Cambridge: Cambridge University Press, 1961); J. R. Partington, *A History of Chemistry*, 2 vols. (London: Macmillan, 1961) (the second volume, covering the sixteenth and the seventeenth centuries, was the first one published).

32. "I am exceedingly sceptical of any attempt to reach a 'synthesis'—whatever this term may mean—and I am convinced that specialization is the only basis of sound knowledge" O. Neugebauer, *The Exact Sciences in Antiquity* [1952; New York: Harper, 1962], v–vi.

problem is sketchy and far too technical for the average historian. Standard histories of physics, chemistry, biology, etc., contain much of the information but it needs to be digested and interpreted in the main stream of scientific ideas. Only the future can tell whether the history of science in the nineteenth century can be presented in a meaningful way for the general historian.[33]

Three years later Marshall Clagett gathered an international group of scholars at the University of Wisconsin to discuss current problems in the history of science. Published five years later, there is no better volume to indicate the state of the field a quarter century ago. The papers presented were heavily slanted toward the physical sciences and concentrate primarily on the period ranging from the late Middle Ages to the eighteenth century. In his preface to the collected papers, Clagett commented:

> It might seem at first glance that we put too little emphasis on developments of the last century. The Committee would certainly agree that this is so. But I would stress that so few historians are doing serious and professional historical work in the history of science of the last few decades, that the presentation of a critical discussion of such problems would be most difficult. It might also seem that we slighted the biological developments in favor of those of the physical sciences. This was not our original intention. But our preliminary efforts to line up a notable group of people in the discussion of nineteenth-century biology was only partially successful. The field of those engaged in active research in biological history is so narrow that when we received some advance refusals, we had as a result to eliminate an additional day we had hoped to devote to biology.[34]

In fact, in the years since that meeting in Madison, historical research in nineteenth-century science has far outstripped that in the period of the Scientific Revolution. However, this research has been somewhat uneven. Great strides have been taken in biological research, which has centered on the history of evolutionary thought, but little has been done to synthesize the research on the history of the physical sciences.

Fully as important as the study of nineteenth-century science has been the realization that the development of science may be

---

33. I. Bernard Cohen, "Some Recent Books on the History of Science," in *Roots of Scientific Thought: A Cultural Perspective*, ed. Philip P. Wiener and Aaron Noland (New York: Basic Books, 1957), 656. Published originally in the *Journal of the History of Ideas*.

34. Marshall Clagett, ed., *Critical Problems in the History of Science* (Madison: University of Wisconsin Press, 1962), vi.

influenced by factors we would not consider to be science at all. One of the first problems to arise related to Isaac Newton. Often praising him as the greatest scientist of all time, his biographers frequently consciously ignored the fact that a large percentage of Newton's papers deal with alchemy and other matters which on the surface seem to have little to do with the foundation of classical physics and the establishment of the Copernican theory. Even more striking had been the neglect of Paracelsus, van Helmont, and their followers. Their work had been heatedly debated in the sixteenth and seventeenth centuries, but rejected as mystical (ergo, nonscientific) by the new scientific establishment of the late seventeenth century. Because of the positivistic bias of historians of science, neither Newton's alchemy nor the mysticism of Paracelsus and van Helmont were "science." The mechanist philosophers of the Scientific Revolution had rightly excluded them from consideration, and we should continue to do so.

George Sarton had dismissed alchemy, astrology, and natural magic as pseudo-science, but his decision to do this could rightly be questioned if historians of science ever chose a different approach to the field. Such a move was, indeed, under way among historians—especially English historians. In 1931 Herbert Butterfield published his influential essay, "The Whig Interpretation of History," in which he argued that historians had, in effect, chosen sides. They had organized their histories from the viewpoint of the present, they clearly favored the Protestant reformers of the sixteenth and seventeenth centuries, and they defined "progress" from that viewpoint. In political terms they were guilty of writing "Whiggish" history. These historians felt the need to give a verdict, and in so doing they oversimplified the rich complexity of their sources. He wrote:

> The value of history lies in the richness of its recovery of the concrete life of the past. It is a story that cannot be told in dry lines, and its meaning cannot be conveyed in a species of geometry. There is not an essence of history that can be got by evaporating the human and the personal factors, the incidental or momentary or local things, and the circumstantial elements, as though at the bottom of the well there were something absolute, some truth independent of time or circumstance. . . . Above all it is not the role of the historian to come to what might be called judgements of value. . . . His role is to describe; he stands impartial between Christian and Mohammedan; he is interested in neither one religion nor the other except as they are entangled in human lives. . . . He is back in his proper place when he takes us away from simple and absolute judgements and by returning to the

historical context entangles everything up again. He is back in his proper place when he tells us that a thing is good or harmful according to circumstances, according to the interactions that are produced. If history can do anything it is to remind us of those complications that undermine our certainties, and to show us that all our judgements are merely relative to time and circumstance.[35]

Butterfield's "manifesto" was a challenge to all historians. In fact, he was later to become interested specifically in the history of science, and we shall return to him shortly.

Among historians of science and medicine, Walter Pagel was one of the first to draw attention to the neglected figures of history.[36] But although his first book on van Helmont appeared in 1930, his widespread methodological influence is more recent, dating from the publication of his *Paracelsus* (1958) and his *William Harvey's Biological Ideas* (1967). Recognizing the fallacy of Sarton's "history of the gradual revelation of truth," Pagel has countered that such an approach "based on the selection of material from the modern point of view, may endanger the presentation of historical truth." Indeed, histories in which "discoveries and theories of the past are taken from their original context to be judged alongside modern scientific and medical entities" are likely to be dangerously misleading.[37]

How then should the historian of science proceed? Referring to his own research, Pagel has suggested that:

Instead of selecting data that "make sense" to the acolyte of modern science, the historian should therefore try to make sense of the philosophical, mystical or religious "side-steps" of otherwise "sound" scientific workers of the past, "side-steps" that are usually excused by the spirit or rather backwardness of the period. It is these that present a challenge to the historian: to uncover the internal reason and justification for their presence in the mind of the savant and their organic coherence with his scientific ideas. In other words it is for the histo-

35. Herbert Butterfield, *The Whig Interpretation of History* (1931; New York: W. W. Norton, 1965), 68, 73, 74, 74–75. For a recent discussion of Butterfield and "Whiggish" history see A. Rupert Hall, "On Whiggism," *History of Science* 21 (1983): 45–59.

36. Walter Pagel, *Jo. Bapt. Van Helmont: Einführung in die philosophische Medizin des Barock* (Berlin: Springer, 1930); *Paracelsus: An Introduction to Philosophical Medicine in the Era of the Renaissance* (Basel: S. Karger, 1958); *William Harvey's Biological Ideas: Selected Aspects and Historical Background* (Basel: S. Karger, 1967).

37. Walter Pagel, "The Vindication of Rubbish," *Middlesex Hospital Journal* (Autumn, 1945): 1.

rian to reverse the method of scientific selection and to restate the thoughts of his hero in their original setting. The two sets of thought—the scientific and the nonscientific—will then emerge not as simply juxtaposed or as having been conceived in spite of one another, but as an organic whole in which they support and confirm each other. There is no other way to lay the savant open to our understanding.

It has thus been Walter Pagel's desire to interpret the facts of medical and scientific history "as the outward expression of their time." When this has been done,

it will then appear that not only certain standards of technical equipment made discoveries possible, but that these can be seen also as the offspring of certain nonscientific ideas and of a particular cultural background. . . . The History of Medicine will then appear much more complicated than it does in the usual perspective of straight lines of progress. Yet we will have to embark on the cumbersome task of reconstructing ancient thought if we wish to write history—and not best sellers.[38]

Pagel once told me that after listening to Koyré lecture on Isaac Newton's physics he rose to ask about Newton's work on alchemy. Koyré dismissed the point by saying that "we are not concerned with that." From his point of view he was right, but for Pagel it is impossible to understand the "total man" unless we examine *all* of his work. Perhaps nothing better illustrates the basic differences between these two scholars than this anecdote.

Important though Pagel's work is, his influence may well have been less than that of the late Dame Frances Yates, who wrote a series of books relating the Scientific Revolution to Hermeticism. A literary historian, Dame Frances first attracted the attention of historians of science with the publication of her *Giordano Bruno and the Hermetic Tradition* in 1964.[39] Here was an attempt to assess the work of Bruno as a sixteenth-century supporter of the heliocentric theory not because he was a forward-looking scientist, but because the sun-centered system best accommodated his mystical, "Hermetic," views of the sun and the universe. This book is surely one of the most influential to have been published in the history of science in the past three decades. And on the whole this influence has been healthy, since she urged historians

---

38. Pagel, *Harvey's Biological Ideas*, 82; "Vindication of Rubbish," 4.
39. Frances A. Yates, *Giordano Bruno and the Hermetic Tradition* (Chicago: University of Chicago Press, 1964).

to cope with a vast body of texts that never should have been ignored in the past.

The Yates influence has also had dangerous side effects. Over whelmed by the importance of Hermeticism, Neoplatonism, magic, and other mystical strands of Renaissance philosophy, Frances Yates went on to ever more daring positions that were based upon less and less solid evidence. In *The Rosicrucian Enlightenment* (1972), she came close to insisting that the entire Scientific Revolution developed from Renaissance mysticism and magic. Here she strove to connect the origins of the Royal Society of London as well as the work of Descartes and Newton with John Dee and the Rosicrucian documents of the early years of the century.[40] Unfortunately, these suggestions have not been upheld by the sound historical evidence they require. They are speculations which must be considered doubtful at best.

The works of Pagel and Yates have generated considerable interest and debate. And it may be worth noting that neither of them represents any of the older, traditional fields in the history of science. Yates may best be described as a literary historian, while Pagel was a classicist and a pathologist as well as a historian of medicine. But they both offer a challenging approach to the history of science—one that may go far toward solving the entire problem of the Scientific Revolution.

Among historians of science the study of the pseudo-sciences has aroused the most conflict in relation to the proper interpretation of the work of Isaac Newton. All would agree that Newton represents the culmination of many strands of early modern physics, mathematics, and astronomy, but how is one to interpret the thousands of folios of alchemical manuscripts he wrote? Among the first to try to integrate them into a total picture of Newton has been R. S. Westfall, who had earlier discussed this author only in terms of the traditional internal history of science. By the early 1970s Westfall had become convinced that the Hermetic mysticism of the seventeenth century was an essential ingredient in Newton's thought and that this "could lead the relatively crude mechanical philosophy of the seventeenth-century science to a higher plane of sophistication." "The Hermetic elements in Newton's thought were not in the end antithetical to the scientific enterprise. Quite the contrary, by wedding the two traditions, the Hermetic and the

40. Frances A. Yates, *The Rosicrucian Enlightenment* (London: Routledge and Kegan Paul, 1972), 113, 171–205.

mechanical, to each other, he established the family line that claims as its direct descendants the very science that sneers today uncomprehendingly at the occult ideas associated with Hermetic philosophy." And, in the most recent contribution to the study of Newton's alchemy, B. J. T. Dobbs goes further to claim not only that much of Newton's most important work derives from his alchemical speculations, but that "in a sense the whole of his career after 1675 may be seen as one long attempt to integrate alchemy and the mechanical philosophy."[41]

It is little wonder that more traditional historians of science have expressed their fears of these new developments. At a meeting at King's College, Cambridge (1968), devoted to new trends in the field, P. M. Rattansi argued the case for contextual history, stating that the "historians' task cannot be that of isolating 'rational' and 'irrational' components, but of regarding it as a unity and locating points of conflict and tension only on the basis of an exploration in considerable depth." In reply, Mary Hesse argued against the inclusion in the field of subjects that were not truly scientific in modern terms. The pseudo-sciences might well belong to history, but they could not be considered as part of the history of science. Anticipating that such an approach might be considered exclusive, she added that it is essential that we should use modern science as a means of weighing the arguments of the past. To use judgments of the past that include nonscientific elements is a waste of our time. Indeed, she concluded, we must be careful what we read or permit ourselves to assess, since by "throwing more light on a picture, we may distort what has already been seen."[42] Hesse's reaction is by far the most extreme yet to surface from the more traditional historians and philosophers of science.

The impasse evident in the exchange between Hesse and Rattansi exhibits the tension currently existing in the field. And yet the role of the so-called pseudo-sciences is hardly the only source

41. Richard S. Westfall, "Newton and the Hermetic Tradition," in *Science, Medicine and Society in the Renaissance: Essays to Honor Walter Pagel*, 2 vols., ed. Allen G. Debus (New York: Science History Publications, 1972), 2: 195; B. J. T. Dobbs, *The Foundations of Newton's Alchemy: or, "The Hunting of the Greene Lyon"* (Cambridge: Cambridge University Press, 1975), 230.

42. P. M. Rattansi, "Some Evaluations of Reason in Sixteenth and Seventeenth-Century Natural Philosophy," in *Changing Perspectives in the History of Science: Essays in Honour of Joseph Needham*, ed. Mikuláš Teich and Robert Young (London: Heinemann, 1973), 150; Mary Hesse, "Reasons and Evaluations in the History of Science," in *Changing Perspectives*, 143.

for this. Perhaps the sharpest debate at the moment concerns the relation of science and society. Only a few years ago this seemed to be relatively unimportant. When Thomas S. Kuhn prepared a history of science for the *Encyclopedia of the Social Sciences* (1968), he compared "internalist" with "externalist" histories of science. The former dealt with technical questions related to the growth of science; the latter were "attempts to set science in a cultural context which might enhance understanding both of its development and its effects." Of special interest was the debate over the thesis proposed by Thomas K. Merton (1938), which sought to explain the success of seventeenth-century science in England by pointing to *(a)* the Baconian emphasis on practical arts and trade processes and *(b)* the stimulus of Puritanism in religion. But if Kuhn argued that internal and external histories of science are complementary, he also felt that this was an older argument made for the most part by scholars who had not succeeded in proving their point. He referred to the "new generation of historians" (that is, for the most part the Koyré inspired historians) who "claim to have shown that the radical sixteenth- and seventeenth-century revisions of astronomy, mathematics, mechanics, and even optics owed very little to new instruments, experiments, or observations. Galileo's primary method, they argue, was the traditional thought experiment of scholastic science brought to a new perfection."

This was far removed from the craft tradition or the new methodology of Bacon which failed consistently. As far as the seventeenth-century is concerned, he suggested that only the "new" sciences such as electricity and magnetism, chemistry, and thermal phenomena borrowed from the craft tradition.[43] The mathematical sciences should continue to be studied by internal methods.

Kuhn's much lauded *Structure of Scientific Revolutions* (1962) is an internalist study seeking to explain scientific revolutions in terms of the replacement of one scientific paradigm with another. With ever-increasing interest in nonscientific factors in the growth of science, this work has not strongly affected historians of science as much as one might expect. Rather, it has appealed most to social scientists, philosophers, and historians who have used it

43. Thomas S. Kuhn, "History of Science," in *International Encyclopedia of Social Sciences*, ed. David L. Sills (New York: Crowell Collier and Macmillan, 1968) 14:76–82.

less as a model for the history of science than to examine the internal development of their own fields.[44]

For Thomas Kuhn the new history of science was to be primarily internalist. However, the late sixties and the early seventies were to see an ever-growing interest in the interrelation of science with society. For this reason the history of science has become a field far more attractive to historians, philosophers, and social scientists, many of whom have had little training in either the sciences or the history of science. These authors argue that significant aspects of scientific history may now be grasped without the technical scientific knowledge that earlier seemed to be essential. There have been mixed results from this, since in fact, technical knowledge does remain important even in some of the most esoteric areas of the history of science. Still, a number of important studies have appeared. For example, Keith Thomas's *Religion and the Decline of Magic* (1971) is a monumental contribution to our understanding of the early modern intellectual scene in England. No less important is the work of Christopher Hill, who has used the recent studies of alchemy and the Paracelsians as an integral key to his understanding of the Civil War in England in his *The World Turned Upside Down* (1972).[45]

In *The Newtonians and the English Revolution, 1689-1720* (1976), Margaret Jacob has argued that the triumph of Newtonian physics may have been due less to the value of Newton's science than it was to the fact that English theologians in the period of the "Glorious Revolution" (1688) sought a powerful ally through their espousal of the Newtonian synthesis: "These churchmen . . . used the new mechanical philosophy in support of Christianity and in their assault on atheism and thus spread the ideas of the

44. Thomas S. Kuhn, *The Structure of Scientific Revolutions* (Chicago: University of Chicago Press, 1962). This book was also issued as vol. 2, no. 2 of the *International Encyclopedia of Unified Science* (Chicago: University of Chicago Press, 1962). As examples of Kuhn's appeal in the social sciences, see the following: Barry Barnes, *T. S. Kuhn and Social Sciences* (New York: Columbia University Press, 1982); Signe Seiler, *Wissenschaftstheorie in der Ethnologie: zur Kritik u. Weiterführung d. Theorie von Thomas S. Kuhn anhand ethnograph* (Berlin: Reimer, 1980); Garry Gutting, ed., *Paradigms and Revolutions: Appraisals and Applications of Thomas Kuhn's Philosophy of Science* (Notre Dame: University of Notre Dame Press, 1980).

45. Keith Thomas, *Religion and the Decline of Magic: Studies in Popular Beliefs in Sixteenth- and Seventeenth-Century England* (1971; Harmondsworth: Penguin, 1973); Christopher Hill, *The World Turned Upside Down: Radical Ideas During the English Revolution* (1972; New York: The Viking Press, 1973) (see especially 231-46).

new science and its concomitant natural philosophy. Without the sermons of the first latitudinarians, science would have remained esoteric and possibly even feared by the educated but pious public." She sees the new science as an explicit rejection of the older mechanical philosophies of Hobbes and Descartes as well as the Aristotelianism of the universities and the radical cosmologies of the mid-century, which had too often been associated with those who rose in rebellion against the Church and State.

> The obvious question of course, is why these liberal churchmen felt impelled to reject one science or natural philosophy and accept another. Historians of science have often presumed that the new mechanical philosophy triumphed in England simply because it offered the most plausible explanation of nature. It may do just that, but in my understanding of the historical process that made it acceptable the supposed correspondence of the new mechanical philosophy with the actual behavior of the natural order is not the primary reason for its early success.

For Jacob the social explanation of the triumph of Newtonianism is to be found in "its usefulness to the intellectual leaders of the Anglican Church as an underpinning for their vision of what they liked to call the 'world politick.' The ordered, providentially guided, mathematically regulated universe of Newton gave a model for a stable and prosperous polity, ruled by the self-interest of men."[46] In short, we see here an explanation of the Newtonian triumph on grounds totally divorced from the fact that Newton's work represents the culmination of nearly a century and a half of scientific discussions and research leading from the *De revolutionibus orbium* (1543) of Copernicus to the *Principia mathematica* (1687).

At a meeting of the American Association for the Advancement of Science held in December 1979, Charles C. Gillispie lashed out against those who followed newer trends in the field. As reported in *Science*, Gillispie complained that "the history of science is losing its grip on science, leaning heavily on social history, and dabbling with shoddy scholarship." He attacked those who discussed scientific problems but who had little or no scientific training.

---

46. Margaret C. Jacob, *The Newtonians and the English Revolution 1689–1720* (Ithaca, N.Y.: Cornell University Press, 1976), 17–18.

Less odious but still troublesome to Gillispie are social histories that ignore science altogether, such as studies that deal with the role of women in a particular scientific institution but omit their actual scientific work. . . . Another trend, he said, is that scholars focus on the personal and anecdotal: Newton on alchemy rather than on motion, Kekulé's snake dance rather than the benzene ring, Darwin's neurosis rather than his marshaling of evidence. Some so-called scholars focus on scandal. . . . "These scholars," says Gillispie, "have a lust for just the sort of thing most rigidly ruled out of court in the science we do now—the irrational, the personal."

Gillispie's plea for a return to the values of Koyré has been dismissed by the social historians, who have replied:

The social history of science has by now established itself within the discipline as a legitimate method of approaching the past. Despite recent rearguard action, notably by C. C. Gillispie, most historians accept that the traditional practices of analyzing theoretical developments within the sciences need to be supplemented by the study of the changing social foundations of scientific activity. The "internal vs. external" debates of the late 1960s are, one hopes, a thing of the past.[47]

A similar debate may be seen currently in the history of medicine, where it used to be considered essential for the scholar to take an M.D. prior to beginning work on a second doctorate in the history of medicine. His research was then expected to center on scientific aspects of medical theory and disease. This tradition continues, but it is no longer in the ascendant. Today the cutting edge of medical history is centered on the social setting of medicine. These historians are most frequently being trained through programs located in departments of history rather than the older departments or institutes of the history of medicine. And since these scholars do not have the medical training of their predecessors, we are witnessing debates in the learned journals relating to the subject matter and the proper training for the history of medicine.[48]

47. William J. Broad, "History of Science Losing Its Science," *Science* 207 (25 January 1980): 389; Paul Wood, "Recent Trends in the History of Science: The Dehumanisation of History," *BSHS Newsletter*, No. 3 (September 1980): 19.
48. See Leonard G. Wilson, "Medical History Without Medicine," *Journal of the History of Medicine and Allied Sciences* 35 (1980): 5-7; Lloyd G. Stevenson, "A Second Opinion," *Bulletin of the History of Medicine* 54 (1980): 135; Ronald L. Numbers, "The History of American Medicine: A Field in Ferment," *Reviews in American History* 10 (1982): 245-64; Gert H. Brieger, "The History of Medicine and the History of Science," *Isis* 72 (1981): 537-40.

At the death of George Sarton the history of science was established as a small field, but one that was recognized by many as having importance. However, because of its historical development it was to be found in the academic world most frequently in the form of programs independent of history or science. Most publishing historians of science twenty-five years ago had been trained as scientists. Sarton recognized this, but believed that in the future the professional historian of science should have at least two master's degrees—one in a science and the other in history—before proceeding on to his Ph.D. in the history of science. However, the influence of Koyré and a trend among philosophers away from the history of philosophy toward the philosophy of science emphasized the growth of independent programs in the history *and* philosophy of science. During the fifties and the sixties there were further discussions of the relationship of the history of science to both history and the sciences.

In 1956 it seemed clear that the history of science required an expertise in the sciences that seemed to set it apart from the training received by all but the most unusual historians. But at this time traditional historians were becoming aware of the tremendous impact of science and technology on our lives, and this gave rise to a certain urgency to learn more of this field. Thus, in a lecture entitled "The History of Science and the Study of History" in 1959, Herbert Butterfield said that, "Although the world had long known that science and technology were important, it is only recently that these things have taken command of our destiny—that destiny which we had learned from our history books to regard as depending so greatly on the wills of statesmen." He argued that historians must take into account the rise of modern science and that when they do this it will "change the whole character of historiography." And yet Butterfield did not challenge the independence of the history of science. In his still influential *The Origins of Modern Science 1300–1800* (1949), he presented the customary positivistic approach to the field that was current in the immediate post-war years.[49] The history of science must be understood by historians, but the field could rightly develop on its own because of the specialized knowledge it required. In fact, Butterfield's call for a greater awareness of science by historians was

49. Herbert Butterfield, "The History of Science and the Study of History," *Harvard Library Bulletin* 13 (1959): 329, 347; *The Origins of Modern Science 1300–1800* (New York: Macmillan, 1952).

heeded. As more and more doctorates were awarded in the history of science in the 1960s and the 1970s, most of these young scholars found themselves hired by departments of history rather than by the older independent programs in the history of science or the history and philosophy of science. This new interest among traditional historians surely accelerated the move toward new areas of research such as those I have already noted, the part played by the pseudo-sciences in the rise of modern science as well as more general topics relating science to society and culture.

The development of the field in recent decades has also reopened the question of the relationship of the history of science to the sciences. In the 1950s few scientists were more influential in arguing reform in scientific education than James B. Conant. World War II had shown clearly the need for more advanced scientific training for American youth. As a result, the method of teaching the sciences was rethought, and at the same time historical case-studies were introduced to give undergraduates not majoring in science the opportunity to see how the sciences have developed. But Conant, in a lecture delivered in 1960, stated that history was just as valuable for the scientist. He believed that scientific education was frequently too narrow and that the use of the case history approach would give students vision that would be broader and more informed. He outlined a new science curriculum that would prepare students first in the history of their own science specialty and then in the history of modern science. These courses were to be followed by others in the history of science taken in its widest possible sense and, only then, cultural and political history, which would be understood in connection with the earlier courses in the history of science. Because of its value for the sciences, Conant argued for strong history of science departments everywhere. He was far less enthusiastic about those who sought to equate the history of science with the social history of science—or the philosophy of science.[50]

Conant's ambitious plans for the historical training of scientists never bore fruit, although the case-history approach to science was extensively employed in American universities in the fifties and sixties. However, eventually these courses were largely abandoned. For scientists they seemed to move too slowly for the mass of material required to be taught. For historians of science

50. James B. Conant, "History in the Education of Scientists," *Harvard Library Bulletin* 14 (1960): 322–23, 325.

they were not historical enough, and for students with little interest in the sciences these courses were often less interesting than a concentrated survey course in a particular science might have been.[51]

Although there are several notable cases in the history of science in which a scientist's knowledge of much older literature led to a breakthrough, these cases are few and far between. I can recall a discussion presided over by Herbert Butterfield in 1959. There were some thirty students and faculty members present, and Butterfield asked if anyone knew of a case in which a knowledge of the history of science proved to be of direct value in a scientific discovery. I was the only one present who answered—and, that was only possible because I had then recently been working on the discovery of the inert gases and knew of Ramsay's reading of the eighteenth-century papers by Cavendish and of their influence on him.

Thomas Kuhn agreed that the sciences might not benefit much from the reading of the history of science. In 1968 he wrote:

> Among the areas to which the history of science relates, the one least likely to be significantly affected is scientific research itself. Advocates of the history of science have occasionally described their field as a rich repository of forgotten ideas and methods, a few of which might well dissolve contemporary scientific dilemmas. When a new concept or theory is successfully deployed in a science, some previously ignored precedent is usually discovered in the earlier literature in the field. It is natural to wonder whether attention to history might not have accelerated the innovation. Almost certainly, however, the answer is no. The quantity of material to be searched, the absence of appropriate indexing categories, and the subtle but usually vast differences between the anticipation and the effective innovation, all combine to suggest the reinvention rather than rediscovery will remain the most efficient source of scientific novelty.[52]

In general I would agree with Kuhn's conclusion that "we should not study the history of science only in the hope of finding long forgotten laws of discoveries still valid today." And yet the history of science does have a real value for scientists as well as nonscientists. Through a study of the earlier literature in his own field the

---

51. This assessment is my own after having taught courses of this genre for four years both at Harvard University and the University of Chicago during the years 1957–1959 and 1961–1963.
52. Kuhn, "History of Science," 81.

student will become aware of the scientific process. He should surely learn to appreciate the fact that the results we accept today were not generally arrived at in a simple manner, and that the same process of debate is part of science today. I have heard historians of astronomy argue that a knowledge of the history of astronomy does help to clarify current astronomical debates. And we find historians of Darwinian evolution active both in the biological sciences and in the heated Creationism debates.

In this discussion I have chosen to illustrate the changes in this rapidly growing field by concentrating on only a few factors: its growth in subject matter, the debates that have occurred over the introduction of the so-called pseudo-sciences and societal factors in the growth of modern science, and the discussion of the relationship of the history of science to both history and the sciences. I might well have turned to other topics, such as the new interest in the history of technology and its relationship to scientific research or the study of science in specific national settings, but I believe that the examples I have chosen will suffice to indicate the types of problems that have engaged the members of the profession over the past few decades.

I sometimes wonder what George Sarton would think of the field if he were still alive. At the time of his death his positivistic views were still dominant. Today they are passé. The history of science has developed to its present state in a relatively short period of time, but this maturity has also been accompanied by a decay of the comfortable sense of progress with which it was once identified. Indeed, the present defensive attitude of some historians of science indicates just how far the interest in new methodologies has penetrated the field. Today, in addition to scientists and historians of science, there are a number of historians, literary critics, and social scientists who are effectively applying the history of science to their own areas of research.

And yet there is really no need to fear—as Gillispie evidently does—that the history of science will lose its need for the technical data of the sciences. The history of science will always require technical research in the sciences and the histories so produced will always have value. But this does not mean that we should be unwilling to go beyond the technical monographic studies and the technical criticism that have characterized much of the post-war scholarship in this field. There must be room for syntheses that lead to a broader understanding of science as a whole as well as its interrelation with other areas of human endeavor. I think that we should learn to apply the method of Walter Pagel to understand discoveries in terms of the entire work of the discoverer and then go on to understand the discoverer in terms of the total intellectual milieu that shaped him. Only when this is done will it be possible for our histories to truly reflect the impact of science on civilization. Only when this is done will we see that there is no real conflict between the traditional internalist and externalist schools of the history of science. And only when this is done will the value of the history of science be universally accepted by historians and scientists alike.

THE SCIENTIFIC REVOLUTION
A Chemist's Reappraisal
Allen G. Debus

I have tried to indicate in the foregoing discussion that the traditional interpretation of the Scientific Revolution presents us with a relatively straightforward picture.[1] In it the rise of modern science is most commonly pictured as a conflict of "ancients" and "moderns," that is, those who remained faithful to Aristotle in natural philosophy and to Galen in medicine against those who espoused a certain "new philosophy" or a "new science" founded on fresh observations and experiments. It is the latter group that is normally associated with the mechanical philosophy of the seventeenth century.

The main thread of this story leads us from one great figure to another, through the work of Copernicus, Tycho Brahe, Kepler, Galileo, and Sir Isaac Newton. Of course, William Harvey is mentioned as well because of his discovery of the circulation of the blood, but, in general, biological developments are secondary to the restatement of Ptolemaic cosmological theory and the gradual solving of the new problems of the physics of motion associated with a moving earth. Bacon and Descartes are normally discussed also, but generally to show that neither of their scientific methodologies are satisfactory for science as we know it today. In short, the student is presented with a story of scientific progress that resulted in the establishment of the Copernican system and the foundation of classical mechanics.

If we hope only to follow the steps leading to the foundation of classical mechanics, then we will see little problem with this tra-

---

1. This essay was drawn heavily from numerous studies of mine written over the past twenty years. I refer the reader especially to "The Chemical Philosophers: Chemical Medicine from Paracelsus to van Helmont," *History of Science* 12 (1974): 235–59. This was based upon part of the manuscript of *The Chemical Philosophy: Paracelsian Science and Medicine in the Sixteenth and Seventeenth Centuries*, 2 vols. (New York: Science History Publications), which was not published until 1977. My view of the relationship of the Chemical Philosophy to other aspects of the Scientific Revolution was discussed in my *Man and Nature in the Renaissance* (Cambridge: Cambridge University Press, 1978).

ditional approach to the field. However, if we seek to understand nature in terms of those scholars who lived in the period of the Scientific Revolution, we may well find the traditional accounts unsatisfactory. If we try to understand their work from their point of view, we will not be able to be as selective in our choice of subject matter, since we will have to be led by their questions as well as our own. In short, we must decide whether we are to be "modernist" or "contextual" in our interpretation.

If we do turn to the broad spectrum of texts written at the time, we soon become aware that the concerns of authors interested in a new philosophy of nature went far beyond astronomy and the physics of motion. I think that there is little doubt that the most hotly debated subjects relate to medicine and chemistry—perhaps not defined in our terms, but rather in terms of a Chemical Philosophy of nature that was proposed as a proper replacement for the works of Aristotle and Galen still being taught at the universities. Even when we speak of "ancients" and "moderns" we must be careful, for when Libavius speaks of the "Philosophia nova," he uses this term to characterize the Paracelsians, whom he attacked. We must then be willing to examine other areas than physics if we wish to reevaluate the Scientific Revolution as a whole.

Of special interest for the historian of chemistry is the work of the Swiss-German physician, Paracelsus (1493–1541), and his followers. Their work is of interest to us today less for specific medical reforms than for their search for a new philosophy of nature based upon chemistry. Paracelsus had been influenced by traditional alchemy, by medical theory and practice, and by Central European mining techniques, but he went beyond all of these to develop an all-encompassing view of nature. He did believe in transmutation, but for him this goal was of far less importance than medical alchemy. This meant the use of chemical methods for the preparation of drugs, but in addition it meant a mystical alchemical approach to medicine that might apply to macrocosmic as well as to microcosmic phenomena.

The Paracelsians of the sixteenth century differ from other nature philosophers of the period in their emphasis on the importance of medicine and alchemy as bases for a new understanding of the universe. Characteristic of the Paracelsians was their firm opposition to the dominant Aristotelian-Galenic tradition of the universities. They rejected logic as a guide to truth (and therefore rejected mathematical abstraction, seeking an alternative to the Aristotelian elements), surely a mainstay of Scholastic natural philosophy, and they found no value in the humoral medicine of the Galenists. Rather, in their firm rejection of the Scholastic tradition, they emphasized the religious nature of their quest for knowledge and they claimed hidden truths they thought had not been fully recognized earlier in the Hermetic and Neoplatonic texts of late antiquity. The Paracelsian was convinced that man must seek an understanding of his Creator through the two books of divine revelation: the Holy Scriptures and the Book of Creation or Nature.[2] The latter would be understood only through fresh and unprejudiced study in the field and in the laboratory, rather than through a rehash of old books in disputations. Thus we find the early Paracelsian, Peter Severinus, telling his readers in 1571 to

> sell your lands, your houses, your clothes and your jewelry; burn up your books. On the other hand, buy yourselves stout shoes, travel to the mountains, search the valleys, the deserts, the shores of the sea, and the deepest depressions of the earth; note with care the distinctions between animals, the differences of plants, the various kinds of minerals, the properties and mode of origin of everything that exists. Be not ashamed to study diligently the astronomy and terrestrial philosophy of the peasantry. Lastly, purchase coal, build furnaces, watch and operate with the fire without wearying. In this way and no other, you will arrive at a knowledge of things and their properties.[3]

Indeed, the Paracelsians constantly called for a new observational approach to nature, and for them chemistry or alchemy seemed to be the best example of what this new science should be.

The Paracelsians were quick to offer an alchemical interpretation of Genesis.[4] Here they pictured the Creation as the work of a divine alchemist separating the beings and objects of the earth and the heavens from the unformed *prima materia*, much as the alchemist might distill pure quintessence from a grosser form of matter. On this basis it was possible to postulate the continued importance of chemistry as a key to nature.

The search for physical truth in the biblical account of the Cre-

2. See Allen G. Debus, "Mathematics and Nature in the Chemical Texts of the Renaissance," *Ambix* 15 (1968): 1–28, 211. On the Aristotelian elements and the Paracelsian principles, see Walter Pagel, *Paracelsus: An Introduction to Philosophical Medicine in the Era of the Renaissance* (Basel: S. Karger, 1958), 82–104; Debus, *Chemical Philosophy* 1:58–59, 69–70.

3. Petrus Severinus, *Idea medicinae philosophicae* (1571; 3d ed., Hagae Comitis, 1660), 39.

4. Ibid., 55–56 and passim.

ation focused special attention on the formation of the elements.[5] Paracelsus regularly used the Aristotelian elements, but he also introduced the *tria prima*—the principles of Salt, Sulfur, and Mercury. The latter were a modification of the old sulfur-mercury theory of the metals employed by Islamic chemists, but they differed from the older concept in that they were to apply to all things rather than be limited to the metals alone. The introduction of these principles had the effect of calling into question the whole framework of ancient medicine and natural philosophy, since these had been grounded upon the Aristotelian elements. Unfortunately, the fact that Paracelsus did not clearly define his principles tended to make this problem an ill-defined one, permitting each chemist to make his own interpretation.

In their attempt to understand the universe through chemical observations or analogies, the Paracelsians followed an old tradition, but one that was secondary in the alchemical literature to both gold-making and the preparation of chemical medicines. For the sixteenth-century Paracelsians it was commonplace to interpret both macrocosmic and microcosmic phenomena chemically. Thus, in the great world they explained meteorological events in terms of chemical analogies. On the geocosmic level they argued over differing chemical interpretations of the growth of minerals and the origin of mountain springs. And in their search for agricultural improvements, they postulated the importance of dissolved salts as the reason for the beneficial result of fertilizing with manure.[6] This theory proved to be the basis of later developments that were to result in a true agricultural chemistry.

It is not surprising that the Paracelsians should have approached their medicine as chemists. They felt assured that their knowledge of the macrocosm might be properly applied to the microcosm. Thus, if an aerial sulfur and niter were the cause of thunder and lightning in the heavens, the same aerial effluvia might be inhaled and generate burning diseases in the body. Humoral medicine was rejected *in toto*. Rather than discuss an imbalance of the bodily fluids leading to disease, as did the Galenists, these physi-

---

5. Ibid., 57–58; see also Pagel, *Paracelsus*, 82–104.
6. Allen G. Debus, "The Pharmaceutical Revolution of the Renaissance," *Clio medica* 11 (1976): 307–17; "Edward Jorden and the Fermentation of the Metals: An Iatrochemical Study of Terrestrial Phenomena," in *Toward a History of Geology*, ed. Cecil J. Schneer (Cambridge: MIT Press, 1969), 100–121; "Palissy, Plat and English Agricultural Chemistry in the Sixteenth and Seventeenth Centuries," *Archives Internationales d'Histoire des Sciences* 21 (1968): 67–88.

cians spoke rather of disease-forming substances entering the body through the air or through food, lodging in some organ, and causing organic disfunction. This was explained most often in terms of internal archei—forces within individual organs operating much as live alchemists in their laboratories.[7] When they failed to operate properly, it would be impossible to properly eliminate impurities from the body and disease would result.

The need for medical reform was underscored by the fact that the Renaissance was a period that witnessed new and violent diseases. The chief of these were the venereal diseases. These chemical physicians stated that their new stronger remedies—often prepared chemically from metals—were essential for the proper cure of these truly terrifying illnesses. There is little doubt that the sixteenth century saw important changes in the chemical preparation of medicines.[8] Paracelsus himself still reflected medieval distillation techniques, and his preparations were largely characterized by the search for a distilled quintessence—frequently this proved to be the original solvent. The true chemical products of the reaction were often discarded. But by the turn of the century such practices were undergoing change. Iatrochemists now turned less to distilled quintessences and more to precipitates and residues in their search for new remedies. This was to be essential for the understanding of chemical reactions.

But interesting as the details of this chemical approach to nature are, they would remain unimportant if they had been ignored at the time. In fact, in the century between 1550 and 1650 conflicts between the Paracelsians on the one hand and the Aristotelians

7. See Debus, *Chemical Philosophy* 1:96–109; Pagel, *Paracelsus*, 104–12.

8. Studies of particular interest include Robert P. Multhauf, "Medical Chemistry and 'The Paracelsians,'" *Bulletin of the History of Medicine* 28 (1954): 101–26; "The Significance of Distillation in Renaissance Medical Chemistry," *Bulletin of the History of Medicine* 30 (1956): 329–46; Wolfgang Schneider, "Der Wandel des Arzneischatzes im 17. Jahrhundert und Paracelsus," *Sudhoffs Archiv für Geschichte der Medizin und der Naturwissenschaften* 45 (1961): 201–15; *Geschichte der pharmazeutische Chemie* (Weinheim: Verlag Chemie, 1972). See also vols. 1, 5, and 14 in the series Veröffentlichungen aus dem Pharmaziegeschichtlichen Seminar der Technischen Universität Braunschweig (Wolfgang Schneider): G. Schröder, *Die pharmazeutisch chemischen Produkte deutscher Apotheken im Zeitalter der Chemiatrie* (Bremen: Veröff. aus d. Pharmaziegesch. Seminar der Technischen Universität Braunschweig, 1957); H. Wietschoreck, *Die pharmazeutisch-chemischen Produkte deutscher Apotheken im Zeitalter der Nachchemiatrie* (Braunschweig: Veröff, aus d. Pharmaziegesch. Seminar der Technischen Universität Braunschweig, 1962); M. Klutz, *Die Rezepte in Oswald Crolls Basilica chymica (1609) und ihre Beziehungen zu Paracelsus* (Braunschweig: Veröff. aus d. Pharmaziegesch. Seminar der Technischen Universität Braunschweig, 1974).

and the Galenists on the other were common. We must establish this point if we are to argue for their inclusion in accounts of the Scientific Revolution. As the tracts of Paracelsus were gradually recovered and published in the middle decades of the sixteenth century, they began to win converts to the new system. Soon systematized condensations of the rambling discourse of Paracelsus—such as that of Peter Severinus—were required for the chemical practitioners.

The growing numbers of chemical physicians made this school the subject of a lengthy attack by the learned Thomas Erastus, who served both as Professor of Theology at Heidelberg and as Professor of Theology and Moral Philosophy at Basel.[9] In his *Disputationes de Medicina Nova Paracelsi* (1572–1574) he pictured Paracelsus primarily as an ignorant man driven by ambition and vanity, a *magus* informed by the devil and evil spirits. He condemned him as an untrustworthy charlatan who continually contradicted himself, a man who knew no logic and consequently wrote in a totally disorganized and incomprehensible manner.

Erastus was wholly opposed to the philosophic system of Paracelsus. It was impious to compare the divine Creation to a chemical separation or to interpret the universe in terms of the macrocosm and the microcosm. Hardly less objectionable were the three principles of Paracelsus, which Erastus asserted, were not at all elementary in nature. Fire analyses and distillation procedures had produced them through the action of heat, and one could therefore rest assured that the Aristotelian elements remained the basic substances of nature.

Erastus objected also to the views of Paracelsus on disease. Here he argued that to assume that diseases are separate entities which enter man from without was unthinkable, and he reaffirmed that the traditional humoral medicine was truly the crowning glory of the Galenists. Hardly less objectionable was the role of innovator assumed by Paracelsus in his chemically prepared medicines. His theory of cure had led to the use of all kinds of minerals and metallic substances (he pointed particularly to the poisonous mercury compounds) which were nothing less than lethal poisons. How then was it possible that so many men were drawn to this medical heresy by the reports of the wonderful cures performed by Paracelsus? The fact is, Erastus answered, that these "cures" were at best temporary ones. In his search through the archives at Basel

9. The work of Erastus is discussed in Debus, *Chemical Philosophy* 1:131–34.

he was gratified to find that all those treated there with Paracelsian methods had died within a year even if they had shown an initial improvement.

In France a conflict between the Chemists and the Galenists resulted in a series of law suits regarding the use of metallic substances internally as medicines.[10] An initial victory by the Galenists in 1566 proved to be premature, and this was followed by bitter dispute in Paris throughout the remainder of the century. At that time a new series of books and pamphlets penned by Joseph Duchesne (1544-1609) in defense of the new chemicals resulted in further controversy on a subject which now inflamed authors from all parts of Europe.

Early in the new century Duchesne published two important books in which he defended the chemical remedies and the Paracelsian approach to nature. Pointedly he contrasted the Galenists with the Chemists. The former, he wrote, follow Galen "and as if by a royal decree where the sentence is firm and without doubt," they pronounce their medical decrees. The Chemists, however, place their faith not in books, but in reason and experience. This is the real basis of chemical medicine and the root of the disagreement between the Galenists and the Paracelsians.

Although Duchesne did pay lip service on occasion to both Galen and Hippocrates, it was clear that he hoped to ground both natural philosophy and medicine on the study of chemistry. It is understandable, then, that his more conservative medical colleagues might well feel threatened. Such indeed was to be the case. Duchesne's books were immediately answered in a condemnation written by the elder Jean Riolan, and the remainder of the decade was to witness the publication of a large number of pamphlets, monographs, commentaries, and volumes that alternately defended and attacked Galenic, Paracelsian and chemical medicine. By 1605 the dispute was widely known beyond the borders of France, and a number of the polemical tracts had been translated into other languages. An English version of Duchesne's books appeared as early as 1605, while in Germany Andreas Libavius (1540-1616) published a lengthy refutation of the censure of the chemists by the Parisian school of medicine. The younger Riolan wrote a response to this work, and this brought forth an *Alchymia triumphans* in 1607, which was a sentence by sentence reply to

10. For the French debate in the late sixteenth and early seventeenth centuries, see ibid., 145-73.

the French physician in a volume over nine hundred pages in length.

Joseph Duchesne died in 1609, but the debate was far from over. Six years earlier the first to defend him publicly had been his friend Theodore Turquet de Mayerne (1573–1655). For this action the medical faculty had forbidden his colleagues to consult with him, while Henry IV was urged to rescind his public offices. Outcast by the medical establishment in Paris, this same Turquet de Mayerne was invited to settle in England as Chief Physician to King James I in 1610.

In London the situation was far different.[11] For several decades the College of Physicians had been discussing the publication of an official pharmacopoeia. Their purpose was perhaps less for the benefit of the medical profession than it was to exert control over the pharmacists, the distillers, and the myriad unlicensed practitioners who preyed on the sick. But regardless of their reasons, it is clear that from the beginning the fellows of the London College were willing to accept those chemicals that proved to be of value medically.

Mayerne was to thrive in his new home. Elected a fellow of the college, he worked diligently for the official acceptance of chemicals in medicine. The result was the first official national pharmacopoeia, which was issued in 1618. The author of the preface (almost surely Mayerne) pointed out that although they venerated the learning of the ancients and listed their remedies, "we neither reject nor spurn the new subsidiary medicines of the more recent chemists and we have conceded to them a place and corner in the rear so that they might be as a servant to the dogmatic medicine, and thus they might act as auxiliaries." The *Pharmacopoeia Londinesis* was a compromise effort, and relatively few of the listed chemicals were highly controversial in nature. Still, their inclusion in the first official national pharmacopoeia clearly gave them a status they had not previously enjoyed, and at the same time the College had asserted its control over the acceptance of specific chemical medicines and the determination of the approved methods of preparation.

If Turquet de Mayerne represents the practical chemist urging

11. The English developments that led to the publication of the *Pharmacopoeia Londinensis* are summarized in ibid., 173–91. Much of the basic research on this publication was done by Georg Urdang. This was summarized by him in his introduction to the reprint of *Pharmacopeia: Pharmacopeia Londinensis of 1618* (Madison: University of Wisconsin Press, 1944).

the adoption of the new medicines, Robert Fludd (1574–1637) represents the mystic. Fludd, no less than Crollius, may be connected with Andreas Libavius. In 1614 and 1615 several anonymous pamphlets ascribed to an otherwise unidentified Rosicrucian Brotherhood presented a call for religious and educational reform.[12] The educational reforms were Paracelsian in tone and oriented toward medicine and chemistry. They were quickly translated into numerous languages and they elicited an astonishing response. Among those who attacked them was Libavius, who favored the new chemical medicines but saw in these works an adherence to the same sort of Paracelsian mystical cosmology that he opposed in the work of Oswald Crollius.

Fludd, on the other hand, hoped for the acceptance of a mystical worldview based on a fusion of Hermetic and Christian doctrine. He was delighted by the Rosicrucian tracts, and he sought to contact the brotherhood by writing a sharp reply to Libavius in 1616.[13] This short *Apologia* was to be the first of a steady stream of publications he was to write over the next twenty years. In these works he described in great detail a universal system founded upon the macrocosm-microcosm analogy, which depended upon the universal life spirit. This was for him the true Chemical Philosophy. I will say in passing that there are a number of aspects of his work that are of interest to all historians of science, but we do not have time to discuss them in detail here. The important point for us is that his mystical interpretation of the Chemical Philosophy became the subject of a heated debate.

The first volume of Fludd's many folios describing the macrocosm and the microcosm appeared in 1617. Here he attacked the Copernican system, and he turned to musical harmonies to explain the solar system. The latter for him was the proper application of mathematics to astronomy. This section was noted immediately by Johannes Kepler, who delayed the publication of his *Harmon-*

12. My views on the work of Robert Fludd and its relationship to the Chemical Philosophy are to be found in numerous articles. Many of these plus additional material are summarized in *Chemical Philosophy* 1:205–93. For a discussion of Fludd and the Rosicrucian literature, see 208–24, and *Robert Fludd and His Philosophical Key: Being a Transcription of the Manuscript at Trinity College, Cambridge*, (New York: Science History Publications, 1979).

13. Robert Fludd, *Apologia compendiaria fraternitatem de Rosea Cruce suspicionis et infamiae maculis aspersam, veritatis quasi fluctibus abluens et abstergens* (Leiden: Godfrid Basson, 1616). This was greatly expanded the following year to the *Tractatus apologeticus integritatem societatis de Rosea Cruce defendens* (Leiden: Godfrid Basson, 1617).

ices mundi (1619) to prepare an appendix directed against Fludd's concept of mathematics.[14] Here and in a second work (1621), Kepler emphasized the sharp distinction to be made between the true mathematician (Kepler), on the one hand, and the chemist, Hermeticist, and Paracelsian (Fludd) on the other. But although this distinction was hardly as clear as Kepler might have wished, it is true that the meaning of mathematics for Kepler was quite different than it was for Fludd. The latter sought mysteries in symbols according to a preconceived belief in a cosmic plan while the latter insisted that his hypotheses be founded on quantitative, mathematically demonstrable premises. If a hypothesis could not accommodate his observations, Kepler was willing to alter it; Fludd would not.

Although the Fludd-Kepler exchange is of considerable interest, the scope of the reaction to Fludd's publications among French scholars was to be much broader.[15] In France the Paracelsian medical debates of the late sixteenth and early seventeenth centuries had been accompanied by a steady flow of new and reprinted chemical texts. A new crisis occurred in 1624 when fourteen alchemical theses were defended at the residence of an influential Hermeticist. The meeting was dispersed on the order of the Parlement of Paris, the Doctors of the Sorbonne officially condemned the theses, and, before the end of the year, Jean Baptiste Morin had published a detailed *Refutation* of the alchemical position.

There may be no more influential figure in early seventeenth-century French science than Father Marin Mersenne (1588-1648). A friend of Descartes, Galileo, and Gassendi, he kept the savants of Europe up to date on current scientific research through his extensive correspondence. In two works published in 1623 and 1625, it is clear that he felt that a truly mathematically based science must first overcome the claims of the Chemical Philosophers. But although he was deeply concerned about the theological implications of the alchemical position, he did not reject alchemy *in toto*. To avoid wild speculations in the future, he sought the establishment of national alchemical academies which could police the field while taking as their goal the improvement of the health of mankind and the reform of science in its entirety. For Mersenne

14. Robert Fludd, *Utrisque cosmi maioris scilicet et minoris metaphysica, physica atque technica* (Oppenheim: T. De Bry, 1617). Debus, *Chemical Philosophy* 1:256-60.

15. The French scene, including Fludd's debate with Mersenne and Gassendi, are discussed in Debus, *Chemical Philosophy* 1:260-79.

a reformed alchemy would steer clear of religious, philosophical, and theological questions. Dreams and speculations such as the chemical interpretation of the Creation must be rejected if the subject was to gain the approval of the Catholic Church.

In the course of his work, Mersenne had singled out Fludd as a heretic and a magician. Deeply wounded, Fludd replied in two monographs in which he again described the analogy of the macrocosm and the microcosm, the harmony of the two worlds, the significance of the vital spirit, and its dispersal through the arterial system. True alchemy, Fludd insisted, has as its goal the establishment of the entire Chemical Philosophy as a basis of explanation for both man and the universe.

It is clear that Fludd's understanding of an "alchemia vera" was precisely what Mersenne sought to avoid. Above all, Fludd was disturbed by Mersenne's warning that alchemists should disassociate themselves from religious matters. This subject is one that seeks to comprehend the Creation and the spirit of life. Nature and supernature are surely united, and chemistry serves as a key to both.

In despair Mersenne sought support among other European scholars against Fludd's system of the world. To this end he sent a collection of Fludd's works to his friend Pierre Gassendi with an appeal for aid late in 1628. Gassendi, of course, rivals Mersenne as a founder of the mechanical philosophy because of his scholarly refutation of the Aristotelian philosophy and his efforts to establish an atomic explanation of matter. In little more than two months after receiving the books from Mersenne, Gassendi had completed his critique. In an impassioned passage Gassendi complained of Fludd's views, which would make "alchemy the sole religion, the Alchemist the sole religious person, and the tyrocinium of Alchemy the sole Catechism of the Faith." It is a devastating attack which is made even more interesting because of Gassendi's rejection of William Harvey's views on the circulation of the blood.[16] Mersenne, already aware of the *De motu cordis*, had sent this book to Gassendi along with the works of Fludd surely believing its author to be a disciple of his adversary. Gassendi rightly distinguished between the experimental work of the one and the "mystical anatomy" of the other. Fludd had earlier

---

16. Allen G. Debus, "Robert Fludd and the Circulation of the Blood," *Journal of the History of Medicine and Allied Sciences* 16 (1961): 374–93; "Harvey and Fludd: The Irrational Factor in the Rational Science of the Seventeenth Century," *Journal of the History of Biology* 3 (1970): 81–105.

written of a mystical circulation of the spirit of life in the body through the arterial system, but Gassendi rejected both Harvey and Fludd because he insisted on the Galenic system of the blood flow. This was the first significant debate on the Harveyan circulation and it is interesting to see Harvey interpreted as a disciple of Robert Fludd in a work centered on the fallacy of the chemical approach to nature.

Among those contacted by Mersenne in his crusade against Fludd was Jean Baptiste van Helmont (1579–1644) who was to carry on a rich correspondence with the French savant. In one of the earliest letters (1630) van Helmont answered a query on the value of Gassendi's then recent reply to Fludd. The Belgian physician-chemist was unequivocal as he referred to the "fluctuantem Fluddum," who was a poor physician and a worse alchemist, a superficially learned man on whom Gassendi should not waste his time. Yet, if van Helmont was at least temporarily included within the Mersenne circle, his work reveals that he had been deeply influenced by that of the earlier Paracelsians. In his first publication (1621) he had praised the macrocosm-microcosm analogy, Paracelsus and his three principles, and he had termed magic "the most profound inbred knowledge of things." This work was to lead to his prosecution for heresy by the Spanish Inquisition and to his imprisonment followed by house arrest. Among other charges he had been accused of following Paracelsus and his disciples in preaching his Chemical Philosophy, thus having spread more than "Cimmerian darkness" over all the world.[17]

Van Helmont's later works show a more critical approach, but there remains much to connect him with his chemical predecessors. Throughout we meet a strong plea for reform. It was necessary to "destroy the whole natural Phylosophy of the Antients, and to make new the Doctrines of the Schooles of natural Phylosophy." Ancient science and medicine were characterized as "mathematical" and logical, and this must be avoided at all costs in favor of a truly observational approach to nature. The new philosophy proposed by van Helmont was one that would seek to

---

17. On van Helmont, see Debus, *Chemical Philosophy* 2:295–379 and, especially for van Helmont's medical views, Walter Pagel, *Joan Baptista van Helmont: Reformer of Science and Medicine* (Cambridge: Cambridge University Press, 1982). J. B. van Helmont, *Disputatio de magnetica vulnerum naturali et legitima curatione, contra R. P. Joannem Roberti* (Paris: Victor Leroy, 1621). An important work, this clearly shows a different man than do the later tracts published in the post-1648 *Opera*. On his prosecution and arrest, see Pagel, 10–13.

reject any concept of nature interpreted primarily through mathematics.[18]

Throughout van Helmont's work may be noted the close association of nature and religion. Once again we are told to look first at the account of Creation in *Genesis*. This—as in the case of Fludd—ascertains the order of Creation and the true elements which are water and air. The *tria prima* may be useful to the practicing chemist, but they are not elementary. The key to nature is to be found in fresh observations—and it is chemistry that offers us our greatest opportunity for truth.

> I praise by bountiful God, who hath called me into the Art of the fire, out of other professions. For truly Chymistry, hath its principles not gotten by discourse, but those which are known by nature, and evident by the fire: and it prepares the understanding to pierce the secrets of nature, and causeth a further searching out in nature, than all other Sciences being put together: and it pierceth even unto the utmost depths of real truth.[19]

Coupled with this was an awareness that quantification—understood here as laboratory weights and measurements rather than mathematical abstraction—might well offer new insight.[20]

Although the willow tree experiment is the best known example, one may also cite his interest in the determination of specific gravities and a more accurate scale of temperatures for laboratory work. In the course of his work he was led to insist on the indestructibility of matter and the permanence of weight in chemical change.

Van Helmont's medicine reflects his background. Unwilling to accept the ancient medical texts, he was also disturbed by those who would accept everything ascribed to Paracelsus. Thus, in these later works, van Helmont rejected a doctrine of the microcosm which postulated man as an exact replica of the greater world. Still, this did not prevent him from calling attention to

18. J. B. van Helmont, *Ortus medicinae. Id est, initia physicae inaudita. Progressus medicinae novus, in morborum ultionem, ad vitam longam* (Amsterdam: Ludovicus Elsevir, 1648; Brussels: Culture et Civilisation, 1966), 6. The relevant texts on van Helmont's new philosophy are cited in Debus, *Chemical Philosophy* 2:312–17.

19. Debus, *Chemical Philosophy* 2:317–22. Van Helmont, *Ortus*, 463 [from the "Pharmacopolium ac dispensatorium modernorum" (sect. 32)]; here I am citing the contemporary English translation by John Chandler, *Oriatrike or Physick Refined* . . . (London: Lodowick Loyd, 1662), 462.

20. Debus, *Chemical Philosophy* 2:327–29.

numerous similarities that were to be found in both man and nature as a whole. For example, he considered disease in man to be a localized phenomenon and, although considerably more complex, similar in many ways to the growth of metals in the earth. Nor was van Helmont less concerned than Fludd with the vital spirit.[21] His belief in its existence in the blood was to be an influential factor in his firm rejection of bloodletting. No less important was his chemical investigation of digestion, which was to lead to the concept of acid-base neutralization and which he described with both physiological and inorganic examples.[22]

Like other Chemical Philosophers, van Helmont sought educational reform. We have noted this demand before, but van Helmont's work appeared in print at a time when numerous plans for educational reform were being proposed and being seriously considered. Convinced that the study of nature was the only goal to medical progress (and of attaining knowledge of our Creator), he wrote bitterly of his own education, which had led to no certainty and which had caused him at one time to decline a master's degree. If we are to progress, he argued, we must reject the Aristotelian studies of the universities and build a new science upon an entirely new educational system. Students should begin their work with simple subjects: arithmetic, geometry, geography, the customs of nations and an examination of plants and animals. After three years of these elementary studies, the young men might then proceed to the important part of their education—the study of nature. But the study of nature for van Helmont may be carried out satisfactorily in only one way, through chemical examination. These studies, carried out for four years, must not be accomplished

by a naked description of discourse, but by a handicraft demonstration of the fire. For truly nature measureth her work by distilling, moystening, drying, calcining, resolving, plainly by the same means, wereby [chemical] glasses do accomplish these same operations. And so the artificer, by changing the operations of nature, obtains the properties and knowledge of the same. For however natural a wit, and sharpness of judgement the Philosopher may have, yet he is never admitted to

21. The most complete discussion of van Helmont's biological ideas and theory of disease is to be found in Pagel, *van Helmont*, 96–198. Van Helmont, *Ortus*, 328; Allen G. Debus, "Chemistry and the Quest for a Material Spirit of Life in the Seventeenth Century," in *Spiritus: IVº Colloguio Internazionale del Lessico Intellettuale Europeo, Roma, 7–9 gennaio 1983*, ed. M. Fattori and M. Bianchi (Rome: Edizioni dell Ateneo, 1984), 245–63.

22. Pagel, *van Helmont*, 129–40.

the Root, or radical knowledge of natural things, without the fire. And so everyone is deluded with a thousand thoughts or doubts, the which he unfoldeth not to himself, but by the help of the fire. Therefore I confess, nothing doth more fully bring a man that is greedy of knowing, to the knowledge of all things knowable, than the fire.[23]

Convinced that the new Chemical Philosophy must supersede the now defunct studies of the schools, van Helmont predicted that it would be a small wonder to see just how much a student educated as he suggested "shall ascend above the Phylosophers of the University, and the vain reasoning of the Schooles."

Van Helmont's call for a chemical reform of education may have been pursued most ardently in England. Noah Biggs demanded a reform of the curriculum of medicine and natural philosophy that was clearly based upon the Helmontian blueprint in 1651, while John French wrote of "a famous University beyond Sea, that was faln into decay" that had been restored to its former glory through the encouragement of chemistry. More important was a debate in 1654 relating to education at Oxford and Cambridge.[24] In that year John Webster, a nonconformist and a chemist, demanded the abolition of scholastic methods at these seats of learning. He argued that divine truths would only be imparted through God's revelation to man in the Bible and also through the study of His created nature. Displaying a broad knowledge of recent work in medicine and the sciences, he called for an emphasis on new techniques in mathematics, the teaching of the Copernican system and the Harveyan circulation, and the use of atomic explanations. But above all, he felt that it was the Paracelsian and the Helmontian chemists who truly offered an observational and experimental program that might be emulated by others. The essential key must be chemistry, for this teaches the unfolding of nature's secrets through the use of manual operations. Like van Helmont, Webster noted that no philosopher is admitted to the root of science without a knowledge of fire. He added that one year of work in a chemical laboratory would prove more beneficial than centuries of disputes over the texts of Aristotle.

---

23. Van Helmont's short autobiography, the "Studia authoris," is printed in all editions of the *Ortus* and the *Opera*. Van Helmont, *Ortus*, 49–50; here I cite the Chandler translation (see note 19 above), 45.

24. John Webster, *Academiarum Examen, or the Examination of Academies . . .* (London: Giles Calvert, 1654); reprinted in Allen G. Debus, *Science and Education in the Seventeenth Century: The Webster-Ward Debate* (London: Macdonald, 1970), 67–192.

For the progress we might demand from this new science, this chemical science, nothing less than the destruction of the scholastic system seemed necessary. And when Seth Ward and John Wilkins rose immediately to challenge Webster on behalf of the current curriculum,[25] they soon found that their own dream of a new science founded on mechanical principles had more in common with the Aristotelians entrenched at the universities than that of the "experimental" chemists. There is no doubt that the chemists were the most vocal proponents of an educational reform based upon a program of the observational and experimental study of nature.

Of course, we all know that neither Oxford nor Cambridge, much less the other universities of Europe, reorganized their curricula to accommodate the reforms demanded by the chemists. The *Philosophia nova* that triumphed was that of the mechanists rather than that of the chemists. This may have been due to the superiority of their science, or it may have been due at least partly—as Jacob has suggested for the English scene—to the rejection of the Chemical Philosophy by latitudinarian churchmen who associated with it the religious enthusiasm and the radical politics that led to the Civil War.[26] We do know that few alchemists or Helmontian Chemical Philosophers were made fellows of the Royal Society of London at its founding in 1662. Nor do we see them being admitted in strength to the other national scientific societies of the late seventeenth or the eighteenth centuries. We know from their many new publications that they continued to be active, but their failure to be admitted to the academies shows clearly that they were not part of the new scientific establishment.

However, this does not mean that they had been unimportant in the century prior to the founding of the scientific academies in London and Paris. In that period there had been an enormous quantity of literature authored by the Chemical Philosophers—and we have shown that these works were widely read among a closely knit European circle of scholars. Erastus, Kepler, Libavius, Mersenne, Gassendi, and many lesser names were fully informed of the publications of the chemists. Their debate with the chemists had touched on a number of key questions related to the establishment of a new science: the value of the ancient philosophers, the

25. See Debus, *Science and Education*, 193-259.
26. Margaret C. Jacob, *The Newtonians and the English Revolution, 1689-1720* (Ithaca, N.Y.: Cornell University Press, 1976).

role of fresh observations and experiments, the use of mathematics in the interpretation of nature as it relates to reasoning, to the study of motion, and to the laboratory. Harvey's views on the circulation of the blood were first debated in this context, and here, no less than in the Copernican debates, the relation of science to religion was an important subject of concern. These subjects, and others besides, must be of interest to all who are concerned with the period of the Scientific Revolution.

The importance of the Chemical Philosophers might be difficult to understand if we limited ourselves only to medicine: the introduction of chemically prepared medicines, the concept of disease, or even the general problems of medical theory. The Paracelsians were not only physicians. They must be understood also as Chemical Philosophers of nature, scholars who consciously sought the replacement of ancient knowledge with a "new philosophy" founded on the twin pillars of true religion and fresh— chemically based—observations. Because of the similarities of the greater and lesser worlds—whether considered literally as with the earlier Paracelsians or metaphorically as with the mature van Helmont—medicine played a central role in their concept of a new knowledge of nature.

It is possible to note the direct influence of these Chemical Philosophers in the general acceptance of the chemical medicines in the course of the seventeenth century, in the persistent chemical search for a vital spirit, and in the widely held chemically oriented systems of physiology proposed by authors such as Willis or de la Böe Sylvius. It is indeed difficult to understand Charleton, Boyle, Mayow, Becher, Glisson, or even Isaac Newton without some knowledge of this then widely accepted approach to nature.[27] Medical topics are frequently discussed and understood in relation to element theory, the chemical theory, and properties of the earth and the generation and growth of metals. Not only must the student of this Chemical Philosophy be prepared to investigate these topics, he should also expect to find in the chemical texts other subjects as widely separated as educational, economic, and agricultural reform.

There are some who would argue that we may safely ignore these works. I referred earlier, for instance, to Mary Hesse's defense of a more traditional interpretation of the Scientific Revolution. She

27. These connections are drawn in greater detail in Debus, *Chemical Philosophy* 2:447–537.

rejected current research on the Hermetic sources and then went on to state that "throwing more light on a picture may distort what has already been seen."[28] We may ask in reply whether the picture we have seen in the past has been distorted and suggest that this might be clarified with additional light. Surely the study of the large body of Paracelsian-Helmontian literature of the seventeenth century will add immeasurably to the complexity of our understanding of the rise of modern science. But can we ignore it if this literature was read and debated at the time? To assume that our ignorance of it will ensure a more accurate interpretation seems to me to be a most remarkable conclusion. Traditional accounts should be called what they are—the history of physics and astronomy in the sixteenth and seventeenth centuries.

If we are to act as responsible historians we must try to judge historical events in the context of the period they occurred. If we do this for the Scientific Revolution, we find that a major debate centered on the acceptance or the rejection of the Chemical Philosophy. For this reason the debate must play a fundamental role in our future histories of science and medicine as well.

---

28. Mary Hesse, "Reasons and Evaluation in the History of Science," in *Changing Perspectives in the History of Science: Essays in Honour of Joseph Needham*, ed. Mikuláš Teich and Robert Young (London: Heinemann, 1973), 143.

ALCHEMICAL DEATH AND RESURRECTION
The Significance of Alchemy in the Age of Newton

Betty Jo Teeter Dobbs

With the study of alchemy one enters into another world, a world with presuppositions so different from those of the twentieth century that they baffle the modern scholar. Even the great historian Herbert Butterfield judiciously omitted alchemy from his classic study of the origins of modern science: "Concerning alchemy it is more difficult to discover the actual state of things, in that historians who specialise in this field seem sometimes to be under the wrath of God themselves; for, like those who write on the Bacon-Shakespeare controversy or on Spanish politics, they seem to become tinctured with the kind of lunacy they set out to describe."[1] One can but hope Butterfield's judgment was not universally accurate, for the present essay is an attempt to reconstruct by historical methods some of the meaning of alchemical texts and illustrations.

The matter indeed is not entirely hopeless if one is willing to accept the guidance of one of alchemy's most distinguished practitioners, Isaac Newton. As is now fairly well known, Newton devoted many years to alchemical studies.[2] Born in 1642 and dying in 1727, Newton is of course better known as a founder of modern science, a great mathematician and physicist who invented the calculus, found the law of universal gravitation, and satisfactorily explained the spectrum of colors in rainbows and prisms. It is certainly true that he did all those things, but he spent most of his time on alchemical and theological studies,[3] and he left behind

1. Herbert Butterfield, *The Origins of Modern Science, 1300–1800*, rev. ed. (New York: Free Press, 1965), 141.

2. See B. J. T. Dobbs, *The Foundations of Newton's Alchemy: or "The Hunting of the Greene Lyon"* (Cambridge: Cambridge University Press, 1975); *The Janus Faces of Genius: The Role of Alchemy in Newton's Thought* (Cambridge: Cambridge University Press, 1992).

3. B. J. T. Dobbs, "Newton as Alchemist and Theologian," in *Standing on the*

large numbers of manuscripts on alchemy and theology that are only now, in this present generation, being seriously studied. It is that Newton, that other Newton, who may guide one into the alchemical maze and out again.

Of the approximately one million words on alchemy that Newton left in manuscript, some of the most enlightening are in a set of papers that now belongs to the Smithsonian Institution and is housed in the Dibner Library of the History of Science and Technology.[4] A generous gift to the nation in 1974 from the Burndy Library of Norwalk, Connecticut, founded the Dibner Library; it was a gift that included manuscripts and books collected by Dr. Bern Dibner over a period of many years. Dr. Dibner had purchased this particular Newtonian manuscript in London during World War II or shortly thereafter.[5] In saving it from the general chaos of that period, Dibner performed a very special service, for it is this manuscript more than any other that provides the clues for an interpretation of early modern alchemy.

Newton left the manuscript untitled and undated, but he probably wrote it about 1672, when he had been studying alchemy for some four years, and its incipit makes an appropriate title: "Of Natures obvious laws & processes in vegetation." In particular, Newton concentrated in this manuscript on the vegetation of metals, but he was convinced that the processes of vegetation were similar in all three kingdoms of nature—the animal kingdom, the

---

Shoulders of Giants: A Longer View of Newton and Halley. ed. Norman J. W. Thrower (Berkeley: University of California Press, 1990), 128–40.

4. Dibner MSS. 1031B, Dibner Library of the History of Science and Technology, Special Collections Branch, Smithsonian Institution Libraries, Washington, D.C. The first public notice of the existence of this manuscript appeared in *A Catalogue of the Portsmouth Collection of Books and Papers written by or belonging to Sir Isaac Newton . . .* (Cambridge: Cambridge University Press, 1888), Section II (1), no. 31, p. 12, where it was described as an "abstract of a treatise on Nature's obvious laws and processes in vegetation." Returned to the family at that time, it was sold at auction in 1936: *Catalogue of the Newton Papers Sold by Order of the Viscount Lymington . . .* (London: Sotheby, 1936), lot 113, p. 17, where it was described as "[Vegetation of Metals: draft of a Short Treatise, *incomplete* (in English)] *about* 4500 *words*, 12 *pp.* autograph, with many corrections and alterations, *sm.* 4 *to."* It is now described as "*Vegetation of metals* [between 1660 and 1727]. [12] p.; 22 cm., Holograph notes on vegetation and the generation of minerals, as well as air, heat, fire, cold and God. Last page only in Latin." *Manuscripts of the Dibner Collection in the Dibner Library of the History of Science . . .* (Washington, D.C.: Smithsonian Institution Libraries, 1985), no. 80, p. 7.

5. Personal communication to the author from Dr. Bern Dibner, 26 July 1977. When subsequently pressed for more details, he responded that it seemed at the time more important to rescue those fragile pieces of paper from the Blitz than to keep records of the transactions, a judgment with which one may heartily agree.

vegetable kingdom, and the mineral kingdom. He said the metals vegetate after the same laws as those observed in the vegetation of plants and animals, and that vegetation is the effect of a latent spirit that is the same in all things.[6] The manuscript continues through twelve closely written pages, with many corrections and alterations as Newton pondered the issues involved in nature's obvious laws and processes in vegetation, and especially in the vegetation of metals, which is what one usually calls alchemy.

Let us follow Newton then into that other and largely forgotten world, to learn something about the incredible treasures the old alchemists thought were hidden at the center of the alchemical maze: the secret of life itself, and also the secrets of perfection and final salvation. The concepts of death and resurrection had, in the age of Newton, a rich alchemical meaning and a deep significance far beyond the popular image of alchemy as misbegotten and superstitious efforts to make gold.

Alchemical Vitalism

The problems that Newton hoped to solve through his study of alchemy were especially intense in the seventeenth century. The so-called mechanical philosophy had been established earlier in the century by Descartes and other philosophers, and by Newton's time the mechanical philosophy was generally accepted by the community of natural philosophers as the most promising way of approaching the study of the natural world. The mechanical philosophy was predicated upon the existence of atoms or corpuscles—discreet particles of matter—that were in constant motion. All events in the natural world were to be explained by matter and motion, by the tiny particles of a passive, inert matter that transferred motion by pressure on, or impact with, other small particles. But because of the general passivity of matter in the mechanical philosophy, certain problems arose regarding cohesion and life. How can passive little billiard balls of matter cohere and stick together in organized forms? How can those tiny passive particles of a common universal matter combine to produce the immense variety of living forms to be found in the world? Intuitively, one perceives the cohesion and differentiation of liv-

6. Dibner MSS. 1031B, f. 1r.

ing forms to be qualitatively different from anything that the mechanical motion of small particles of matter might produce.[7]

It was Newton's conviction that the passive particles of matter could *not* organize themselves into living forms. Their organization required divine guidance, the latent spirit that he said was present in all things, a vitalistic and active spirit that could guide the particles of passive matter into all the beautiful forms of plants and animals and minerals that God had ordained. It was a "vital agent," or a "fermental virtue," as he sometimes called it, or in the Smithsonian manuscript, the "vegetable spirit."[8] It was the secret of this spirit of life that Newton hoped to learn from alchemy.

Vitalism seems to belong to the very origins of alchemy. In the early Christian centuries, when alchemical ideas were taking shape, metals had not been well characterized as distinct chemical species. Metals were thought then to have variable properties, somewhat like modern metallic alloys that vary in their properties according to what is in the mixture. Or perhaps more frequently at that time, metals were conceived as similar to a mix of bread dough—a homely but effective analogy. The injection of a leavening agent such as yeast into a mixture of flour and water brings about desirable changes by a process of fermentation; perhaps a metallic mixture could also be induced to ferment, by the introduction of a suitable leaven, and then ripen into the desired form of gold. Sometimes, apparently, the alchemists also thought of their metallic mixtures as similar to a material matrix or womb of unformed or immature matter, a female principle into which the injection of an active male sperm or seed might lead to a process of generation and the creation of the more perfect metal, gold. By analogy, alchemists referred to this critical phase of the alchemical process as "fermentation" or "generation," and the search for the vital ferment or seed became a fundamental part of their quest.[9]

---

7. Dobbs, *Foundations,* 100–105; B. J. T. Dobbs, "Newton's Alchemy and His Theory of Matter," *Isis* 73 (1982): 511–28.
8. Dibner MSS. 1031B, f. 4r. See also Dobbs, "Newton's Alchemy and His Theory of Matter."
9. Marcellin Pierre Eugene Berthelot, *Les origines de l'alchimie* (1885; reprint, Paris: Librairie des Sciences et des Arts, 1938), 240–41. Similar ideas occur in Aristotle (*De generatione animalium*, 1.1, 715b26; 1.16, 721a8; 1.2, 716a17; 2.3, 736b30; 2.4, 738b23) and were commonplace in Newton's time; see Rosalie L. Colie, *Light and Enlightenment: A Study of the Cambridge Platonists and the Dutch Armenians* (Cambridge: Cambridge University Press, 1957), especially 117–44. For a pictorial representation of the alchemist sowing seeds of gold in "white foliated

Newton was confident that the vital agent was in some sense divine, for it was so defined against passive matter as an "active" principle in the time-hallowed traditions of both Platonism and Stoicism. Inspired by his interest in this divine active principle, he sought in alchemy the source of all the apparently spontaneous processes of fermentation, putrefaction, generation, and vegetation—that is, everything associated with normal life and growth, such as digestion and assimilation, for the word "vegetation" was originally from the Latin *vegetare*, to animate or enliven. Such processes produced the endless variety of living forms and simply could not be explained by the mechanical action of inert corpuscles. Mechanical action could never account for the process of assimilation, in which food stuffs are turned into the bodies of different animals, vegetables, and minerals, Newton said. Nor could it account for the sheer variety of forms in this world, all of which had somehow sprung from a common lifeless matter. [10]

As illustrative of what Newton meant by his vegetable spirit, one may select some familiar examples from the work of the nineteenth-century painter Vincent van Gogh. Van Gogh was keenly aware of the exuberant forces of vegetation in the world around him. One need only recall the writhing sunflowers and the rhythmic dance of stately irises, none quite like another; the vibrant fields of grain from which surprising birds fling themselves into the air; the wind-tormented pines; the brooding cypresses; the coiled fire of stars. A "life force" seems to hover over van Gogh's later canvases as he struggled to express its apparently insatiable appetite for variety, for richly differentiated forms, for color, for unexpected activity. [11] One should not discount the young Isaac Newton's sensitivity to similar scenes, for he was after all a coun-

earth," see Emblema VI of Michael Maier's *Atalanta fugiens* (1618), recently reproduced in Stanislaus Klossowski de Rola, *The Golden Game: Alchemical Engravings of the Seventeenth Century* (London: Thames and Hudson, 1988), 74, 98.

10. See Dobbs, "Newton's Alchemy and His Theory of Matter"; and B. J. T. Dobbs, "Newton's Alchemy and his 'Active Principle' of Gravitation," in *Newton's Scientific and Philosophical Legacy*, ed. P. B. Scheuer and G. Debrock, International Archives of the History of Ideas, no. 123 (Dordrecht: Kluwer Academic Publishers, 1988), 55–80; Dibner MSS. 1031B, ff. 5v–6r. See also Dobbs, *Janus Faces*, chap. 2.

11. See, for example, the following paintings reproduced in A. M. Mammacher, *Genius and Disaster: The Ten Creative Years of Vincent van Gogh* (New York: Harry N. Abrams, n.d.): *A Wheat Field* (1887), 29; *Sunflowers* (1888), 78; *Irises* (1890), 117; *The Enclosed Field* (1890), 119; *The Starry Night* (two versions, 1889), 120–21; *Storm-beaten Pine Trees against a Red Sky* (1889), 123; *Wheat Field with Cypresses* (1889), 127; *Road with Cypresses* (1890), 135; *Cypresses with Two Figures* (1889), 149; *Crows over the Wheat Field* (1890), 175.

try boy. Could one obtain such beauty and such natural variety from the gray mechanical motion of particles of inert matter? No. Hence the inference that the guiding divine principle of life has been at work in their organization and direction. That divine guiding spirit was Newton's vegetable spirit, the active agent of the alchemical work.

The same spirit was at work in the organization of matter in the original creation, and the work of creation was often treated in the early modern period as a chemical or alchemical process. Figure 1 is an alchemical emblem of creation that appeared with a collection of alchemical treatises in 1678.[12] The alchemists often compared the alchemical work to creation, quoting the critical passages from the first chapter of Genesis: "In the beginning God created the heaven and the earth. And the earth was without form, and void; and darkness was upon the face of the deep. And the Spirit of God moved upon the face of the waters. And God said, Let there be light: and there was light."[13] The light then became God's agent for the remainder of the work of creation, operating upon the original chaos to separate out the earthly globe (fig. 1, roundel 5); to separate the elements of earth, air, fire, and water from each other and to create plant life (roundels 6 and 7); to organize the heavenly bodies—the sun to rule by day and the moon by night, and the stars also (roundel 8); to call forth "every living creature that moveth"—whales and fishes in the sea, winged fowl, the beasts of the earth (roundel 9); finally, Adam and Eve themselves (roundel 10).[14]

12. "Janitor Pansophvs, Seu Figura Aenea Quadripartita Cunctis Museum hoc Introeuntibus, Superiorum ac Inferiorm Scientiam Mosaico-Hermeticum, analyticè Exhibens," Figura III, in *Musaeum Hermeticum reformatum et amplificatum, omnes sophospagyricae artis discipulos fidelissimè erudiens . . .* (Francofurti: Apud Hermannum à Sande, 1678). A modern facsimile reprint exists, introduced by Karl R. H. Frick (Graz-Austria: Akademische Druck-u. Verlagsanstalt, 1970), and Arthur Edward Waite's English translation of 1893 has been reprinted in 2 vols. (New York: Samuel Weiser, 1973). See also Fludd's numerous and imaginative illustrations of Creation, now conveniently gathered in Joscelyn Godwin, *Robert Fludd: Hermetic Philosopher and Surveyor of Two Worlds* (Boulder, Colo.: Shambhala, 1979).

13. Genesis 1:1–3. For the alchemical use of this passage, see, for example, Eirenaeus Philalethes, *Secrets Reveal'd: or, An Open Entrance to the Shut-Palace of the King . . .* (London: W. Godbid for *William Cooper,* 1669), 9. For a survey of the general predilection of early modern chemists and alchemists to interpret creation as a chemical or alchemical process, see Allen G. Debus, *The Chemical Philosophy: Paracelsian Science and Medicine in the Sixteenth and Seventeenth Centuries,* 2 vols. (New York: Science History Publications, 1977).

14. Genesis 1:4–27.

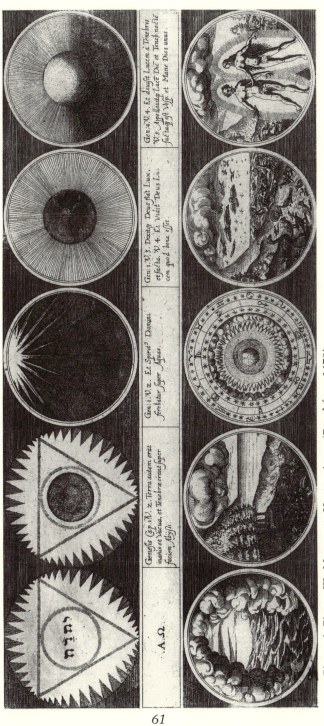

Figure 1. Figure III, *Musaeum Hermeticum* (Frankfort, 1678).

The light that was God's creative agent in the beginning could thus be identified with the active alchemical agent. Newton made that identification explicit, saying that the vegetable spirit might be the body of light, and many of the alchemists used the term "illumination" to describe the alchemical activation of matter.[15]

In summary, then, one may say that the creation itself was widely viewed in the sixteenth and seventeenth centuries as a chemical or alchemical process, and that the alchemists compared the illumination or activation of lifeless matter in alchemy with God's use of light at the beginning of the world. The alchemical emblem in figure 1 also expresses that same sense of the bursting vitality of creativity that one sees in van Gogh's vegetable world—an urgent description of life and growth, of the multiplication and ramification of life into the unexpected, the unpredictable, and the new, as God's creative fiat works his will upon the original creation. That emblem gives the viewer a vivid representation of divine cosmic creativity and it also expresses something of what the alchemists hoped to achieve themselves in their creative alchemical opus.[16]

Alchemical Death and Resurrection

So far this essay has stressed alchemical vitality, alchemical life at the microcosmic level that one sees in all the ramifying and incredible variety of what one would now call the biosphere, and also at the cosmic level in the divine creative surge of activity in the original week of creation. It is now time to consider the themes of alchemical death and resurrection, which are best understood against the background of alchemical vitalism.

Illumination, or the activation of matter, had a symbolic, metaphorical significance in alchemy. Light represented the power of God to activate or reactivate *lifeless* matter. The alchemical usage was closely akin to the iconographic tradition of representing the divine power by light rays. In many Annunciations the Christ

15. Dibner MSS. 1031B, f. 4r. For an example of this use of *illumination*, see Eirenaeus Philalethes, *Secrets Reveal'd*, 73, 108.
16. For the perennial sense of the ever-ramifying living spontaneity of the cosmos restated in terms of modern cosmogonic theory, see J. McKim Malville, *The Fermenting Universe: Myths of Eternal Change* (New York: The Seabury Press, 1981).

child entered Mary's womb on a beam of light.[17] The same iconographic tradition holds in the representation of the alchemical
process in figure 2, where divine power enters the alchemical flask
by means of the rays of the sun and the moon.[18]

The activation of lifeless matter by divine power was a common
concept in early modern Europe. As in alchemy with regard to the
activation of mineral matter by God's power, so also in questions
of generation in the other kingdoms of nature. Spontaneous generation had been an accepted fact for time out of mind, sanctioned
by Aristotle and vouched for by a host of pre-microscopic empirical observations.[19] Yet even though in the sixteenth and seventeenth centuries it was an almost unquestioned natural event,
spontaneous generation was still thought to need a precipitating
trigger—the warmth of the sun or an act of God, or perhaps both.
In addition to the authority of Aristotle and of observation, there
was the authority of Genesis. God had said, "Let the earth bring
forth," and it was so.[20] What God had done in the beginning, He
could still do. The most orthodox interpretation of the generation
of eels from mud, or of maggots from putrefying flesh, was that
God's creative power had brought them forth, that the power of
God had activated lifeless matter.

In sexual generation, the authority of the great seventeenth-
century physician William Harvey stood foursquare behind the
same concept. It is not the cock's semen per se, in and of itself,
that conveys fertility to the hen, Harvey said. Rather, it is "the
spirit and virtue of a divine agent" with which the semen is
imbued.[21]

The spirit and virtue of a divine agent, without which there will
be no new life—how similar Harvey's statement was to much of

17. James Hall, *Dictionary of Subjects and Symbols in Art*, rev. ed. (New York:
Harper and Row, 1979), s.v. "Annunciation." See *The Annunciation* by the Florentine Bicci de Lorenzo (1373-1472), *The International Style: The Arts in Europe
around 1400* (Baltimore: Walters Art Gallery, 1962), 2-4 and plate 29. An especially good example is the Annunciation in the central panel of the Mérode altar-
piece by the Master of Flémalle, New York, Metropolitan Museum of Art, Cloisters
Collection.

18. Frontispiece, A. T. Limonjon (Sieur de St. Didier), *Le triomphe hermetique,
Ou La Pierre Philosophale victorieuse . . .* (Amsterdam: Chez Henry Wetstein,
1689).

19. John Farley, *The Spontaneous Generation Controversy from Descartes to
Oparin* (Baltimore: Johns Hopkins University Press, 1977), 1-15.

20. Genesis 1:11.

21. William Harvey, *Anatomical Exercises on the Generation of Animals*, vol.
28 of *Great Books of the Western World* (Chicago: William Benton for *Encyclo-
paedia Britannica*, 1952), 404.

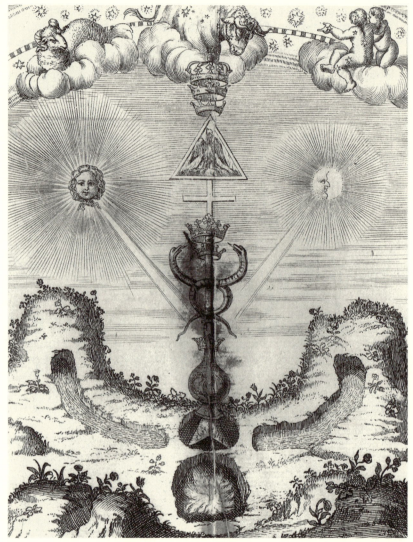

Figure 2. Frontispiece, A. T. Limonjon (Sieur de St. Didier), *Le triomphe hermetique* (Amsterdam, 1689).

what one finds in alchemy on the activating, vegetative principle without which the life of metals is lost. As Newton had observed, the vital agent was the same in all three kingdoms.

As vegetative spirit, as the agent of fertility, the alchemical agent was associated especially with the light received by the earth during the season of spring, the season of resurrection and new life. The presence of the alchemical spirit in fact was often symbolized by the spring zodiacal signs, as it is at the top of figure 2: Aries, Taurus, Gemini—the Ram, the Bull, and the Twins. One may explain that association by quoting from Virgil's *Georgics*, as William Harvey did, a passage that would then have been familiar to every educated person:

> Earth teems in Spring, and craves the genial seed.
> The Almighty father, AEther, then descends
> In fertilizing shower, into the lap
> Of his rejoicing spouse, and mingling there
> In wide embrace sustains the progeny
> Innumerous that springs. The pathless woods
> Then ring with the wild bird's song, and flocks and herds
> Disport and spend the livelong day in love.[22]

There are, however, other significant symbols employed in this emblem, several of which point even more directly to death and resurrection. In the flask there is a pelican. The habits of the pelican were explicated in the anonymous bestiary *Physiologus*, perhaps written as early as the second century A.D. in Greek and later to become the model for many Latin bestiaries. According to *Physiologus*, the pelican is a bird that pierces its own breast in order to feed its young ones with its own blood. The pelican became a symbol of the sacrifice of Christ on the cross, where Christ shed his blood to redeem mankind.[23] That motif is repeated in the central figure of the entire composition, the cross, which similarly points to Christ's redemptive sacrifice. The cross has an even broader significance, to which one must return later, but just above the cross one finds the phoenix enclosed in a triangular space. A fabulous creature of great beauty discussed by Herodotus, Ovid, the elder Pliny, and others, the phoenix was

22. Virgil, *Georgics*, 2. 323–29, quoted in Harvey, *Anatomical Exercises*, 346. See also the more extended contemporary discussion of these ideas in chapter 3 of book 2 of Thomas Burnet, *The Sacred Theory of the Earth*, 2d ed. (1690–1691; reprint, Carbondale, Ill.: Southern Illinois University Press, 1965), 148–49.

23. Hall, *Dictionary*, s.v. "Pelican," and "Crucifixion," 86; George Ferguson, *Signs and Symbols in Christian Art.* (New York: Oxford University Press, 1966), s.v. "Pelican" (where one notes that the pelican also symbolized the Eucharistic Sacrament). On *Physiologus*, see Jerry Stannard, "Natural History," in *Science in the Middle Ages*, ed. David C. Lindberg, Chicago History of Science and Medicine, Allen G. Debus, ed. (Chicago: The University of Chicago Press, 1978), 429–60.

thought to live to the great age of three to five hundred years, only finally to burn itself upon a funeral pyre. From the ashes of its self-sacrifice, a new, young phoenix arose and began a fresh cycle of life. Christians adopted the phoenix as a symbol of resurrection as early as the first century, using it on funeral stones, and it later became more specifically a symbol of Christ's resurrection.[24]

The emblem in figure 2 is one that is supposed to contain the entire alchemical process of the perfection of matter, and so one must read it in the ascending mode. That style of alchemical presentation is not only appropriate for describing a transformation of more lowly forms into higher ones, but it also bears a strong resemblance to a non-naturalistic device used by medieval painters to indicate the relative importance of various figures in a composition by placing the most important figure in the highest position.[25] In figure 2 the reading from bottom to top is also made imperative by the placing of the crowns: the lowest crown is single; then there are two; finally at the top is a triplet of crowns, each more noble than the last. The sequence of crowns offers a clear representation of increasing levels of perfection. With the understanding that the emblem is to be read from bottom to top, one is in a position to examine a more general signification inherent in its construction.

At the bottom is the earth, in the interior of which metals grow naturally, just as plants grow naturally on its surface. One alchemical doctrine regarding the growth of metals in the bowels of the earth drew upon an Aristotelian theory of two exhalations within the earth, one vaporous and one smoky. The proportions of the one to the other, coupled with the relative degree of purity of the matrix in which the two exhalations met, plus the degree of maturation of the product, were the theoretical constructs that served the alchemists in their attempts to explain the differences between the metals. Perfect proportions, a pure matrix, and full maturation yielded gold; imperfection in any area yielded a lesser, or more base, metal. Islamic alchemists identified two abstract chemical principles, Mercury and Sulfur, with, respectively, the vaporous and smoky exhalations, making Mercury and Sulfur the constituents of all metals, and that identification passed into the

24. Hall, *Dictionary*, s.v. "Phoenix"; Ferguson, *Signs*, s.v. "Phoenix."
25. See the discussion of "Flight into Egypt, Grain Miracle" from the Hours of the Rohan Master (first quarter of the fifteenth century) in Pamela Berger, *The Goddess Obscured: Transformation of the Grain Protectress from Goddess to Saint* (Boston: Beacon Press, 1985), 123–25.

alchemy of the Latin West, where it was often a dominant theme.[26] The cutaways in the earth in figure 2 probably represent the flow of the mercurial and sulfurous principles in the earth, with the earth's central fire (bottom center) serving to join them and assist in their maturation.

However, the natural process in the earth might take a thousand years to accomplish what the alchemist could do in a day, and along the central pole of the picture the alchemist follows nature but accelerates her work. First, the two requisite forms of lowly, earthly matter are assembled and sacrificed. What is in the flask is then dead, but it is reactivated by the divine power streaming in from heaven and achieves the first crown of perfection. Next, by a process not made explicit, the alchemist produces the perfectly pure mercurial principle, represented by the two snakes twined about the pole that echo the form of the alchemical symbol for Mercury. With the preparation of that special Mercury, the process has reached the second level of perfection represented by the double crown. Above the double crown appears the form of the alchemical symbol for Sulfur, the triangle with a crossed stem. When the alchemist is also able to prepare the perfectly pure sulfurous principle and join it with his perfectly pure Mercury, then the process reaches the third level of perfection represented by the triple crown. Perhaps at that stage the alchemist has indeed made gold from his two perfect principles, but atop the final crown is one last symbol that may be emblematic of the philosopher's stone: a small globe bearing a cross on its upper surface.[27] Such a globe is also emblematic of power, imperial or divine dignity and sovereignty, or of Christ as *Salvator Mundi*, the Saviour of the world.[28]

Most of these are Christian symbols of death and resurrection, but one must also realize that even more ancient symbols are present in figure 2. The cross itself is a Christian adaptation of the primitive world-tree, the axle pole of the world that reaches from earth up to heaven, which in addition, with its subterranean roots, serves to unite the underworld with earth and heaven as well.[29]

26. E. J. Holmyard, *Alchemy* (1957 reprint, Harmondsworth: Penguin Books, 1968), 21–24, 74–75.

27. De Rola, *The Golden Game*, 304, 307.

28. Ferguson, *Signs*, s.v. "Globe"; Hall, *Dictionary*, s.v. "Globe" and "Salvator Mundi."

29. Buffie Johnson, *Lady of the Beasts: Ancient Images of the Goddess and Her Sacred Animals* (San Francisco: Harper and Row, 1988), 51 and plate 16 (an Egyp-

The tree was also an ancient symbol of the earth's fecundity in religions much older than Christianity. Through its seasonal dying and renewal, the tree had the meaning of resurrection, as did the snakes twined about it here. The snakes also are pre-Christian, signifying fertility, wisdom, and the power to heal. Because the snake sloughs its skin, it is a symbol of rebirth; because it emerges mysteriously from the earth, it brings messages from the underworld; because of its association with water, it carries an aura of cosmic creativity. The two snakes twined about the rod are reminiscent of the Caducean rod of Mercury or Hermes, ancient deities employed as messengers of the gods. The Caduceus with the two snakes entwined about the rod is of course still used by the medical profession as an emblem of healing.[30]

Although some of the symbols here derive from archaic times, in fact this emblem was published in Christian Europe in the seventeenth century, and its overall thrust calls attention to Christ. The cross of Christ was a version of the cosmic tree at the center, uniting the underworld, earth, and heaven, and was often so used in Christian art.[31] That cross is the central image in this alchemical emblem, and it is topped, as already noted, by a symbolic representation of Christ as *Salvator Mundi*. In the seventeenth century and for several centuries before, there was a widespread identification of Christ with the active alchemical agent of perfection, the philosopher's stone, an identification that rested upon a typological exegesis of two references to stones in the Old Testament. Psalm 118 refers to the stone that the builders rejected but that later became the essential cornerstone, "the head stone of the corner," and Isaiah spoke of the Lord of hosts, who would be a sanctuary for those who sanctified him but "a stone of stumbling"

---

tian tomb painting of 1600–1400 B.C. showing the Tree Goddess feeding the dead from her sacred sycamore); Roger Cook, *The Tree of Life: Image for the Cosmos* (1974; reprint, New York: Thames and Hudson, 1988), 9–12, plates 7 and 8 (showing Buddhist stupas as cosmic trees). Mircea Eliade associated cosmic trees with all the religious symbolism of the center. See, for example, his *The Myth of the Eternal Return; or, Cosmos and History*, trans. Willard R. Trask (Princeton: Princeton University Press, 1971), 12–21; *Myths, Dreams and Mysteries: The Encounter between Contemporary Faiths and Archaic Realities*, trans. Philip Mairet (1960; reprint, New York: Harper and Row, 1975), 18–19, 63–66; and *A History of Religious Ideas*, trans. Willard R. Trask, Alf Hiltebeitel, and Diane Apostolos-Cappandona, 3 vols. (Chicago: University of Chicago Press, 1978–1985), 2:399–403.

30. Johnson, *Lady of the Beasts*, 122–86; Hall, *Dictionary*, s.v. "Caduceus" and "Snake"; Marija Gimbutas, *The Goddesses and Gods of Old Europe, 6500–3500 B.C.: Myths and Cult Images*. (Berkeley: University of California Press, 1982), 93–101.

31. Cook, *Tree of Life*, 20–21, 102–03, and plate 49; Eliade, *Eternal Return*, 16–17.

for others.[32] In the New Testament both uses of *stone* are taken to refer explicitly to Christ.[33] Thus, any symbolic representation of the alchemical work of achieving the philosopher's stone may also be read as instructions for finding Christ, for achieving personal salvation and the salvation of the world.

That concept may also be grasped at the level of cosmic creativity, where again there is biblical justification for it. In the opening verses of the first chapter of the Gospel according to John, there are phrases that point to Christ's activity in the creation of the world: "In the beginning was the Word, and the Word was with God, and the Word was God. The same was in the beginning with God. All things were made by him; and without him was not any thing made that was made."[34] "All things were made by him"— the Word, or Logos, or Christ. One may see that concept expressed in figure 3, where Christ is engaged in separating the elements out from the original chaos of creation;[35] the four traditional elements of which all things were made—earth, water, air, and fire— are each in their own corners of the illustration. The late fifteenth-century book on the nature of things from which the picture comes was not a treatise on alchemy at all, and the illustration demonstrates the general cultural conviction that Christ was that person of the triune godhead acting in the creation of the world. Given, then, that the alchemists thought the creation was itself an alchemical process, it was only natural that they would identify Christ with the active agent that worked to convey God's creative power in the alchemical flask. As one may see later, the identification of Christ as the divine actor in alchemy lent cosmic meaning to alchemy, and especially in the sixteenth and seventeenth centuries the practice of alchemy assumed apocalyptic overtones.

The issue of alchemical death must first be considered in more detail, however, for it was thought to be an essential stage early in the alchemical process, and the active alchemical agent was as much an agent of death and putrefaction as it was of life and vegetation. The alchemical worldview was a dynamic one, evoking a great cyclical interchange of matter that involved life, death, and continual rebirth or resurrection. Based ultimately on a primitive perception of the yearly seasonal cycle of life, death, and resurrec-

32. Psalm 118:22; Isaiah 8:13–14.
33. Acts 4:11; I Peter 2:4–8.
34. John 1:1–3.
35. Bartholomeus Anglicus, *De proprietatibus rerum*, trans. John Trevisa (London: Wynkyn de Worde, [1495]), sig. e iii recto.

Figure 3. "Christ among the elements," Bartholomaeus Anglicus, *De Proprietatibus Rerum*, (London, 1495) fig. sig. e iii r.

tion in the vegetable kingdom, alchemical death was a necessary prelude to alchemical resurrection and perfection.

One of the most fundamental presuppositions of alchemy was that of the undifferentiated first matter from which all things could be derived, the so-called "philosophical chaos." In several papers Newton argued that the mode of acting of the alchemical agent was *first* to putrefy and confound into chaos, *then* to proceed to generation of new forms.[36] The chaos is the essential ana-

36. See, for example, Isaac Newton, "Propositions," Keynes MS. 12A, King's College, Cambridge, ff. 1v–2r; and Dibner MSS. 1031B, f. 5r, v.

logical element linking the alchemical work to cosmogony on the one hand and to spontaneous and sexual generation on the other, and one may look a little more closely at the concept of the chaos that seemed in the sixteenth and seventeenth centuries to make all those processes fundamentally similar. In spontaneous generation the analogies with the "philosophical chaos" of alchemy and with the initially unformed matter of creation are both reasonably clear. Decaying flesh and stinking mud seem to be in a state of putrefaction, in a process of degradation from organized forms into an inchoate mass from which new, unrelated forms might spring.

The analogue of an unformed primal matter in sexual generation is now not quite so easy to grasp, for one now conceives organized life to pass in an unbroken chain from parent to offspring with no intervention of death and decay. But in the early modern period, there was, on the contrary, just such a sense of discontinuity as is now lacking. Although there were competing theories as to whether male or female emissions were more important, it was rather generally agreed that after coition there was a mingling of male and female "sperms" (or perhaps male semen and female menstrual blood). This confused mass underwent decay and resolution into a "primordium"—simple and undifferentiated—from which the new life arose, but only after divine activation. Harvey was at pains to deny the ancient theories because his anatomical researches revealed none of the required masses.[37] Harvey's conclusion—that the vector of life was a divine spirit—nevertheless emphasized a fundamental discontinuity between the generations in the animal kingdom.

The accepted paradigm for generation in the vegetable kingdom was somewhat different, for there an analogy was made between the seeds of plants and the male animal's "seed," or "sperm," with the earth herself assigned the female role of receptive womb.[38] But the belief that death and decay preceded new life in the fields was common also, and indeed had Biblical authority, for Jesus had

---

37. Harvey's arguments against the ancients are well summarized in Elizabeth B. Gasking, *Investigations into Generation, 1651-1828* (Baltimore: Johns Hopkins University Press, 1967), 19-24.

38. See John Farley, *Gametes and Spores: Ideas about Sexual Reproduction, 1750-1914* (Baltimore: Johns Hopkins University Press, 1982), 22, for a discussion of that analogy in *Aristotle's Compleat and Experienc'd Midwife*, a compendium of sexual information that remained popular into the eighteenth century. This analogy was quite common in alchemical literature.

said, "Except a corn of wheat fall into the ground and die, it abideth alone: but if it die, it bringeth forth much fruit."[39]

Many alchemists quoted that passage from John to explain the necessity for death and putrefaction in the mineral kingdom before the alchemical work could proceed to the generation of new and more perfect forms.[40] In alchemy, metallic putrefaction was considered to be essential at an early stage. It produced a chaotic, dark, unformed matter—a chaos such as had existed at the beginning of the world. Upon it the spirit of God moved, and as light had come upon the first creation, the alchemical matter was "illuminated" and endowed with the potentiality of life and growth.

One may now return to the more cosmic meaning of alchemy. In addition to constituting a prefiguration of the alchemical process, the week of divine creativity as recounted in the first chapter of Genesis also provided an adumbration of the course of all of human history. And if the "philosophical chaos" of alchemy was similar to the original chaos of creation, so was the beatific conclusion of the alchemical process similar to the anticipated end of history in a new Beatitude, the New Jerusalem, the Millennium, comparable to the seventh day of the week of creation, when God rested and all was good. The divine actor expected to usher in the Millennium was related to the agent in alchemy too, for it was the Second Coming of Christ that was to announce the end of time. After the Reformation of the Church began in the sixteenth century, there was a strong belief that the End of Days was approaching. The purification of the Church seemed to many Protestants to mark the beginning of the end. The Church, as the Body of Christ on earth, was being purged and cleansed and made ready to receive her leader.[41]

That concept found a ready parallel in the practice of alchemy, where matter was purged and cleansed and exalted, and among many early modern alchemists there was the general expectation that the end of time would bring the final redemption of matter just as it would bring the final redemption of mankind. All nature had fallen with Adam and Eve at the time of their original sin, but

---

39. John 12:24.
40. See Dobbs, *Foundations*, 30–31, and the literature cited there.
41. Stanton J. Linden, "Alchemy and Eschatology in Seventeenth-Century Poetry," *Ambix* 31 (1984): 102–24; Eliade, *History of Religious Ideas* 3:255–61; Herbert Breger, "*Elias Artista:* A Precursor of the Messiah in Natural Science," in *Nineteen Eighty-Four: Science between Utopia and Dystopia*, ed. Everett Mendelsohn and Helga Nowotny (Dordrecht: D. Reidel, 1984), 49–72.

nature would be restored at the end. Alchemy reached its height of popularity in the sixteenth and seventeenth centuries, and there was great appreciation for the words of Paul in the third chapter of the Acts of the Apostles, a text that pointed to the restitution of *all* things: "And he shall send Jesus Christ, which before was preached unto you: Whom the heaven must receive until the times of restitution of all things, which God hath spoken by the mouth of all his holy prophets since the world began."[42]

The Ripley Scrolls

One is now in a position to explore a late sixteenth-century representation of the alchemical process in some detail, where all of these themes of life, death, resurrection, and restitution are reflected, in one of the Ripley Scrolls. There are a number of these magnificent exemplars of the alchemical imagination still extant, all thought to date from the sixteenth and early seventeenth centuries.[43] The one reproduced here in figures 4–7 (continuous sections of the manuscript from bottom to top) is now held by the Huntington Library and probably dates from about 1570.[44] The Ripley Scrolls are not exactly identical but have quite similar illustration accompanied by English or Latin verses and tags that purport to explain the illustrations. As in the case of the alchemical emblem explored in figure 2, the scrolls claim to represent the entire alchemical process, but the scale of the representation is dramatically enlarged (the Huntington Scroll is ten feet and eight inches long), so on them several quite different but still enigmatic

42. Acts 3:20–21. Not all strains of Protestantism accepted the concept of universal grace and redemption, however; see Alan Rudrum, "Theology and Politics in Seventeenth-Century England," *The Clark Newsletter: Bulletin of the UCLA Center for Seventeenth- and Eighteenth-Century Studies*, no. 15 (Fall 1988): 5–7.

43. See Linden, "Alchemy and Eschatology," 122, note 13. Parts of those held by the British Library are reproduced in C. A. Burland, *The Arts of Alchemists* (New York: MacMillan, 1968); and in Stanislas Klossowski de Rola, *Alchemy: The Secret Art* (London: Thames and Hudson, 1973). One held by Yale University is reproduced in its entirety in *Alchemy and the Occult: A Catalogue of Books and Manuscripts from the Collection of Paul and Mary Mellon given to Yale University Library*, comp. Ian Macphail, 4 vols. (New Haven: Yale University Library, 1968–77), 3, 271–88. Professor Linden is preparing a systematic scholarly study of the several scrolls.

44. Huntington MS. HM 30313, Henry E. Huntington Library, San Marino, California. The present writer has also examined the one held by the Fitzwilliam Museum, Cambridge (Fitzwilliam MS. 276*), which is twenty-two feet long.

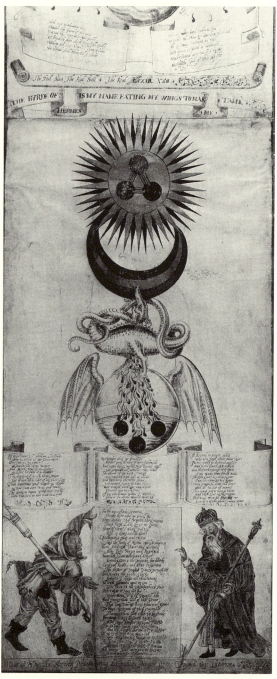

Figure 4. Ripley Alchemical Scroll, bottom section.
The Huntington Library, MS. HM 30313.

Figure 5. Ripley Scroll, second section.

Figure 6. Ripley Scroll, third section.

Figure 7. Ripley Scroll, top section.

pictures are employed. As before, one must read up, since the exaltation of the matter is being described.

In the first bottom illustration (fig. 4), the dragon declares his name to be the "*Serpent* of *Arabia*" and says he "somtyme was both wood and wild," but now he is "both meeke and mild." He is a symbol for the vital agent, the vegetable spirit, for he says he "is leader of all this game."[45] As a dragon, he is related also to the universal Gnostic dragon that referred to undifferentiated chaos and to the universal solvent "that passes through all things," for he claims "*Omogeni*" as father, "*Magnesia*" as mother, "*Azot*" and "*Kibrick*" as sister and brother.[46] The *Oxford English Dictionary* notes that the prefix *omo* is an erroneous and obsolete rendering of the prefix *homo;* thus the dragon has declared his father's name to be "Homogeny," or homogeneity, and the other obscure alchemical names for his kin may be somewhat similarly interpreted. The writer of the Scroll thoughtfully adds the instruction for the practitioner to know "ere thou begin" what the dragon is "and all his kin." He has many names, but "all is but one Nature," a phrase reminiscent of certain passages Newton wrote in the late 1660s describing the vital agent.[47] The vital agent is diffused through all things in the world, Newton said, and "it accommodates itself to every nature."

45. Because the Huntington Scroll is framed and hangs high above a stairwell and so is inaccessible for close study, I have utilized the verses from a different scroll, published by Elias Ashmole in 1652: "Verses Belonging to an Emblematic Scrowle: Supposed to be invented by Geo: Ripley," in *Theatrum Chemicum Britannicum Containing Severall Poeticall Pieces of our Famous English Philosophers . . . ,* (Sources of Science, no. 39 [New York: Johnson Reprint Corporation, 1967], 375–79. Modern descriptions of the scrolls that I have studied, Fitzwilliam MS. 276* and Mellon MS. 41 in *Alchemy and the Occult,* 3:272–85, start with the top illustration and work down. Ashmole, however, who was himself a participant in the early modern alchemical tradition, starts at the bottom and works up, which reinforces the argument above that this is the correct way to read the process. I have, however, compared Ashmole's transcriptions with the appropriate verses from Fitzwilliam MS. 276* and from Mellon MS. 41. Ashmole's transcriptions are in somewhat less archaic language, and it is possible that he partially modernized his exemplar; however, the sense seems to be the same in almost all cases. The quotations in this paragraph are from *Theatrum Chemicum Britannicum,* 375. In "A Table explaining the Obscure, Obsolete, and mis-spell'd words used throughout this Worke" (unpaginated, found at the end of the volume), Ashmole noted that Woode meant "mad."

46. J.E. Cirlot, *A Dictionary of Symbols,* 2d ed., trans. Jack Sage (New York: Philosophical Library, 1981), s.v. "Dragon" and "Ouroboros"; *Theatrum Chemicum Britannicum,* 375.

47. *Theatrum Chemicum Britannicum,* 376.

From metallic semen it generates gold, from human semen men, etc.
And it puts on various forms according to the nature of the subject.
In metals it is not distinguished from the metallic substance, in men,
not from the human substance, etc.[48]

The dragon says his wings had taken him everywhere, but now
they pull him down. He hangs there on the globe that represents
the earth, and of the blood and water issuing from him, he says:

> Of my blood and water I wis,
> Plenty in all the World there is.
> It runneth in every place;
> Who it findeth he hath grace.[49]

With those words the dragon assimilates himself to Christ, to the
redeeming blood and water that issued from Christ on the cross,
and also to the redeeming alchemical agent that the alchemists
often claim is to be found everywhere if one only knows how to
look for it.[50]

The first part of the scroll, including the dragon and the moon
and sun above him, seems to be a preview of the entire process.
The writer indicates that the operator is to divide the dragon (homogeneity personified) into three parts:

> And then knit him as the Trinity:
> And make them all but one,
> Loe here is the *Philosophers Stone*.[51]

The three parts indicated are the feminine and masculine principles, represented here by the moon and the sun, and the vital,
fructifying agent itself, without which there can be no new life.
The moon and the sun perhaps also comprise a subtle reference to
the entire course of human history, for Augustine had compared
the Old Testament to the moon and the New Testament to the
sun: the Old shines only by reflecting the light of the New, thus
organizing salvation history into periods.[52] Within the sun in this
illustration is a trinitarian image that probably represents the re-
united principles of the philosopher's stone, "knit . . . as the Trin-

---

48. Keynes MS. 12A, ff. 1v–2r.
49. *Theatrum Chemicum Britannicum*, 375–76.
50. John 19:34.
51. *Theatrum Chemicum Britannicum*, 376.
52. Hall, *Dictionary*, XV, s.v. "Crucifixion"; Augustine, *City of God*, 4.33, and
16.26; *Against Faustus*, 6.9.

ity," and may also reflect the presence of the Triune Godhead in historical time.

Moving up after the preview of the whole process, one finds the first stage described (fig. 5). A large bird with a human head, standing on the globe, announces that he is the Bird of Hermes: "The *Bird* of *Hermes* is my name, Eating my wings to make me tame." The bird had had wild wings, repeating the figure of the winged dragon or serpent below, but now it becomes clear that the operator is to capture, stabilize, and fix this agent of putrefaction and vivification so it can be used later in the process. The scroll notes that the bird is "Eating his Wings variable, And thereby maketh himselfe more stable."

> When all his Fethers be agon,
> He standeth still there as a stone;
> Here is now both White and Red,
> And also the Stone to quicken the dead.[53]

Above the bird is the sun, here called "Phoebus" (radiant). Internal name references in the verses back to "*Omogeny*" and "*Magnesia*" indicate that Phoebus is the first agent now prepared for use, likened to the sun that illuminates matter and "causeth Nature forth to spring." Phoebus is called "Father to all living things, Maynteyner of Lyfe to Crop and Roote."[54] And so the first part of the process is complete, with the active alchemical agent captured in a usable form.

Now one enters the stage of putrefaction. The agent of vivification is also the agent of putrefaction, and matter is now to be reduced to chaos: as Newton said, the *first* action of the agent is to confound formed matter into an inchoate state. The first image in this sequence is that of the reducing fire, guarded by two lions. No mention is made in the verses of the two lions, one red and one green, and they may be simply symbolic of the matched pairs of formed matter that are to be merged into unformed material. On the other hand, their presence may be intended to emphasize the sacred nature of the fire, for in prehistoric periods the lion, because of its physical strength and divine vitality, assumed the role of guardian for the Great Goddess in several areas, serving the Goddess also in birth and death. The Egyptian lion-headed goddess,

---

53. *Theatrum Chemicum Britannicum*, 376.
54. Ibid., 377.

Sekmet, epitomized the heat of the sun, so fierce in that desert country, and although she was a goddess of fertility, she was also a goddess of war and destruction. The guardian lions on the scroll, however, are in an attitude most reminiscent of those guarding the Great Goddess in the civilizations of Crete and Mycenae.[55] Since alchemy undoubtedly carried much archaic symbolism into Christian Europe, it is entirely possible that these alchemical lions were intended as emblematic of death, life, and divinity.

Above the fire and its attendant lions, one sees again the dragon or serpent, the active agent, now ready to act upon the material in the well (fig. 6). Around the central vessel are the four elements (the corner posts) that are to be reduced to chaos—earth, water, air, fire.

> The Fire with Water brent shalbe,
> And Water with Fire wash shall he;
> Then Earth on Fire shalbe put,
> And Water with Air shalbe knit,
> Thus ye shall go to Putrefaccion,
> And bring the *Serpent* to reduction.[56]

The liquid in the well may itself be symbolic of the chaotic state, but lest the lesson of putrefaction be lost upon the viewer, the artist made it triply clear by including three additional figures standing in the water. They represent the three essential divisions of formed matter—body, soul, and spirit—and are so labeled. They probably also represent the trio of chemical/alchemical principles added to contemporary matter theory by Paracelsus in the sixteenth century—Salt, Sulfur, and Mercury—which were considered by the Paracelsians to be equivalent to the body, soul, and spirit of formed matter. The three emblematic persons here are in any case being totally reduced, for they are drooping, indicating that they are dying and entering into putrefaction.

The symbolism of the toad that seems to emerge from the dragon's mouth is less obvious. The verses say that the dragon first "shalbe Black as any Crow, And downe in his Den shall lye full lowe." The state of the dragon becomes like the swelling of a toad,

---

55. Johnson, *Lady of the Beasts,* 100–111, and especially drawing 122 and photograph 123 on p. 108.

56. *Theatrum Chemicum Britannicum,* 378. Fitzwilliam MS. 276* reads "redemceone" rather than "reduction." Mellon MS. 41 also appears to have a variant of "redemption" here.

swelling so much it finally bursts: "And thus with craft the *Serpent* is slaine." The dragon will then show many colors and afterward turn white, whereupon the operator should wash him to remove his sin.

> With the Water that he was in,
> Wash him cleane from his sin:
> And let him drinke a litle and a lite,
> And that shall make him faire and white,
> The which Whitnes is ever abiding
> Lo here is the very full finishing.[57]

The toad might, if pictured with a skull or skeleton, be emblematic of death, but since no bones are here displayed, that signification is cast in doubt.[58] A toad gnawing at a woman's genitals suggested lust, but neither is that interpretation in order here.[59]

If one considers the archaic significance of the toad, however, its presence in the alchemical process becomes more intelligible, for in prehistoric times it was associated with fertility, apparently because of the resemblance of a one- or two-month-old human embryo to a toad and because the real cause of conception was not then understood. Gimbutas records numerous instances from the civilizations of Old Europe (6500–3500 B.C.) of hybrid woman/toad figurines that may best be interpreted as the Great Goddess in her life-giving aspect. Even after the dissolution of those early civilizations under the impact of the Indo-European invasions, the toad continued to be associated with birth, pregnancy, and the womb, especially in southern and central Europe, where pre-Indo-European mythologies remained strong. A Bronze Age "Lady Toad" has been discovered in lower Austria, and toads from Etruscan, Greek, and Roman sanctuaries and graves have been reported, many of them carved in expensive materials such as amber and ivory, showing the high esteem accorded the toad well into historical periods. Even in the twentieth century ethnographers report toads of wax, iron, silver, and wood given as votive offerings to the Virgin Mary in churches in Bavaria, Hungary, Moravia, and Yugoslavia, intended as a protection against barrenness and to insure safe pregnancy.[60] Certain attributes of the prehistoric Great Goddess have been assimilated by the Virgin Mary and the female

57. *Theatrum Chemicum Britannicum,* 379.
58. Hall, *Dictionary,* s.v. "Toad."
59. Cirlot, *Dictionary,* s.v. "Toad."
60. Gimbutas, *Goddesses and Gods,* 174–79.

saints, as is now well understood,[61] but, even so, the appearance of votive toads in twentieth-century Christian churches is a remarkable instance of the persistence of ancient conceptions and misconceptions, and it lends credence to the suggestion that the alchemical toads on the early modern Ripley Scrolls were intended to be emblematic of the life-giving powers of the active alchemical principle.

If the toad is indeed best understood as a symbol of fertility, it provides the transition from the well of dissolution and putrefaction to the next image above, a vat or well in which the water is green, the color indicating that the material is now ready to vegetate—that is, that it is alive. The association of the color green with vegetability must be based on universal human experience with the vegetable kingdom, but one may note also its ancient historic association with resurrection. Mummies of the Egyptian Old Kingdom (2613–2182 b.c.) sometimes had facial details added in green paint on the outside of their wrappings, green being the color of resurrection.[62] The material in the new well, one may infer, is not only alive but has been resurrected, and since the new well of life seems to grow out of the old well of death, these images constitute an appropriate rendition of the dynamic worldview of alchemy, in which life, death, and resurrection continually succeed one another.

In the well of life appear the feminine and masculine principles, symbolized by human figures of female and male but also by the feminine moon and the masculine sun. They are identical in meaning with the mercury and sulfur, the feminine and masculine metallic principles of figure 2. Seven alchemists stand around, each with an egg-shaped flask containing the precious cosmic fluid of vivification. The egg shape associates the flasks with the primordial egg of cosmic creativity, the egg from which the whole universe and all the gods emerged. Versions of the myth of the cosmic egg have been preserved in the mythologies of a great many cultures, and Gimbutas had traced its origins back into the Paleolithic era.[63] For the alchemical flask to be shaped like an egg affili-

61. Berger, *Goddess Obscured*; Marina Warner, *Alone of All Her Sex: The Myth and the Cult of the Virgin Mary* (reprint 1976; reprint, New York: Random House, 1983).
62. A. J. Spencer, *Death in Ancient Egypt* (1982; reprint Harmondsworth: Penguin Books, 1984), 38. See also Ferguson, *Signs*, s.v. "Colors: Green," where it is noted that green was the color of water in pagan initiation rites.
63. Gimbutas, *Goddesses and Gods*, 101–7.

ates its contents with the cosmic beginnings of life. The alchemists, then, pour in their vivifying waters in seven imbibitions, and the female and male become fruitful, the life emanating from them signified by the vine and by the Tree of Life itself.

Above them on the Tree of Life is their offspring, more noble than themselves. As Newton said in his *Commentary* on the *Emerald Tablet* of Hermes Trismegistus, the chemical/alchemical principles of the metals "unite like male and female," "and they act on each other, and through that action they are mutually transmuted into each other and procreate a more noble offspring to accomplish the miracles of this one thing."[64] The baby, occasionally called "the philosophical infant" in alchemical literature, is further ennobled by additional spirit coming down to him from above, the heavenly quintessence.[65] The odd creature slithering down the tree is presumably the bearer of that divine grace. Burland characterized a somewhat different but similarly placed creature on one of the Ripley Scrolls he studies as the Melusina, but since the Melusina was a fairy who did rather defective work and was perhaps even malignant, one may doubt that our alchemical artist meant to employ her as a heavenly messenger.[66] Rather more likely is the prospect that this particular epiphany in the Tree of Life has a pre-Judeo-Christian meaning stemming from a period when women, trees, and serpents were sturdy partners in wisdom, fertility, healing, and spirituality—before the story of their supposed encounter in the Garden of Eden sundered their ancient union in Western consciousness and made both snake and woman into symbols of evil.[67] The archaic unities more appropriately explicate this alchemical vision, as the newborn infant receives his heavenly nimbus and benediction.

The "philosophical infant" probably symbolized the white stone of the philosophers, an intermediate grade of perfection. The white stone was reported to change base metals to silver, cure

---

64. King's College, Cambridge, Keynes MS. 28, f. 2r, v. See B. J. T. Dobbs, "Newton's *Commentary* on the *Emerald Tablet* of Hermes Trismegistus: Its Scientific and Theological Significance," in *Hermeticism and the Renaissance: Intellectual History and the Occult in Early Modern Europe*, ed. Ingrid Merkel and Allen G. Debus (Washington: Folger Shakespeare Library, 1988), 182–91, especially 184–85.
65. F. Sherwood Taylor, "The Idea of the Quintessence," in *Science, Medicine, and History: Essays on the Evolution of Scientific Thought and Medical Practice Written in Honour of Charles Singer*, ed. E. Ashworth Underwood, 2 vols. (London: Oxford University Press, 1953), 1:247–65.
66. Burland, *Arts*, 72; Cirlot, *Dictionary*, s.v. "Melusina."
67. Johnson, *Lady of the Beasts*, 182–91.

some illnesses, and promote longevity. Above the sequence of illustrations that led to the production of the infant, there is a single line of large letters informing the viewer that "This is ye last of the whit stone & ye beginning of ye red," and directing attention to the last illustration on the scroll, where the operations involved in the production of the red stone are to be explained.

The final illustration (fig. 7) has two levels of meaning, one microcosmic and one macrocosmic. At the first, microcosmic, level the figures inside the giant flask symbolize what the alchemists called "reiteration." Taking the white stone from the previous process and going through all the stages again, the alchemist expected finally to achieve the red stone—the highest level of perfection. The red stone was thought to have the power to change base metals into gold, the most perfect metal. It was also a universal medicine or panacea, curing all ills and conferring immortality. There are eight roundels inside the big flask; each contains a representation of some part of the process. They are chained in the center to a book that presumably contains all the divine secrets needed for the art.

But the other meaning of this last illustration is a cosmic one. All of the small figures are themselves inside the large alchemical flask that represents the cosmic egg of the universe that is in the hands of God.[68] The alchemist writ large who broods over the egg is the second person of the Trinity, the cosmic Christ, who is so often identified with the final achievement of the philosopher's stone and who will bring the entire course of history to a beatific end at the end of time. This aspect of the picture thus represents the Second Coming of Christ that will usher in the Millennium in joyful fulfillment of the Reformation expectations that ran so high in the sixteenth century, when the alchemical process was widely thought to be a representation of cosmic history and to lead not only to the perfection of matter but to the moral and religious restitution of humanity.

With the achievement of the philosopher's stone and with the Second Coming of Christ, then will both alchemy and history be at an end, but a good end. As Hermes Trismegistus, the most famous alchemist of all, said in his *Emerald Tablet*, then will all

---

68. Although Linden did not exactly make this connection, I owe this insight to his excellent article "Alchemy and Eschatology," in which he analyzed a series of alchemical illustrations with divine figures in them, including this final image from the Huntington Scroll.

need and all grief flee from you.[69] And as one reads in the Book of Revelation, in John's vision of the New Jerusalem, "And God shall wipe away all tears from their eyes; and there shall be no more death, neither sorrow, nor crying, neither shall there be any more pain: for the former things are passed away."[70] The end of death; the end of all need, all grief, all pain; the achievement of final perfection and final salvation—that was the ultimate significance of alchemy in the age of Newton.

Conclusion

The meaning of alchemical texts and illustrations is often obscure to modern scholars, at least partly because of the prescientific—even archaic—assumptions that undergird alchemical thought and practice. Rather than dismiss alchemy as irrational and incomprehensible, however, one may attempt to recover alchemical meaning by historical methods, decoding its obscure symbolism by analyzing its premodern presuppositions about life, death, and resurrection.

In the remarkable alchemical studies of Isaac Newton, one may locate many clues that assist in that decoding. Because of the problem of explaining life under the rubric of the mechanical philosophy—the multiplicity and variety of life forms, their beauty, cohesiveness, and purposefulness—Newton turned to a study of alchemy in an attempt to find the secret of life, the divine agent of fertility, the "vegetable spirit." His analyses of the older alchemical literature often laid bare the hidden assumptions of alchemical theory regarding life and death. Although modern scientific knowledge invalidates many of those assumptions, they are nonetheless understandable in terms of ancient conceptions and misconceptions.

One often finds that alchemical symbolism is based on a primitive understanding of life, death, and resurrection in the vegetable and animal kingdoms, on the universal annual cycle of changes in wild animals and forests, then in both flocks and fields with the development of agriculture. The yearly miracle of birth and rebirth in the springtime captured the religious imagination of many peoples, and in a period when there was little accurate knowledge of

---

69. See Dobbs, "Newton's *Commentary.*"
70. Revelation 21:4.

the continuity of life from generation to generation, it led to a belief in a divine principle of fertility necessary to initiate and sustain new plants and animals. Applied to the mineral kingdom, such a belief also sustained centuries of alchemical doctrine.

Many religious rituals centered on human efforts to promote and encourage the divine principle of fertility in the earliest civilizations, and primitive conceptions regarding life, death, and resurrection were enshrined in archaic religious beliefs. From thence they passed naturally into alchemical doctrine in its formative period early in the Christian era, giving alchemy a natural affinity with older religions but also with the Christian religion, which absorbed variants of the same beliefs at about the same time. In the Europe of the early modern period, then, alchemy was often at least a semireligious pursuit and shared many symbols with the dominant Christian religion, especially symbols of the sacrificial death that promotes life and symbols of resurrection.

Although alchemy also still utilized much pre-Christian religious symbolism, it became rather dramatically entangled with apocalyptic expectations after the Reformation. The conviction that the End of Days had been initiated by the Reformation of the Church was widespread, as was the conviction that the salvation of all things was at hand—the "restitution of all things," matter as well as humanity. Christ was identified with the philosopher's stone; both were after all conceived as agents of redemption and immortality. Thus the affiliation of alchemy with religious belief in the approaching End and the Second Coming of Christ led to heightened expectations of alchemical success, and alchemy was never more popular than it was in the sixteenth and seventeenth centuries, just before its demise. At that time, as the alchemical symbols studied here reveal, alchemy was thought to carry the secret of life itself, and with it the secrets of resurrection, of immortality, of perfection, of final salvation and Beatitude. Though ultimately doomed to failure, the alchemical quest in the early modern period was a noble one indeed, sustained by some of the very highest human hopes and aspirations.

SCIENCE, THE *PRISCA THEOLOGIA,* AND MODERN EPOCHAL CONSCIOUSNESS

Stephen A. McKnight

One of the long-standing debates among historians is whether the modern age began with the Renaissance or with the Scientific Revolution. The advocates of the first position maintain that the recovery of human dignity and the reemergence of the *studia humanitatis* paved the way for the breakdown of the medieval "dark age" and ushered in the modern age of human dignity, autonomy, and creativity.[1] The defenders of the latter position hold that the modern age began with the new epistemology that replaced theology as the queen of the sciences.[2] It is not the purpose of this essay to become embroiled in this debate. Rather, the purpose is to develop an alternative line of inquiry, and in order to do so, I want to reformulate the basic question. Rather than debate the influence of science on modernity, I want to examine the influence of the concept of modernity on the development of science. Or to be more precise, I want to examine the extent to which the concept of a new, modern age contributes to the institutionalization of science as the soteriological means of controlling nature and improving "man's estate."

Because this way of posing the question takes us off the familiar track, I probably should sketch the path we will take. First, I want to describe three features of modernity that are implicit in the current debates over the relative influence of science and humanism. Then I want to trace the origins of this epochal pattern in both the humanist revival of the *studia humanitatis* and in the Neoplatonic recovery of the *prisca theologia.* Since the latter is less familiar and likely to be more controversial, I will spend more time with its development. And then I will briefly relate this ep-

---

1. See, for example, William Kerrigan and Gordon Braden, *The Idea of the Renaissance* (Baltimore: Johns Hopkins University Press, 1989), which attributes the success of this pattern of interpretation to Burckhardt and Cassirer.
2. Herbert Butterfield, for example, claimed that the Scientific Revolution is comparable in civilizational significance to Christianity.

ochal pattern to the development of science through a brief discussion of Francis Bacon's *Great Instauration* and *New Atlantis*.

Modernity as an Epochal Break with the Dark Ages

The most distinctive feature of modernity is the underlying conviction that an epochal break separates it from the preceding medieval period. This break or separation from the past represents more than simply the present as opposed to what had happened before. There is a qualitative judgment made about the present age, and it carries implications for the nature and character of the preceding age. The character of this new age is reflected in the symbols created for it. There is the symbol of Renaissance, marking a rebirth after a period of stagnation and death, and there is later a symbol of enlightenment which stands in stark juxtaposition to the preceding dark age. Integral to this epochal consciousness is a new confidence in man's capacity for self-determination, and this in turn derives from the conviction that an epistemological breakthrough provides man with the capacity to change the conditions of his existence. As we follow the stages in the development of the concept of modernity, we also find a break down of distinctions between sacred and secular history that leads to a reformulation of the traditional pattern of Western historiography. And this reformulation plays a major role in shaping the cultural use of science as the soteriological means of controlling nature and perfecting society.

It is my contention that there are two Renaissance sources for the reformulation of the ages of darkness and light, or of birth and death. One is the revival of the *studia humanitatis* and the other, which has been virtually ignored, is the Neoplatonic revival of the myths and symbols of the *prisca theologia*, or Ancient Wisdom.

The first major figure to express the new epochal consciousness was Petrarch (1304–1374), who juxtaposed the dawn of the new age to the dark age that was at last coming to an end. Petrarch also provided the first formulation of a three-phase history moving from a classical period through a Christian dark age to the modern age of humanity's rebirth and renewal.[3] In an effort to reawaken the

---

3. Petrarch is, of course, not the only developer of a three-stage construction of history that has formal connections with eighteenth- and nineteenth-century progressivist constructions. Scholars have also shown important parallels with Joachim of Fiore's (ca. 1132–1202) famous three stages of spiritual evolution and

consciousness of the dignity and the creativity of man reflected in the grandeur of the monuments from the Roman imperial age, Petrarch proposed to prepare a history that would highlight this period and distinguish it from the period of darkness (età tenebrae) that followed "the celebration of the name of Christ in Rome."[4] This formulation was extraordinary for his era; it was the first time that the term dark age was used to refer to the period of the Christian empire. In fact, this characterization inverted the standard periodization of history that contrasted the age of Christianity to the preceding age of pagan darkness. In his famous poem, the Africa, Petrarch developed this imagery further: "My fate is to live amid varied and confusing storms. But for you perhaps, if as I hope and wish you will live long after me, there will follow a better age. This sleep of forgetfulness will not last forever. When the darkness has been dispersed, our descendants can shine again in the form of pure radiance."[5] In expressing this hope, Petrarch distinguished three periods in Western history—the classical age, the dark age, and the emerging modern epoch.

In developing this pattern Petrarch introduced two major innovations in Western historiography. First, he changed the conventional model that divided Western history into two epochs, the ancient and the modern. Second, he transformed the site and source of the basic epochal distinction. In conventional history, the coming of Christ and the establishment of Christianity as an ecumenic religion divided the ancient and modern periods. In this formulation the period before the birth of Christ was referred to as a dark age. In Petrarch's conception, the age of darkness began with the establishment of the Christian religion in Rome, and the modern period began with a reawakening consciousness of the grandeur of Western civilization and the majesty of the human spirit.

---

perfection. Petrarch is, however, the first to develop the historical pattern with the specific features we are examining, that is, a qualitative break between the Christian "dark age" and the modern age in which the source of meaning and purpose in history is transferred to man. Joachim, on the other hand, describes three progressive stages of spiritual enlightenment. For a discussion of Joachim's concept of history and its influence, see Marjorie Reeves, Joachim of Fiore and the Prophetic Future (London: SPCK, 1976); Eric Voegelin, The New Science of Politics (Chicago: University of Chicago Press, 1952), 110–121; and Karl Löwith, Meaning in History (Chicago: University of Chicago Press, 1949), 145–59.

4. See Theodor Mommsen, "Petrarch's Concept of the 'Dark Age,'" in Medieval and Modern Studies, ed. Eugene Rice, Jr., (Ithaca: Cornell University Press, 1959), 127.

5. Petrarch, Africa, 9:451–57; quoted in Mommsen, "Petrarch's Concept of the 'Dark Age,'" 127–28.

Petrarch's formulation, then, was the first instance of the three-stage pattern of history that separates two periods of light by a period of darkness. Petrarch's reconceptualization would not be of great significance if it remained restricted to his own work or even to his own time. But this characterization supplied the root symbols of the Enlightenment and introduced the historical pattern that has dominated Western historiography down to recent times.

While Petrarch viewed his own time as the tenuous beginning of the transition from darkness to light, later Renaissance humanists spoke confidently of their own age as one of "rebirth" and even proclaimed the accomplishments of its greatest figures to be superior to achievements during the classical age.[6] The historian who first used the term *la rinascita* to distinguish his age from the preceding age of sterility and death was the sixteenth-century historian Vasari.[7] His *Lives of the Most Excellent Italian Painters, Sculptors, and Architects* is more than the first "modern art history," as it is often described. For Vasari and many of his contemporaries, art represented the highest form of human creativity.[8] Therefore, his record of the achievements of Leonardo and Michelangelo, whom he regarded as the greatest artists who ever lived, is a demonstration of a burgeoning human creativity that would lead to a thoroughgoing cultural renewal and revitalization.

Vasari's designation of this new era as a period of renaissance marks another significant appropriation of religious imagery and another blurring of categorical distinctions between the sacred and the secular. Petrarch had borrowed and reversed the distinction between the age of darkness and the age of light. Vasari drew upon the conversion imagery of resurrection and rebirth but applied it to a cultural rather than a spiritual revitalization. Prior to Vasari's formulation, there had been references to other cultural renewals (for example, the Carolingian era), but contemporary interpreters regarded these as a revitalization (*renovatio*) and not as

6. For a discussion of Renaissance historiography, see W. K. Ferguson, "The Interpretation of the Renaissance," in *Renaissance Essays: From the Journal of the History of Ideas*, ed. P. O. Kristeller and P. P. Wiener (New York: Harper and Row, 1968); and Erwin Panofsky, *Renaissance and Renascences in Western Art* (Stockholm: Almqvist and Wiksell, 1960), especially Chap. 1, "Renaissance: Self-Definition or Self-Deception."

7. See Panofsky's discussion in *Renaissance and Renascences*, 31–35.

8. For a discussion of the Neoplatonic view of the artist as magus, see E. H. Gombrich, *Symbolic Images: Studies in the Art of the Renaissance*, 2d ed. (Oxford: Phaidon, 1978); and Erwin Panofsky, *Studies in Iconology: Humanistic Themes in the Art of the Renaissance* (1939; reprint, New York: Harper and Row, 1962).

a revolutionary epochal break. The basic framework in which society was understood was not questioned, and the conventional
historical pattern was not broken by these events. Vasari's formulation, by contrast, presented the new age as a radical departure from the Christian (Gothic) period. Moreover, his application of the language of salvation to secular developments marked
an extraordinary inversion of sacred and secular history, parallel-
ing Petrarch's inversion of the periods of darkness and light.

Another important feature of Vasari's historiographical innovations is his alteration of the conventional analogy of the history of
a culture to the biological cycles of birth and death. Greek and
Roman historians had traced the rise and fall of known cultures,
referring to movement from infancy through childhood to adult-
hood and finally old age and death. Vasari traced the infancy of the
Renaissance from the work of Giotto through the transition in
Masaccio (*adolescentia*) to its maturity in the work of Leonardo
and Michelangelo. There is no discussion of the fourth and final
stage (*senectus*), however, because Vasari finds no inherent reason
that this extraordinary artistic achievement would go into decline.[9] The only precedent for Vasari's treatment is found in Christian salvation history (*Heilsgeschichte*), which purposely used the
truncated pattern to mark the essential contrast between sacred
and profane history. Tertullian, for example, described three phases
of religious and spiritual evolution culminating in "the Paracletan
period," a period of spiritual maturity that will endure forever.
Saint Augustine contrasted the City of God to the City of Man by
stopping the cyclical pattern with the third stage of maturity because the City of God can never reach a period of senility and
death.[10] With Vasari, then, we find another instance in which the
modern epochal consciousness is expressed in a historical pattern
that had been reserved for religious history. For Vasari, Petrarch,
and other Renaissance revisionists seeking to mark the uniqueness
of the events unfolding in their own time, conventional secular
historical patterns were inadequate. Their experience could only be
expressed in the language of conversion and spiritual awakening.[11]

---

9. Vasari does express some anxiety that another period of barbarity might disrupt this age. But such a threat is external. In terms of the biological analogy, it is
like saying an adult would never die unless murdered.

10. For a brief discussion, see Erwin Panofsky, *Meaning in the Visual Arts: Papers in and on Art History* (Garden City, N.Y.: Anchor Doubleday, 1955), 218–19.

11. This meaning and use of the term carries into the famous histories of Burckhardt and Michelet.

The importance of this pattern has been recognized by Theodor Mommsen and Irwin Panofsky. There is another pattern that is equally important but for the most part has been entirely neglected as a model for historical reinterpretation.[12] This pattern comes from the *prisca theologia* or Ancient Wisdom tradition. This Ancient Wisdom is a collection of a wide array of pseudo-scientific and esoteric religious traditions revived by the Neoplatonists as part of the recovery of ancient learning. The *prisca theologia*, or Ancient Wisdom, was regarded by Ficino and other Neoplatonists as the record of God's revelation to non-Christian theologians of the ancient Near East and Mediterranean—for example, Zoroaster, Hermes Trismegistus, Pythagoras, and Orpheus. Ficino and other theologians were drawn to it for two primary reasons. First, these revelations, when studied comparatively, offered the prospect of establishing the essential core of the non-Christian revelation. Second, the establishment of an essential core could then serve as the basis for integrating this non-Christian revelation with Christian truth. This comparison with Christianity would, in turn, accomplish two additional purposes: (1) the linking would make clear and emphatic the superiority of Christianity over these partial, fragmented traditions and (2) the establishment of the essential core could provide the key to resolving the dispute over the merits of Aristotelian and Platonic thought and their compatibility with Christianity.

One of these Ancient Wisdom traditions, the Hermetic, appeared to be especially suited to the reconciliation of ancient learning with Christianity. This was because Hermes Trismegistus was believed to have been the teacher of both Plato and Moses. His work, therefore, held the promise of reconciling Judaism and ancient philosophy with the tenets of Christianity. A clear indication of the high regard for Hermes Trismegistus is the fact that Ficino, the head of the Platonic Academy, set aside his work on Plato to analyze newly found Hermetic materials. The reasons for giving primacy to Hermes Trismegistus are made clear in the *argumentium* to the *Pimander.* The *argumentium* begins by establishing Hermes as one of the earliest and greatest of the *prisci theologi:* "Moses was born during the age of Atlas the astrologer, who was the brother

---

12. There is no mention of it in Wallace Ferguson's classic study, *The Renaissance in Historical Thought: Five Centuries of Interpretation* (Boston: Houghton Miflin, 1948), or in the more recent book by William Kerrigan and Gordon Braden, *The Idea of the Renaissance* (Baltimore: Johns Hopkins University Press, 1989).

of Prometheus the natural philosopher [physici] and maternal uncle of Hermes the greater [Majioris] whose nephew was Hermes Trismegistus. . . . They say that he [Hermes Trismegistus] killed Argus, ruled the Egyptians and gave them laws and letters."[13] In subsequent passages, Ficino notes that Hermes received the title "Thrice-Great," (Trismegistus) because he was the greatest philosopher, the greatest priest, and the greatest king to have ever lived; and he attained such a godlike status that temples were dedicated to him and the open speaking of his name was forbidden.

Ficino then indicates that Hermes progressed from natural philosophy to a study of the gods and finally to contemplation of and teaching about the majesty of God, the orders of demons, and the transmigration (*mutatianubus*) of souls. For that reason, he is called the "first author of theology" (*Primus igitur theologia appellatus*). Ficino next provides a theological genealogy that shows that Hermes is the originator of the Platonic wisdom:

> Orpheus, following Hermes, became the second of the ancient theologians. Aglophemus was initiated into the teachings of Orpheus and was succeeded by Pythagoras in theology, Philolaus, the teacher of our divine Plato, was his disciple. In this way, a *prisca theologia*, completely coherent with itself, was developed by six marvelous theologians, beginning with Hermes and culminating in Plato.[14]

The most important points to note about this genealogy is that it establishes the harmony of the ancient revelations by tracing them to a single line of transmission, and it also traces Plato's teachings to a divine source. Ficino then notes that two of Hermes' writings are most divine, the *Asclepius* and the *Pimander*, and he explains that the purpose of these books is to teach other men how to rise above the deceptions of sense and fantasy and open their minds to the divine Mind (Mens) so that we can contemplate the order of all things as they exist in God.

Two segments of the *Corpus Hermeticum* are particularly sig-

13. The translations and abbreviated paraphrases of the *argumentium* offered here are my own. The Latin text used is in the *Opera Omnia*, 2d. ed., 4 vols., (1576; reprint Torino, 1959), 4:1836.

14. Ibid. For a useful examination of this and other genealogies of the Ancient Wisdom developed by Ficino, see D. P. Walker, "The Prisca Theologia in France," *Journal of the Warburg and Courtauld Institutes* 17 (1954): 204–59. In every instance Hermes is either first or second (following Zoroaster)—for example, the *Theologia Platonica*—or contemporaneous with Zoroaster—for example, the *Plotinus commentaries*.

nificant for our current analysis. The first is in Book One of the *Pimander*, called "The Egyptian Genesis." As the account opens, Hermes is deeply troubled by his inability to understand the meaning of existence and is further confused by the learned ignorance of the theologians. After he falls into a deep sleep, the divine messenger Pimander appears and indicates that God has sent him to answer the existential questions troubling Hermes. When Hermes expresses his desire to know the true nature of man and the world, Pimander begins with the *true* account of creation. The supreme God and the divine Father of mankind instructed the Demiurge to create the natural world. Man, however, was created directly by the divine Father and in his image. Man, therefore, is beautiful and shares in the creative powers of divinity. When primal man viewed the creation being fashioned by the Demiurge, he yearned to use his own creative powers and obtained permission from the Father to assist the Demiurge. The Demiurge, who loves this son of God, teaches him the essential nature of the created order, and man is thereby able to participate in the creation.

> And he [Man] who had full power over the world of things mortal and over the irrational animals . . . having broken through the [celestial] vault showed to lower Nature the beautiful form of God. When [Nature] beheld him who had in himself inexhaustible beauty and all the forces of the Governors combined with the form of God, she smiled in love; for she had seen the reflection of this most beautiful form of Man in the water and its shadow upon the earth. He too, seeing his likeness present in her, reflected in the water, loved it and desired to dwell in it. At once with the wish it become reality, and he came to inhabit the form devoid of reason. And Nature, having received into herself the beloved, embraced him wholly, and they mingled: for they were inflamed with love. And this is why alone of all the animals on earth man is twofold, mortal through the body, immortal through the essential Man.[15]

The second passage is from the *Asclepius* and contains a detailed explanation of the various deities governing the world, and this is followed by the well-known and controversial passage which celebrates man's capacity to make gods:

15. *Corpus Hermeticum*, 4 vols., edited with French translation by A.J. Festugieve (Paris: Librairie Lecoffre, 1949–1954). The passage is from 1:13; the English translation is found in Hans Jonas, *The Gnostic Religion: The Message of the Alien God and the Beginnings of Christianity*, 2d ed. (Boston: Beacon Press, 1963), 150–51.

Having spoken of the society which unites gods and men (that is, hav-ing discussed the celestial influences), you must know, O Asclepius, the power and force of man. Just as the Lord and Father is the creator of the gods of heaven, so man is the author of the gods who reside in the temples. Not only does he receive life, but he gives it in his turn. Not only does he progress towards God, but he makes gods.

These statues, the text continues, are animated statues full of *sensus* and *spiritus*, who can accomplish many things, foretelling the future, giving ills to men and curing them. From the context, it is clear that these images or talismans are the means man uses to draw down the power of the heavens and help in the ongoing creative process. A later passage underscores the use of astral magic by again referring to man as the great miracle and claiming that his most marvelous ability is his ability to make gods. In this passage, Hermes, who is conveying what he has learned through divine revelation, explains that "what we have said about man is already marvelous, but most marvelous of all is that he has been able to discover the nature of the gods and to reproduce it. . . . [The magi] mingled a virtue, drawn from material nature, to the substance of the statues, and . . . evoked the souls of demons or angels into their idols."[16] This magical power enables man to par-ticipate in the maintenance of cosmic order and to create a micro-cosmic social order.

The Hermetic view of man as magus, as God's designated emis-sary appointed to maintain the macrocosm and to perfect the mi-crocosm, is further developed in *Picatrix*, a textbook of magical procedures.[17] The fourth book's discussion of talismans and im-ages also offers an account of the marvelous city of Adocentyn, which was founded and governed by the supreme magus, Hermes Trismegistus. "Hermes was the first who constructed images by means of which he knew how to regulate the Nile against the motion of the moon" and protect his city against flooding. He also invoked spirits into the statues guarding the city walls. At each gate

16. *Corpus Hermeticum*, 2:325–6, 347–49. Translations are from Frances Yates, *Giordano Bruno and the Hermetic Tradition* (Chicago: University of Chicago Press, 1964), 37. Man is also referred to as the *magnum miraculum* in the *Corpus Her-meticum* 2:301–2.

17. The *Picatrix* is not attributed directly to Hermes Trismegistus, though it refers to him as one of the greatest magi. The text reached Europe in an Arabic edition and was a basic source for Ficino's understanding of magic and Hermetism.

he introduced spirits which spoke with voices, nor could anyone enter the gates of the City except by their permission. There he planted trees in the midst of which was a great tree which bore the fruit of all generation. . . . Near the City there was abundance of waters in which dwelt many kinds of fish. Around the circumference of the City he placed engraved images and ordered them in such a manner that by their virtue the inhabitants were made virtuous and withdrawn from all wickedness and harm.[18]

According to this text, Hermes used the knowledge made available to him to establish a perfect social order operating in harmony with the divine cosmos. In this brief passage we find that man first controls those events in nature that adversely affect him—for example, the flooding of the Nile. The second creative act is to use the knowledge of the natural order to produce an abundant supply of food to meet man's physical needs. The third is to protect the inhabitants of the city from external threats.

But now we come to the epochal dilemma. If this is man's true nature and the true relation of the cosmos to God and man, why is there such a profound existential ignorance and why has man so thoroughly forgotten his role as magus? (Remember that Pimander has come to Hermes because Hermes has been driven to distraction by the educated confusion of his day.) The *Asclepius* does not offer an explanation of the epochal shift but does forecast the coming of an age when chaos and despair will fill the world. Egypt, the holy land that Hermes has served as priest-king, will be overrun by barbarians who will destroy the true religion, and the gods will leave the earth and go back to heaven, leaving only evil angels who will goad men to commit every conceivable crime.[19] "Then the earth will lose its equilibrium, the sea will no longer be navigable, the heaven will no longer be full of stars . . . the earth will molder, the soil will be no longer fertile, the air itself will grow thick with a lugubrious torpor." The lament does not explain the origin of this time of troubles except to say that it will occur when barbarians who do not understand the true religion overrun Egypt. Instead, the purpose of this passage is to provide a reassurance that the condition is only temporary and that God will intervene to renew the world and man.

18. *Picatrix*, book 4, chap. 3. This translation is taken from Yates, *Giordano Bruno*, 54, which also contains a useful analysis.
19. See *Corpus Hermeticum* 2:326.

Such will be the old age of the world, irreligion, disorder, confusion of all goods. When all these things have come to pass, O Asclepius, then the Lord and Father, . . . will annihilate all malice, either by effacing it in a deluge or by consuming it by fire, or destroying by pestilential maladies diffused in many places. Then he will bring back the world to its first beauty, so that this world may again be worthy of reverence and admiration, and that God also, creator and restorer of so great a work, may be glorified by men who shall live then in continual hymns of praise and benedictions.[20]

The lament, then, offers a reassurance that the current confusion will be overcome (through the teachings of Hermes) and mankind will thereby regain its primordial humanity. When man realizes his true nature, it will be possible to restore the world to its first beauty so that it will again be worthy of reverence and admiration and man can rebuild the utopian city of Adocentyn.

It is clear from the writings of Ficino and other Neoplatonists that they believed that their rediscovery of the Ancient Wisdom was the beginning of a new age of light, namely, the new age promised by Asclepius. So here we find another historical pattern prevalent in the Renaissance: two ages of light are separated by a dark age of ignorance and confusion. This notion of the recovery of the knowledge that had been lost, I believe, has a fundamental bearing on the early modern notion of a rebirth or an enlightenment.

Ficino and Pico

The influence on Ficino is obvious in two of his major works: the *Theologia Platonica* (1469–1474) and *De vita triplici* (1489). In the dedicatory preface, Ficino explains that one of the primary purposes of the *Theologia Platonica* is "to present a new understanding of human nature." His principal contention is that man is the most extraordinary of God's creatures because of the unique union of the spiritual and physical in his soul. According to Ficino, proper understanding of the soul's composition enables man to draw upon the spiritual element to overcome the limitation of the physical and to escape Fate. This process of spiritualization transforms man from a determined creature like all others into the greatest of God's miracles—a terrestrial god. Ficino's new understanding of human nature is developed further in *De vita triplici.* Here Ficino describes magical procedures designed to "overcome

---

20. *Corpus Hermeticum* 2:327–28. The translations are from Yates, *Giordano Bruno,* 39.

Fate" and allow man to reform the world. The key to these procedures is a new understanding of the world. Ficino presents a
view in which the natural and spiritual elements of the cosmos
are linked by the world soul (*anima mundi*) and the world spirit
(*spiritus mundi*). According to Ficino, the Ancient Wisdom reveals
how to draw upon the power of the world spirit to enhance man's
physical and spiritual condition and to control the powers of nature in the way the *prisci theologi* did. Ficino's prescriptions for
these magical operations extend from procedures for improving
physical health and intellectual aptitude to elaborate operations
that allow man to participate directly in the restoration of order to
the natural world and to emulate the utopian achievements described in the *Asclepius*.

Pico, Ficino's best known pupil, begins his famous *Oration* by
indicating that he intends to develop a new perspective on the
nature of man and his place in God's creation. His point of departure is the affirmation by Hermes Trismegistus and other *prisci
theologi* that man is the greatest miracle of creation. The difficulty is that conventional views of man do not explain why or
how he can be the *magnum miraculum*. In fact, other beings—
angels and star demons, for example—appear to hold a far loftier
position than does man. In order to set the record straight, Pico
offers a new myth of creation:

> God the Father, the supreme Architect, had already built this cosmic
> home we behold, the most sacred temple of His godhead, by the laws
> of His mysterious wisdom. The region above the heavens He had
> adorned with Intelligences, the heavenly spheres He had quickened
> with eternal souls, and the excrementary and filthy parts of the lower
> world He had filled with a multitude of animals of every kind.

Having finished his creation, God longed to have "someone to
ponder the plan of so great a work, to love its beauty, and to wonder at its vastness." He therefore decided to create man:

> He finally took thought concerning the creation of man. But there was
> not among His archetypes that from which He could fashion a new
> offspring, nor was there in His treasure-houses anything which He
> might bestow on His new son as an inheritance, nor was there in the
> seats of all the world a place where the latter might sit to contemplate
> the universe. All was now complete; all things had been assigned to
> the highest, the middle, and the lowest orders.[21]

21. Quotations are from the Elizabeth Forbes translation, which appears in Ernst

Because man could not be given special or unique features, God gave him a composite nature with unlimited potential to be whatever he decides. "He therefore took man as a creature of indeterminate nature and, assigning him a place in the middle of the world, addressed him thus: 'Neither a fixed abode nor a form that is thine alone nor any function peculiar to thyself have we given thee, Adam, to the end that according to thy longing and according to thy judgment thou mayest have and possess what abode, what form, and what functions thou thyself shalt desire.'" All other beings, even the celestial demons, have a fixed nature.

> Thou, constrained by no limits, in accordance with thine own free will, in whose hand We have placed thee, shalt ordain for thyself the limits of thy nature. We have set thee at the world's center that thou mayest from thence more easily observe whatever is in the world. We have made thee neither of heaven nor of earth, neither mortal nor immortal, so that with freedom of choice and with honor, as though the maker and molder of thyself, thou mayest fashion thyself in whatever shape thou shalt prefer.

Here we have another instance of a myth of man's true, primordial nature that has been lost. Pico does not explain why but instead offers a path of recovery. Pico implores his fellow men to use their full potential: "Let a certain holy ambition invade our souls, so that, not content with the mediocre, we shall pant after the highest and (since we may if we wish) toil with all our strength to obtain it." But how do we go about our redivinization? According to the *prisci theologi*, the first step in the process is "washing away the filth of ignorance and vice, cleanse our soul," through natural philosophy. But Pico adds that "It is not . . . in the power of natural philosophy to give us in nature a true quiet and unshaken peace but that this is the function and privilege of her mistress, that is, of holiest theology." The theology that Pico refers to is the collected wisdom of the *prisci theologi*. For those capable of understanding these teachings, the path to divinization is sure and certain. Pico draws not only on the Judeo-Christian mystical teachings but on the full range of ancient theology to verify his contention that following this path of knowledge entitles mankind to "become He Himself Who made us."[22]

Cassirer, P. O. Kristeller, and J. H. Randall, Jr., eds., *The Renaissance Philosophy of Man* (Chicago: University of Chicago Press, 1948), 224–45.
  22. Ibid., 229, 231.

Having established the path to be taken from natural philosophy through the occult teachings of the ancient theologians, Pico
describes his own knowledge system and its contribution. First,
Pico claims the notable achievement of having assembled an extraordinary library of documents of the Ancient Wisdom. This
recovery of these precious documents will in itself serve as a
means of overcoming the ignorance and error that have afflicted
human philosophizing and theologizing. But Pico says that his
achievement is not simply as collector. His distinctive accom-
plishment is that he has drawn together and reconciled the essential core of these various teachings into a single coherent system
of philosophy and magic "by means of which whoever holds them
will be able . . . to answer any question whatever proposed in natural philosophy or divinity."[23] Pico then devotes a long segment to
an explanation of how to move from the present alienated state of
existence to the full recovery of our humanity through the use of
magic.

It is evident that Pico's *Oration* is indebted to the creation account found in the *Corpus Hermeticum*. In the *Pimander*, or *Poimandres*, Hermes Trismegistus has revealed to him the true nature of the world and of man. The Demiurge created the world,
but the divine Father created man. So man is beautiful and shares
in the divine power. As primal man looks down on the universe,
he expresses his wish to use his divinely given creative powers and
obtains permission from God to assist the Demiurge in creation
of the natural order. Primal man is taught the essence of the workings of the universe, and he is thus able to become a creator as
well. Pico has modified this story, eliminating the Demiurge and
having God perform both acts of creation, but the essence of the
story remains. Man is a special creation of God with divine powers. When Pico's full narrative in the *Oration* is taken into account,
there is a strong suggestion that the magus is the reincarnation of
primal man. He has the power to create in the physical world because he has been empowered by God and because the lesser orders
of being that control the operations of the natural world taught
him nature's secrets.

We have in Pico, then, a parallel construction of an ancient period of high achievement, a period of darkness and confusion, and

---

23. Ibid., 234. Pico adds that his system is "other than we are taught in that
philosophy which is studied in the schools and practiced by doctors of this age"
(234).

a new age of rebirth and life. This construction is also found in
Agrippa, who was regarded as one of the wisest men of his age.

Agrippa

An early work entitled *De triplici ratione cognoscendi Deum*
(1516) describes the widespread corruption and spiritual disorder
in the Church as evidence that Christianity has lost its anchoring
in the primary revelations of God. Agrippa (1486–1535) identifies
two principal sources for this state of alienation and confusion.
His primary criticism is directed toward the scholastic effort to
make theology commensurable with classical philosophy. For
Agrippa, this enterprise shows a failure to recognize the distinction between the knowledge provided through direct revelation by
God and the informed opinions derived from man's sensory experience and deductive reasoning. Agrippa is also highly critical of
the revival of the Latin humanist tradition, which also places
undue emphasis on human reason and imagination.

In describing the three paths open to man, Agrippa places the
conventional approaches in juxtaposition to the true understanding revealed in the ancient teachings. In its broadest application
this is a contrast between the intellectual disorder resulting from
Adam's squandering the highest forms of esoteric knowledge and
the magus's using that knowledge to become a terrestrial god.
From this perspective, nature—the first of Agrippa's three paths
to true knowledge—can only be understood properly if one follows the occult teachings of the Ancient Wisdom. On this point
Agrippa's position is similar to Ficino's effort to develop a cosmology that links the physical and the spiritual worlds and connects man's knowledge of the cosmos with the power to restore
nature and to perfect the human condition. His perspective on the
law, the second path, derives from the Cabalist tradition, which
he is convinced provides the power to ascend through the orders of
nature to direct communion with God.[24] Thus, man gains full

24. Pico was a principal contributor to the development of a Christianized
Cabala. See Frances Yates, *The Occult Philosophy in the Elizabethan Age* (London:
Routledge and Kegan Paul, 1979), especially chap. 2. For a discussion of Agrippa's
Cabala, see Yates, *Occult Philosophy*, chaps. 5 and 6. For a general discussion of
the development of the Christianized Cabala, see J. L. Blau, *The Christian Inter-
pretation of the Cabala in the Renaissance* (Port Washington, N.Y.: Kennikat Press,
1944); and François Secret, *Les Kabbalistes chrétiens de la Renaissance* (Paris:
Dunod, 1964)

knowledge of the workings of nature and the operative power to change the conditions of existence. The return to the gospel, the third path, is through a reading of the Ancient Wisdom traditions, finally clarifying the role God wants man to assume.

This brief discussion demonstrates that Agrippa continued the efforts of Ficino and Pico to establish the unifying core of the revelations given by God and to use it to recover the full understanding of man's nature. For Agrippa, man's true condition had been described in the Egyptian Genesis. God created man to be a terrestrial god. For reasons that are never clear, however, man became disoriented and alienated from his true nature. To guide man back, God provided the *prisca theologia*. Again for unexplained reasons, man lost the ability to understand and use it. Now, however, recovering the hidden truth of the Ancient Wisdom would allow Agrippa and other wise men to gain a comprehensive understanding of these revelations and thereby recognize the source of man's alienation and overcome it. It is with this conviction that Agrippa undertook his famous text *De occulta philosophia libri tres* (1510), which established his international reputation as the master magician of his age.

In a later work, *De incertitudine et vanitate scientiarum et artium* (1526), Agrippa again criticized conventional philosophy and theology and the revival of humanism, but he criticized the distortion and corruption of God's revelation in the Ancient Wisdom as well. Little needs to be said about Agrippa's criticisms of the first two categories, since his stance is consistent with that in the *De triplici ratione*. The criticisms of the occult wisdom, however, do need explanation. A closer examination of his criticisms of the Ancient Wisdom show that they are directed at two elements. The first is astrology and other divinatory systems. Like Ficino and Pico, Agrippa rejected astrology because its basic premise is that man's fate is knowable because it is determined by the stars. Agrippa maintained that man could use astral magic to manipulate the stars and other celestial divinities to serve his own purpose and to alter his fate.

The second element of the Ancient Wisdom criticized by Agrippa is the Hermetic and Cabalistic materials. Here he does seem to be making a significant departure from the *De occulta*, but closer examination shows that this is not the case. In Agrippa's view the Hermetic materials are important, but they are not the primary source of ancient learning. Therefore, when he claims in the *De vanitate* that these materials in themselves are not a sufficient guide to knowledge and that if used by themselves they lead to sin, he is not significantly altering his opinion. His attack on the Cabala also turns out to be consistent with his earlier position. Here he criticizes particularly those elements of the Jewish Cabala that developed after the coming of Christ and show a deliberate disregard for the higher truth revealed by the Messiah. He continues, however, to value those elements of the Cabala that point toward the fuller Christian revelation. This position is consistent with that taken in both the *De triplici ratione* and the *De occulta*. Throughout his life, Agrippa was convinced that the key to this revelation was not in the literal words of the gospel but in their secret, esoteric meaning that could be brought to light by use of the Cabala and other Ancient Wisdom traditions.

It is also important to note that Agrippa's views of the source of knowledge and the concept of man are not altered in the *De vanitate*. Magic is not included in the sciences that he criticizes. In fact, it is the "highest peak of natural philosophy." This magic is the key to restoring man as a terrestrial god and the means for overcoming the alienated state produced by Adam's sin. Further evidence that Agrippa's position remained basically unchanged in his later years is an important letter that Charles Nauert has called attention to. In this letter, written two years after the *De vanitate*, Agrippa acknowledges that there are "natural sciences, metaphysical arts, and occult devices . . . whereby one can licitly defend kingdoms, increase wealth, and cure sickness."[25] This description is consistent with Agrippa's earliest position—that is, on the recovery of knowledge that enables man to transform the conditions of his existence and to perfect society.

If we now briefly review Agrippa's fundamental concerns, it becomes clear that they are comparable to those of the other religious reformers and visionaries of the period. His attacks on the corruption of the Church and the ignorance and error of scholastic philosophy and humanism are similar to those of Luther, for example. What is more, both see the solution to the present disorder in a return to a pure form of gospel Christianity. Their understanding of what constitutes this pristine course, however, is very different: for Luther, it is realigning the teachings and practices of the Church with primitive Christianity; for Agrippa, it is recovering the hidden wisdom of the gospel revelations. Luther and

---

25. Charles G. Nauert, *Agrippa and the Crisis of Renaissance Thought* (Urbana, Ill.: University of Illinois Press, 1965), 216.

Agrippa also hold fundamentally different views of man's proper relation to God. Luther sees a gulf separating sinful man from his righteous God, and only divine action can bridge it. While Agrippa agrees with Luther's description of the human condition after Adam's sin, he is convinced that this unnatural state can be overcome through a recovery of the Ancient Wisdom. When man makes the effort to reorient his soul and recover his true nature, he will be restored as a terrestrial god capable of finding his purpose and fulfillment through his action in the world. The basic contrast between the two is most concisely expressed in their respective views of Adam's sin: For Luther, it is man's desire to gain knowledge to be like God; for Agrippa, it is in man's choosing a sentient life in which he worships the creation rather than the Creator and thereby disregards the higher forms of knowledge that can put him in direct communion with God and enable him to be an active participant in the creation.

Bruno

There is a long-standing view of Bruno (1548–1600) as a martyr to the cause of modern science.[26] Thanks primarily to the work of Frances Yates, it is now clear that Bruno's interest in and commitment to the defense of the Copernican system stemmed from a very different source than Galileo's. For Bruno the Copernican system represented a recovery of the Ancient Wisdom's view of the universe and signaled the beginning of a general recovery of the ancient tradition which would produce a thoroughgoing religious and political reformation. Our purpose in this brief analysis is to develop Bruno's vision of the beginning of a new age and his view of the messianic role he was to play in ushering it in. We begin with one of his early writings, *Cena de le ceneri* (1584), which is his account of a dinner at Oxford in which he defended the Copernican view against the "pedantry" of the university's philosophers and theologians. This account may initially seem to be similar to Galileo's famous *Dialogue Concerning the Two Chief World Systems*, in which the Copernican theory is defended against philosophical and theological criticisms. Closer examination of Bruno's work makes it clear, however, that the intent of

26. This analysis of Bruno and Campanella closely follows my *Sacralizing the Secular*, 79–90.

the two works are markedly different. In his dialogue Bruno criticizes the general state of learned ignorance of university philosophers and church theologians in ways that recall Agrippa's criticisms in the *De triplici ratione* and *the De vanitate*. Also like Agrippa, Bruno maintains that there is a way out of this state of ignorance and disorientation through the teachings of the "Chaldeans, of the Egyptians, of the Magi, of the Orphics, of the Pythagoreans and other early thinkers." Bruno reveres Copernicus's work because he thinks it is inspired by this Ancient Wisdom tradition and therefore signals a recovery of the true understanding of the cosmos. "Who then would treat this man [Copernicus] and his labours with such ignoble discourtesy as to forget all his achievements and his divinely ordained appearance as the dawn which was to precede the full sunrise of the ancient and true philosophy after its agelong burial in the dark caverns of blind and envious ignorance." From subsequent passages it becomes clear that Bruno regards the development of the Copernican theory as a first step in a wholesale recovery of the Ancient Wisdom and that Bruno will lead the way to the full recovery. Examination of Bruno's description of his own achievement in relation to that of Copernicus suggests that he regarded Copernicus as a sort of John the Baptist who paved the way for his messianic role.

> The Nolan . . . has freed the human mind and the knowledge which were shut up in the strait prison of turbulent air. . . . [The mind's] wings were clipped so that it could not soar and pierce the veil of the clouds to see what was actually there. It could not free itself from the chimera of those who, coming forth with manifold imposture from the mire and pits of earth (as if they were Mercuries and Apollos descended from the skies), have filled the whole world with infinite folly, nonsense and vice, disguised as so much virtue, dignity and discipline. By approving and confirming the misty darkness of the sophists and blockheads, they extinguish the light which make the minds of our ancient fathers divine and heroic. . . . Thus, by the light of his senses and reason, he opened those cloisters of truth which it is possible for us to open with the key of the most diligent inquiry; he laid bare covered and veiled nature, gave eyes to the moles and light to the blind . . . he loosed the tongues of the dumb . . . [and] he strengthened the lame who could not make that progress of the spirit which base and dissoluble matter cannot make.[27]

From this passage and from his previous reference to the signifi-

27. Giordano Bruno, *The Ash Wednesday Supper*, trans. and ed. Edward A. Gosselin and Lawrence S. Lerner (Hamden, Conn.: Archon Books, 1977), 89–90.

cance of Copernicus, we can see that Bruno regards his heliocentric system as heralding "the full sunrise of the ancient and true philosophy after its agelong burial in dark caverns." In a subsequent passage, Bruno indicates that his recovery and promulgation of the Ancient Wisdom can serve as the means for overcoming the present dark age of personal, social, and political order and disorientation because the Ancient Wisdom produced men who were

> moderate in life, expert in medicine, judicious in contemplation, unique in divination, miraculous in magic, wary of superstition, lawabiding, irreproachable in morality, godlike in theology, and heroic in every way. All this is shown by the length of their lives, their healthier bodies, their most lofty inventions, the fulfillment of their prophecies, the substances transformed by their works, the peaceful deportment of their people, their inviolable sacraments, the great justice of their actions, the familiarity of good and protecting spirits, and the vestiges, which still remain, of their amazing prowess.[28]

In another of his works, *Spaccio della bestia trionfante* (1584), Bruno presents a brief mythic description of the end of an age of darkness and the beginning of enlightenment.[29] This text contains a scene in which the celestial powers that control the world convene to remedy the disorder that plagues it. In an elaborate mythic description of a realignment of planetary influences, the celestial powers are depicted as initiating this plan of action in order to renew or regenerate the creation. Following this description, Bruno comments that these efforts of the gods must be matched by the magus who can use the new celestial alignments to help usher in the age of regeneration. This text makes it clear that the efforts of the magus are essential in overcoming human ignorance and in installing a perfect social order that will bring an end to the present state of turmoil.

In the early 1590's Bruno repeatedly expressed his conviction that he would be the spiritual messiah who would join with political leaders to effect a religious and political reformation. Drawing upon the *Sommario* documents of his trial, Frances Yates demonstrates that "the legend that Bruno was prosecuted as a philosophical thinker, was burned for his daring views on innumerable

---

28. Ibid., 96.
29. Bruno, *The Expulsion of the Triumphant Beast*, trans. and ed. A. D. Imerti (New Brunswick, N.J.: Rutgers University Press, 1964).

worlds or on the movement of the earth, can no longer stand."[30] It is now clear that Bruno was condemned for his belief that the Egyptian religion was the highest religion given by God, reversing the view of Ficino and others that the ancient theology pointed the way to the fuller, revelation of Christianity. Moreover, his later years make clear that he understood his mission as one of a religious reformer who would be an instrument in the purging of the Church and in the institution of a new age of enlightenment based on Hermeticism and magic.

We have, then, in Bruno a further demonstration of the mounting criticism of orthodox Christianity as a source of darkness and disorder and the concurrent affirmation of the *prisca theologia* as the means of overcoming alienation and installing an enduring political order. Another key figure in perpetuating the vision of a utopian order founded on the principles of Hermeticism and magic is Campanella (1568–1639).

Campanella

The year 1600 signaled for Campanella the beginning of a new age in which the world would be renewed and religious strife and political turmoil put to an end. Like Bruno, Campanella believed he had a messianic role to play in ushering it in. In 1599 Campanella attempted to establish a new capital for the worldwide religious and political reform in Calabria in southern Italy. This effort at rebellion against the Spanish monarchy and the papacy led to an imprisonment which cost twenty-five years of his life. It did not, however, destroy his dream of the renewal of society and the world, nor did it diminish his conviction that he was to play a signal role in ushering in the new age of light. While in prison Campanella wrote *The City of the Sun (Città del Sole)*, for which he is best remembered. As Frances Yates rightly notes, "The City was thus a complete reflection of the world as governed by the laws of natural magic in dependence on the stars. The great men were those who had best understood and used those laws, inventors, moral teachers, miracle workers, religious leaders, in short, Magi, of whom the chief was Christ with His apostles." The head of the city was a priest-king who was a master of natural magic. Through his administration "the people of the City lived in broth-

---

30. Yates, *Giordano Bruno*, 386–87.

erly love, having all things in common; . . . They encouraged scientific invention, all inventions being used in the service of the
community to improve the general well-being. They were healthy
and well skilled in medicine. And they were virtuous. . . . there
was no robbery, murder, incest, adultery, no malignity or malevolence of any kind."[31]

During this time he also wrote first to the Spanish monarch and
then to the pope, describing the "natural" signs that foretold their
destiny as leaders of a universal reform that would end the present
state of ignorance and alienation.[32] Upon his release from prison,
he went to Rome and was well received by Pope Urban VIII and
was even credited with performing astral magic that overcame the
hostile configuration threatening the pope's life. Shortly afterward, Campanella went to France where he was also well received
by Louis XIII and Richelieu because he proclaimed that the French
monarch was to lead the reformation of the world.

In 1638 when Louis XIII's son was born, Campanella prepared
an eclogue to commemorate the occasion. The eclogue is consistent with his vision of the French monarchy's restoration of universal harmony and is modeled after the famous messianic Fourth
Eclogue of Virgil. The eclogue opens in a fashion similar to the
proclamation made to herald the Calabrian revolt—that is, astrological signs show that a renewal of the world is at hand and that a
new reign of religious vitality and social tranquility is about to
begin. Campanella then refers to the Dauphin as the "French Cock
destined to rule with a reformed Peter a united world. In this coming dispensation, labour will be a pleasure amicably shared by all;
all will recognize one God and Father and love will unite all; all
kings and peoples will assemble in a city which they will call
Héliaca, the City of the Sun, which will be built by this illustri-
ous hero."[33] It is evidently from this reference that Louis XIV
gains the title "le roi Soleil."

These events in Rome and in Paris in the last part of Campanella's life marked the full emergence of the Hermetic magical
tradition. With Campanella the emphasis on the magus as the
creator of the perfect social order reemerged completely. In Hermes
Trismegistus's idealized city of Adocentyn, all human physical,
emotional, and spiritual needs were met through the efforts of the

31. Ibid., 369.
32. Tommaso Campanella, *Monarchia di Spagna* (1620) and *Monarchia Mes-
siae* (1633).
33. Quoted in Yates, *Giordano Bruno*, 390.

magus. This utopian element reemerged most fully in the work of Bruno and Campanella, who were drawn to the Hermetic prophesies of a new age in which the *prisca theologia* would be recovered and man and society thereby transformed. In the sixteenth and seventeenth centuries, epistemological, religious, and political issues were inextricably interconnected. For Campanella the coming reformation was both a restitution of a true religion and the institution of a perfect social order. The *prisca theologia* offered an alternative religion and a redefinition of human nature that identified the present Christian disorder as a cause of ignorance and alienation. And it proposed either to completely discard Christianity or to rediscover its true essence through esoteric means. If we look briefly at Francis Bacon's work, we can see how this cultural climate contributed to the understanding of the role of science as a source of enlightenment in society.[34]

Francis Bacon

In the eighteenth and nineteenth centuries Francis Bacon (1561–1626) was lauded as a patriarch of science and a great field general in the battle of the ancients and moderns. Such praise is certainly understandable. More than any other seventeenth-century thinker, he led the attack on traditional learning and developed a thoroughgoing overhaul of the premises of philosophical and scientific inquiry. In addition to his theoretical work, he helped create the idea of a new scientific society (the Royal Society) to advance the understanding of the natural world and enhance the development of technology and the mechanical arts.[35] Moreover, in laying the groundwork for a new form of scholarly collaboration, he set forth some of the most basic guidelines for scientific research —for example, the sharing of theories and experimental results on an international basis and the testing of theories through independent experimental verification. In addition, there are the many passages in Bacon's writings that link the prospects of a utopian social order to the advancement of the new learning. Bacon made it

---

34. The Paracelsian tradition is an important part of the transmission of the *prisca theologia* tradition in England and the continent in the sixteenth and seventeenth centuries. For a useful discussion, see Allen G. Debus, "An Elizabethan History of Medical Chemistry," *Annals of Science* 18 (1962; published 1964): 1–29; and "History with a Purpose," *Pharmacy in History* 26 (1984): 83–96.

35. On Bacon and the institutionalization of science, see Tore Frängsmyr, ed., *Solomon's House Revisited: The Organization and Institutionalization of Science* (Canton, Mass.: Watson Publishing International, 1990).

clear that in order to build the new edifice for the new learning it would be necessary to tear down and clear away the clutter of the present educational system. And, there is Bacon's emphasis on knowledge as power and on the extraordinary developments in applied science that were opening new frontiers and expanding the horizons beyond anything conceived by the ancients.

The "frontispiece" of *The Great Instauration* (1620), which depicts a ship sailing beyond the Pillars of Hercules, is emblematic of the new epochal consciousness. First of all, it symbolizes the expansion and discovery underway since the fifteenth century that expanded the horizons beyond any known or imagined in previous times. This image also has a mythical significance as well. In the ancient world the Pillars of Hercules marked the boundaries between the known, familiar world of man and the forbidden and treacherous ocean (*okeanos*) beyond man's knowledge or grasp. This symbolism between the familiar, habitable world and the unfamiliar and treacherous beyond was a complement to the concept of the ancient cosmos in which man had a definite place in the order of things. Knowledge in this conception depended on discovery of the boundaries of man's nature so that he did not fall into a tragic life of wanton and animalic behavior or of sinful pride that caused him to overstep his boundaries and come into conflict with the gods. In fact, the Greek word often translated as *fate* derives from the term *moira*, whose original and primary meaning is a boundary, a division that walled off one segment from another. In this construction, knowledge is knowledge of one's place in the hierarchy of things, and overstepping the boundaries is symptomatic of ignorance, error, or sin. Bacon's image fundamentally transforms that ancient mythic understanding. It portrays the new man heroically sailing beyond the confines that had restricted other generations to unnaturally restricted existence. By sailing beyond those boundaries, man transcends those boundaries that had held him short of what he could be, and symbolically he enters into the realm of the higher beings.

While the emphasis on the new learning and on progress are obvious and important elements of Bacon's thought, Charles Whitney argues that they have been taken out of their religious/political context and a distorted picture of Bacon has, therefore, emerged.[36] The distorted picture of Bacon has led, in turn, to a distorted un-

---

36. Charles Whitney, *Francis Bacon and Modernity* (New Haven, Conn.: Yale University Press, 1986).

derstanding of modernity. For Whitney the effort to make Bacon the patriarch of science and secularization requires interpretations to discount the importance of the religious language that permeates Bacon's writings as "the husk that surrounds the kernel." This image, of course, identifies the substance of Bacon's writings—that is, the call for a new learning, the linking of knowledge with power, the urging of man to regain dominion over the world—as the elements that are truly modern and the religious language as the inessential.

In juxtaposition to this view, Whitney develops a lengthy analysis of the central term *instauration* as it applies in Bacon's work. In an important essay in the *Journal of the History of Ideas*, Whitney has shown that the term had wide general usage from the ancient period up to Bacon's time.[37] The important context for the term as Bacon uses it, however, is connected with the Vulgate edition of the *Bible*, particularly the account of the instauration of the Temple of Solomon during the time of King Josiah. During the reign of Solomon (ca. 1000 B.C.), the Hebrews enjoyed unprecedented prosperity and freedom from religious or political interference by neighboring powers in the ancient Near East. After Solomon, however, the Hebrew nation was overrun and lost its political autonomy and religious freedom. In 624 B.C. pressure from neighboring powers waned, and the young king Josiah was able to institute political and religious reforms, including the rebuilding of the Temple of Jerusalem. During reconstruction, the Temple's Mosaic law code (the Deuteronomic code) was rediscovered, and this was understood to be the beginning of a renewed covenant with God.

The specific context for this symbol is important for several reasons:

1. The instauration of the Temple is a religious reform as well as a political reform, and as subsequent analysis will show, Bacon links the rebuilding to a rebuilding of nature.

2. The reference to Solomon has a poignancy in Bacon's time because King James I referred to himself as the new Solomon who would bring the new Jerusalem, and this was the primary motif in his coronation ceremonies.

3. Bacon was evidently hoping to emulate the role of Josiah's chancellor by being King James's chancellor who urged him to the reform and provided him the means for accomplishing it.

---

37. Charles Whitney, "Bacon's *Instauratio*," *Journal of the History of Ideas* 50 (1989): 23–64.

4. The rebuilding of the Temple by Josiah represents the dual action of innovation and recovery. In order to build the new edifice, it is necessary to tear down the damaged existing structure. So the building of the Temple is a new endeavor that can only be accomplished by clearing away what has existed. At the same time, however, the intent is to build something that has existed before. At the symbolic level, the attempt involves creating in the present a more perfect rendering of the eternal ideal. This is a motif that needs much further development, and the key is in the Ancient Wisdom tradition.

5. This image of renewal and reformation of the Temple contains a clue to other writings of Bacon where he proposes or describes the restoration of man to his condition prior to the Fall. Bacon agrees with the biblical text that the original sin was in attempting to gain knowledge that God had denied him. Bacon, however, contends that this is the knowledge of ethics or morality that is tied to salvation. This knowledge is different from the knowledge of nature that God had given man in order that he might have dominion over the world. Bacon, therefore, argues that a confusion over the nature of sin and the limits of human knowledge has left man enervated unnecessarily. God had intended man to know the cosmos and have dominion over the world. This differentiation is also found in writings where Bacon wants to separate religion from the arts and sciences that are concerned with knowledge of the world.

6. The theme of instauration also occurs in Bacon's description of the rebuilding of the temple of knowledge. Passages in *The Advancement of Learning* (1605) offer sharp criticism of the present state of knowledge and call for a radical building that will open up avenues never known before. But in those same passages there is a reference to throwing off the present corrupt state of affairs so that the ancient truths can reemerge. This emphasis on recovery of ancient truth is central to the analysis of the influence of the *prisca theologia* tradition.

The discussion of the theme of innovation and recovery suggests parallels with the Ancient Wisdom tradition's influence and use in the sixteenth century. The criticism of metaphysics and theology and the call for an abandoning of the vanities of knowledge (Bacon presents himself as a humble person reattuning himself to the natural world) recall Agrippa's condemnation of the present state of learning. His call for an abandonment of the false traditions of learning in order to discover deeper levels of truth also has a general connection with the theme of the *prisca theologia* tradition. More direct connections can also be made. There is, first of all, the remythologizing of pre-Adamite existence. This reinterpretation of the biblical myth has close parallels to the myth in the *Corpus Hermeticum*. Bacon wants to underscore the God-given right to dominate the world and to possess godlike knowledge of the natural world.

Another key connection is the emphasis on the House of Solomon in the *New Atlantis* (1627). Whitney is right to connect it with the biblical tradition and to the circumstances with James I. But the Solomon that Bacon is interested in is the Solomon who knew the secrets of nature and had a reputation for wisdom like that of the *magus*. This tradition is not part of the biblical account and is not part of what was understood by the writers of Chronicles in the biblical account of the recovery by Josiah. This is part of an occult or esoteric tradition that parallels the mythical or occult tradition regarding Moses. According to this tradition, the Cabala contained the secret teachings that God gave Moses on Mount Sinai. Moses stayed on Mount Sinai for forty days and forty nights in order to absorb the hidden mysteries and teachings. The Ten Commandments were given to those who were ordinary and who needed a clear set of principles for conducting ordinary life, but the highest levels of truth were for those who could know and understand them. Similarly, there was an esoteric tradition that Solomon was the wisest of men because of his knowledge and ability to manipulate and gain direct access to the celestial powers through knowledge of their Hebrew names.[38]

It is apparent that Bacon was aware of this tradition and used it in his utopia, the *New Atlantis*. There the source of order and stability and the source of the new discoveries that solve the basic problems of existences come from the College of Solomon. This is a direct tie to the Ancient Wisdom tradition. Moreover, the symbol of the New Atlantis is itself another image of a primordial or pristine condition existing before the world became corrupted by philosophy and theology. The restoration of Atlantis is a rebuilding of a secular city that is analogous to the rebuilding of the Temple of Solomon. It parallels Bacon's call in his other writings

---

38. S. M. Butler, *The Myth of the Magus* (Cambridge: Cambridge University Press, 1948); *Ritual Magic* (Cambridge: Cambridge University Press, 1949); and *The Fortunes of Faust* (Cambridge: Cambridge University Press, 1952).

for James I to become the new Solomon. The call to build the new temple evokes James's identification with Solomon and the new Jerusalem, and the *New Atlantis* offers him the blueprint of what is possible if the new learning, which is the old learning, is used. It will take English society away from the ignorance and error that plagues Europe and create the conditions that existed before man became alienated and overwhelmed by erroneous interpretations of his finitude and his sin.

In the context of this discussion, it is important to underscore Whitney's argument that it is not necessary to be able to prove that Bacon was a devout Christian in order to demonstrate the importance of the prophetic and apocalyptic imagery in his works. Similarly, it is not necessary to make Bacon a *magus* in order to demonstrate the influence of the *prisca theologia*. Just as there is a substantial body of scholarship that now details the prevalence of apocalyptic and millenarian imagery in Bacon's time, there is a growing body of scholarship that demonstrates the pervasiveness of Hermetic and Rosicrucian symbols in the sixteenth and seventeenth centuries.

This is obviously not a full examination of Bacon and the complex issues shaping his age; it does suffice, however, to bring us to the last part of our discussion because we can now begin to see that it is as important to examine the influence of modern epochal consciousness on the development of science as it is to investigate the influence of science on modernity. Our brief analysis has demonstrated that conventional assumptions about the modern age and about the pattern of historical development connected to the concept have obscured or prevented an accurate and adequate examination of modern epochal consciousness. There is, as we have seen, an epochal pattern emerging from the humanist revival and articulated by Petrarch, Vasari, and to some extent Erasmus. Another comes from the *prisca theologia* as it is developed in the work of Ficino, Pico, and Agrippa. Though we have not made it a subject of study, there is also the important influence of apocalyptic and millenarian strands in Christianity. These come to prominence in the sixteenth-century theological, ecclesiastical, and political clashes between various factions of Christendom.

Each of these contributed to the growing sense of longing or expectation of an end to the darkness and disorder. Each of the three portrayed the coming of a new modern age that would so profoundly change the human condition that it must employ the language of salvation—that is, rebirth and enlightenment. Even orthodox Christian millenarianism directed severe criticism toward the ignorance, error, and disorder within Christendom that would have to be overcome by a return to the fundamental truths of the faith. The humanist and Neoplatonic strands were significantly different from the Christian in one fundamental aspect, however. The humanist tradition emphasized human dignity, autonomy, and creativity. The *prisca theologia* did as well. The Ancient Wisdom especially portrayed the coming of a new age in which man will regain his role as a terrestrial god, possessing the knowledge to control nature and perfect society. It is this magical emphasis on knowledge as power that profoundly influenced Bacon and other early moderns to see science as the new source of soteriological power in the world. And it is the Hermetic myths alone that portrayed man as the primary actor in the salvation drama of the modern age.

What is new in this research is that it demonstrates that Bacon saw science as an instrument for religious renewal and revitalization. Reason/science offered the means rather than revelation. Recent studies by Charles Whitney and others have also demonstrated that there is a strong millenarian dimension to Bacon's position. Whitney has shown, for example, that the language of a great instauration ties Bacon's England to one of the great renewal episodes in the Judeo-Christian tradition. In more controversial interpretations, Frances Yates and Paolo Rossi have pointed to the strong presence of esoteric symbols in the work of Bacon. The *New Atlantis* is a prime example. The symbol itself comes from one of these mythic reconstructions of history that we have already noted. The *New Atlantis* is that part of ancient civilization prior to the deformation through classical philosophy and subsequently Christian religion. The *New Atlantis* is a reinstitution of that ancient learning. This paradigm is much like the Hermetic myths. In this utopian society, the College of Solomon, a collection of scientists, is responsible for the welfare of the society, and as we have already noted, this symbol of the College of Solomon is a key esoteric symbol.

What we see in Francis Bacon, then, is a view of modernity that depended heavily on science for the achievement of the cultural aims of the modern age. Francis Bacon was a modernist in that he was convinced that a new age was about to emerge that would overcome the age of darkness, disorder, and turmoil. He was convinced that man would play a key role in this effort through the subjugation of nature and the perfection of society. He was also modern in that he saw science as the means for attaining these goals.

If this emphasis on the cultural context for the institutionalization of science is as crucial as it appears, then, there is a tremendous amount of work that needs to be done on the origins of the concept of modernity, the patterns of history that accompany its development, and the influence the concept has on the role science assumes—or is given—in early modern society.

MILLENARIANISM, HERMETICISM, AND THE SEARCH FOR A UNIVERSAL SCIENCE

Klaus Vondung

Previous essays in this collection have shown that the Scientific Revolution, the revival of Hermeticism, and a new sense of apocalyptic expectation were fundamental aspects of the intellectual ferment of the early modern period. The purpose of this essay is to demonstrate how apocalypticism and Hermeticism contribute to another key development in the seventeenth and eighteenth centuries—the search for a "universal science," that is, a holistic understanding of all spiritual, social, and natural phenomena which would enable modern man to comprehend, if not dominate, reality. The search for a universal science can be seen as a response to the differentiation and disintegration of sciences, but not of sciences alone. If reality in its different dimensions—nature, society, the human body and soul—is no longer experienced as a comprehensive whole, but as incoherent and independent realms of reality which require different instruments to deal with adequately, and if on top of that, the condition of one or the other of these disconnected realms seems unsatisfactory, there is even more reason to seek a universal instrument of knowledge which would encompass all dimensions of reality and heal any particular deficiencies.

It is not surprising that the seventeenth and the eighteenth centuries were a period when such a longing for a universal science sprang up. The sciences, especially philosophy and the natural sciences, emancipated themselves from theology, which once had provided the ultimate answers to all questions. The natural sciences—in particular astronomy, physics, and mechanics—offered new insights into the structures and laws of material nature and set new standards for scientific objectivity and exactitude. A new philosophy developed which disconnected body and soul, body and reason, and dealt with the former in accordance with the mechanistic model. Other disciplines, like chemistry, medicine, and law, specialized more and more and gained independent prestige.

Theology, by contrast, was clinging to orthodox dogmatism, which offered little to intelligent and open-minded Christians.

At the same time, the seventeenth and eighteenth centuries were a time of severe political and social grievances, which made the world seem to be deteriorating. Numerous wars, beginning with the Thirty Years' War, devastated Central Europe, particularly Germany. The Holy Roman Empire was, after the Thirty Years' War, not much more than a hollow shell; Germany disintegrated step by step into independent states. Within these states the rise of absolutism added to the grievances of the population. The subjects of the system of absolutism most often had reason to regard it as unjust and immoral. The peasants frequently were exploited or sold as soldiers; and the middle class, which in the eighteenth century slowly recuperated from its losses in the Thirty Years' War and regained some self-esteem, was hindered from emancipating itself politically and socially. The churches, especially the Protestant church, were subjugated by the absolute state and made to serve its purposes. This induced many believers to defect and join sects or semi-independent denominations, especially pietist ones.

Thus, the concepts of a universal science which were developed during that period could have varied motives and, in consequence, different accents and scopes. Sometimes they were only by-products, as it were, of a more general, overriding longing for salvation. In the following I will outline, by way of example, two major versions of the concept of universal science, the first being motivated by the seemingly deficient state of the world, the second by the split between religious belief and scientific reason.

Universal Science as an Anticipation of the Millennium

From the twelfth to the eighteenth century there was a continuous tradition of millenarian movements in most of the West European countries, especially in Germany. Their endeavors usually combined the longing for spiritual salvation with political or social protest. During the time of the Reformation, this tradition, represented by movements like the Anabaptists or by apocalyptic prophets like Thomas Münzer, reached a critical point. The Protestant orthodoxy, which in the following centuries allied itself with the absolute state, warded off apocalyptic speculation, as the Catholic church always did. Nevertheless, this type of speculation flourished underneath the official doctrine, in Germany most

often connected with Pietism. It was motivated by such grievances as mentioned above: spiritual dissatisfaction at the official
church, political and social depression, crises and wars. In short,
the authors of these apocalyptic visions and millenarian speculations regarded the present state of the world as being absolutely
deficient, and they despaired of the meaning of history in general.
As a consequence, they predicted that the world would come to an
end soon and that the Sabbath of world history, the Millennium,
would begin. They constructed a "course" in history, a "divine
economy" underlying the seemingly inconsistent historical events
and developments, in order to figure out the exact date of the beginning of the Millennium and in order to give meaning back to
history. The seventeenth and eighteenth centuries are full of such
prophecies and speculations. Their authors were learned men,
most often pastors or professors of theology. Important represen-
tatives in Germany were Kuhlmann, Serrarius, Alsted, Comenius, Coccejus, Bengel, and Oetinger.

Since the millenarians devised their speculations on the course
of history as comprehensive interpretations of the meaning of
human existence in time, they tended to regard their systems as a
key to all knowledge or to develop, within their visions of the
Millennium, the concept of a universal science. The first millenarian to claim explicitly that his speculation on history would dominate all sciences was Quirinus Kuhlmann (1651–1689). Among
the numerous visionaries who in the seventeenth century prophesied the imminent end of the world, he excelled particularly in
missionary zeal. He tried to convince the princes of Germany as
well as the theologians of the German universities that Germany
had been chosen to prepare the world for the Final Judgment and
for the universal renewal to take place in the "Fifth Monarchy."
When he did not find acclaim in Germany he traveled to almost
all of the major residences in Europe—to London, Amsterdam,
Paris, Constantinople, and Moscow—in order to offer salvation.
In Moscow, finally, he became a victim of his missionary fervor
and was burnt as an agitator.

Kuhlmann found the basis of his speculation on history in the
works of Jakob Böhme. He compiled Böhme's prophecies and related them to his own time in such a way that they seemed to be a
confirmation of his speculation and its universal pretension:

From our Germany's new disciple of heaven I perceived my own arguments, which the Highest of All has marvelously shown to me, or

rather solid proof of them, so that I intended, in honor of God and for the knowledge of men, after having exposed false doctrines, to enrich all sciences with many thousand inventions, and to disclose the difference between true and false Christian as well as heathen knowledge in a kind of doctrine hitherto unheard of, in which the great center of the world is hidden.[1]

After Kuhlmann the tendency grew even stronger to make the millenarian interpretation of history govern all sciences and to draw a future universal science from the comprehensive view of the world and history. The pastor and theologian Johann Albrecht Bengel (1687–1752) was convinced that he had gained knowledge of "things" and "times" through insights into the "divine economy."[2] This knowledge not only had theoretical value, but also conveyed an orientation of the present life toward the end of history: "By that the congregation of the Lord has a complete instruction so that always one can know where one stands."[3] Bengel had found out, by a complicated system of interpreting the Revelation to John, that the Millennium would begin in the year 1836. He was so overwhelmed by this knowledge of "times," that he did not draw any further conclusions for the knowledge of "things."

But Bengel's disciple Friedrich Christoph Oetinger (1702–1782) made the pretension explicit which Bengel's knowledge of "things" and "times" had contained only implicitly. Oetinger did not take pains to prove that the Millennium "was not far away anymore, because I take this as granted by Bengel's calculation." He laid more stress on the necessity "that one gets prepared for it." And this preparation was to follow the "model of the Golden Age" (*die güldene Zeit*), as he called the Millennium.[4]

Oetinger designed the Millennium as a perfectly ordered society on this earth, with social equality, political justice, and moral integrity. This design reveals the motives behind the speculation: social, political, and moral protest against the conditions in the

---

1. Quirinus Kuhlmann, *Neubegeisterter Böhme: begreiffend Hundertfünftzig Weissagungen . . .* (Leiden: Loth de Haes, 1674), 91. All translations of quotations from German sources are my own.
2. Johann Albrecht Bengel, *Erklärte Offenbarung Johannis . . .* (Stuttgart: Christoph Erhardt, 1740), 96.
3. Johann Albrecht Bengel, *Sechzig erbauliche Reden . . .* (Stuttgart: Christoph Erhardt, 1747), 6.
4. Friedrich Christoph Oetinger, "Die güldene Zeit" (1759), in *Abhandlungen von den letzten Dingen*, ed. Karl Chr. Eberhard Ehmann (Stuttgart: J. F. Steinkopf, 1864), 7.

absolute state of his time. Oetinger formulated the description of the Millennium like a political program of general significance:

> In any kingdom, true happiness has three conditions: first, that despite all multiplicity, which is not against order, and despite all differences of rank, the subjects have equality among each other, as we have learned from the distribution of Israel where the equal share of land reminded everybody not to pride himself above others. Everybody is to find his happiness in the happiness of his neighbor, his joy in the joy of all the other people, and by that everybody is to be a free lord among others; secondly, that they have a community of goods and not take delight in goods because they are a property; thirdly, that they demand nothing from each other as an obligation. Because, if everything would be available in abundance, there would be no need of government, property, and of no liabilities forced and extorted by government.

Between the lines, Oetinger threatened the princes of Germany with the approaching end of history, and explicitly he admonished them, "on the grounds of getting prepared for the final period of time, to regard their subject's welfare for their own, and to undertake reasonable reforms."[5]

So far, Oetinger's outlook on the Millennium reflected the political, social, and moral grievances of the time. But the matter did not rest there. His demand that we prepare ourselves "according to the model of the Golden Age" had an even wider meaning. In Oetinger's opinion the spiritual and social order of the Millennium would flow from a single principle, the "priesthood of Jesus," which Oetinger defined as "the basis and source of all true science." Thus, there would be only one science, which would comprise all sciences. And this universal science will be accessible for everybody by intuition, because Jesus will "present everything scientific very clearly and make it easily comprehensible, and he will abolish everything that is superfluous and confused in the sciences; . . . all gifts of the spirit will be manifest." Therefore, the best preparation for the Millennium would be to lay the groundwork now for the future universal science by abolishing the present fragmentation of the sciences. Oetinger deplored, in particular, the fragmentation of the sciences dealing with the physical nature of the world, with the order of society, and with the human body and soul:

5. Ibid., 29, 32.

With regard to the juridical science and the science which attends to the life of the body and soul, we propose to equalize what is uneven and humpy so that these three sciences, namely jurisprudence, theology, and medicine, are but one science out of one basic wisdom. Because the laceration of the sciences is a result of the corrupted time; the unification of the sciences is part of the preparation for the Golden Age.[6]

Later on, Oetinger added other sciences to his program of unification; he enumerates "the science of logic, which is the doctrine of reasoning, of ontology, which is the doctrine of general notions, of cosmology, which is the science of the world, of pneumatology, which is the science of the spirits, of psychology, the science of the soul, of theology, astronomy, physics, ethics, arithmetic, geometry, and algebra," and he predicts that "they all will stand together in perfection and intuitively will be seen by the children of God."[7]

The concept of the universal science anticipated spiritually the expected state of perfection. The universal science was to fulfill this function by comprising all dimensions of reality and by interpreting their meaning. Therefore, it would bring the state of deficiency to an end, at least in the consciousness of the adepts, and it would abolish ignorance, insecurity, and despair. It is important that this concept of a universal science was a result of a speculation on the meaning of history. Bengel and Oetinger understood history as a process of revelation which unfolds itself gradually until it reaches comprehensive knowledge of "things" and "times," and thus makes it possible, as Oetinger concluded, to devise a universal science.

Bengel and Oetinger were of decisive influence on Schelling and Hegel.[8] Both Schelling and Hegel intended, although in different ways, a universal science as spiritual anticipation of perfection. In both cases this intention was a result of an interpretation of history, that is, the universal science was regarded as the manifestation of the meaning of history. Schelling repeated statements of Bengel and Oetinger almost literally when in 1804 he defined his-

---

6. Ibid., 28, 141, 9.
7. Ibid., 139.
8. See Ernst Benz, *Schellings theologische Geistesahnen*, Abhandlungen der Akademie der Wissenschaften und der Literatur in Mainz, no. 3, 1955; Ernst Benz, "Johann Albrecht Bengel und die Philosophie des deutschen Idealismus," *Deutsche Vierteljahresschrift für Literaturwissenschaft und Geistesgeschichte* 27 (1953): 509–28.

tory as a "successively developing revelation of God,"[9] and like them he described the end of this process as the unification of all sciences, especially of the natural sciences with the humanities. In his view the universal science anticipates the state of perfection: "The peace of the Golden Age [*das Goldne Zeitalter*] will be made known first through the harmonious unification of all sciences."[10] Like apocalyptic visionaries, Schelling expected that this state would be reached soon; only "a short period of time" would pass until the universal science could be established: "It seems that it was reserved for our age to open the path to this objectivity of science."[11]

Hegel, although differing from Schelling in many respects, established the meaning of all being by means of a similar interpretation of history. For him history was a process of a gradually developing revelation—that is, the process of self-realization of the spirit: "World history is . . . the exegesis and realization of the general spirit."[12] The individual consciousness, in this case Hegel's, partakes in this process and fulfills it insofar as it achieves the "absolute knowledge" of the philosophical system. In this state the subjective consciousness and the objective process of realization of the spirit are reconciled and the spirit grasps "the principle of unity of divine and human nature, the reconciliation of objective truth and freedom as appearing within self-consciousness and subjectivity."[13] Thus, the "absolute knowledge" of Hegel's philosophical system is meant to make the state of perfection and, consequently, the meaning of history spiritually manifest, and therefore can be regarded as a universal science.

Having the meaning of history expressed by a universal science was not confined to German thought. The idea of progress which aims at perfection and regards the spirit, be it divine or human, as the agent of progress, also developed in France in the eighteenth and nineteenth centuries. Condorcet, in his *Esquisse d'un tableau historique des progrès de l'esprit humain*, designed a univer-

9. Friedrich Wilhelm Joseph Schelling, "Philosophie und Religion" (1804), in *Schellings Werke*, ed. Manfred Schröter (München: C. H. Beck, 1927), 4:47.

10. Friedrich Wilhelm Joseph Schelling, "Die Weltalter" (1813), in *Schellings Werke* 4:582.

11. Ibid., 581.

12. Georg Wilhelm Friedrich Hegel, *Grundlinien der Philosophie des Rechts*, ed. Georg Lasson (Leipzig: Felix Meiner, 1911), § 342.

13. Georg Wilhelm Friedrich Hegel, *Phänomenologie des Geistes*, ed. J. Hoffmeister (Hamburg: Felix Meiner, 1952), 26–28; Hegel, *Grundlinien der Philosophie des Rechts*, § 358.

sal science as the peak of progress of the human spirit and as the epitome of the final period of world history. In his view this science—that is, the new philosophy of *raison*—would become, on the basis of mathematical methods, a "universal instrument (*instrument universel*)," and this instrument would disclose the principles and universal truths which "determine the unchangeable and necessary laws of justice and injustice." Condorcet held the opinion that the "universal instrument" could "be applied to all matters of the human spirit."[14] A few decades later Auguste Comte determined the meaning of history to again be a process aiming at a universal science. After the sciences as well as the political constitutions of nations have passed through a "theological-fictitious" and a "metaphysical-abstract" period, they will arrive at the third and final state of "positivity," which is to be the universal instrument of the sciences as well as of the foundation of social order.[15] Also Marx and Engels, who resumed both German and French traditions, entertained the idea that the "pre-history of the human society" was close to its end. They further contended that a universal instrument would be developed at the end of this "pre-history"—namely, their dialectical and historical materialism—which would make the whole of human existence and of history intelligible.[16]

The concepts of a universal science which originated in connection with or as a result of apocalyptic visions of the end of history and the beginning of the Millennium (or of the "Golden Age," the "Age of Positivism," the "Realm of Freedom"), were rather pretentious. The authors of these visions were incorporated in their concepts: they were not only the illuminated prophets who foretold the end of the world; at the same time, and in consequence of their preview of the Millennium, they were the inaugurators of the new universal science "hitherto unheard of," as Kuhlmann put it. This high self-esteem and this pretension were the logical results of apocalyptic interpretations of the world and history. If the end is near and if one knows how the state of perfection will look, such a position suggests itself. However, this is not the only way of arriving at the concept of a universal science. There is an-

14. Condorcet, *Esquisse d'un tableau historique des progrès de l'esprit humain: Entwurf einer historischen Darstellung der Fortschritte des menschlichen Geistes,* ed. Wilhelm Alff (Frankfurt: Europäische Verlagsanstalt, 1963), 267, 299.
15. Auguste Comte, *Cours de philosophie positive, (1830-1842),* ed. E. Littré (Paris: Bachelier, 1864). For Condorcet's influence on Comte, see 4:185.
16. Karl Marx and Friedrich Engels, *Werke* (Berlin: Diez, 1956), 13:9–14.

other, more modest one, modest in the sense that its authors do not pretend to have insights "hitherto unheard of." On the contrary they want to renew an ancient knowledge. On the other hand, this variety of universal science holds pretensions, too, insofar it is supposed to be superior to and more comprehensive than the modern natural sciences.

Universal Science as a Renewal of Ancient Wisdom

Friedrich Wilhelm Joseph Schelling had prophesied a future objective science, reconciliating the humanities and the natural sciences, as a consequence of his speculation on history. In this respect he came close to the apocalyptic belief most clearly pronounced by Oetinger. On the other hand, Schelling also developed a more systematic theory about the unification of what was called at his time ontology, transcendental philosophy, and philosophy of nature. This systematic theory, which he did not bring to completion, was holistic, as we would say today. To a high degree it drew upon a tradition which sprang from different sources than the millenarian one: the tradition of Hermetic religion and philosophy. Also Hermeticism was brought to Schelling's attention by Oetinger, who was an expert in all sorts of esoteric knowledge, although this connection has not yet been investigated satisfactorily.

Schelling's main intention was to overcome the split between the "Ego," or subject of cognition, and nature, or object of cognition. This split had dominated transcendental philosophy since Descartes and was maintained most sharply by Fichte in Schelling's time. Fichte defined nature as the "Non-Ego," which means that nature, as a mere object of our cognition, is not recognized as a reality of its own. Schelling realized that this theory makes nature appear as dead material with no other purpose than being used and dominated by us. He criticized Fichte for having made "egoism [*Ichheit*] the principle of philosophy," and for having reduced nature to a "mere mechanism." This theoretical understanding of nature, which in Schelling's eyes had governed "physics as a science" since Descartes, had the practical consequence that nature was subjugated to the destructive purposes of men, "because insofar nature has to serve human purposes, it will be killed."[17]

17. Friedrich Wilhelm Joseph v. Schelling, *Sämmtliche Werke*, ed. K. F. A. Schelling (Stuttgart: Cotta, 1856–1861), 7:11, 17–19, 26–27, 108–12.

In opposition to the dichotomic theory of cognition and the mechanistic theory of nature, Schelling developed an understanding of nature as a living and active cosmos which permanently produces and renews itself in the three potencies of matter, light, and organism by synthesizing its own polar forces of attraction and repulsion.[18] Human beings as the subject of cognition are participants in the comprehensive whole. This theory made use of major ideas of Hermeticism.

Schelling was not the only one in the decades around 1800 who took up the Hermetic tradition. Toward the end of the eighteenth century, there was growing dissatisfaction with the deepening split between traditional philosophy and the natural sciences, between theory of cognition and philosophy of nature, and also between science and religion. In this situation, Hermeticism was discovered, or rediscovered, as a worldview which again could integrate the conflicting perspectives. Goethe as a young man, for instance, was strongly influenced by the Hermetic tradition, which he used to forge both his own "personal religion" and a comprehensive, organic worldview.[19] The very first, however, to make extensive scholarly use of Hermeticism to bridge the gaps and ruptures which bothered so many intellectuals of the time, was Herder.

Johann Gottfried Herder was one of the most original and versatile minds in eighteenth-century Germany. He influenced his contemporaries (for example, Goethe) and stimulated new developments in the literature and philosophy well into the next century. Despite his importance and the attention he has received, little note has been taken of the Hermetic influence on Herder or of how his adaptation of Hermeticism influenced Romantic literature, the philosophy of nature (probably also Schelling's), and the philosophy of history.

It will be useful to give an impression of what Hermeticism meant in the seventeenth and eighteenth centuries, and how Herder encountered this tradition. The term *Hermeticism* refers to a religious and philosophical tradition which goes back to a collection of Greek scriptures from the end of the third century (in parts probably older): the *Corpus Hermeticum*. The central figure in these scriptures is "Thrice-Great Hermes" (Hermes Trismegistus),

18. Ibid., 4:13, 29–32. See *Klassiker der Naturphilosophie*, ed. Gernot Böhme (München: C. H. Beck, 1989), 247–55.
19. Rolf Christian Zimmermann, *Das Weltbild des jungen Goethe: Studien zur hermetischen Tradition des deutschen 18. Jahrhunderts*, 2 vols. (München: Wilhelm Fink, 1969, 1979).

from whom the name for the collection as well as for the doctrine was derived. Hermes is identified with the Egyptian god That, Thot, or Theut, the god of wisdom and inventor of numbers and writing. The Hermetic scriptures are presented as revelations of the god Hermes/That or of the god Nous to Hermes, in order to give them the appearance of primordial wisdom. In fact, however, they are a syncretistic product of the first centuries A.D. which in many respects resembles Gnosticism. Before I describe the main characteristics of Hermeticism, I first want to show how it was transmitted into the eighteenth century and, in particular, to Herder.

Although Hermeticism was an esoteric doctrine which for a long time lived in the intellectual underground, it never was entirely forgotten, not even in the Middle Ages. One reason for that was the attention paid to it by the church fathers Lactantius and Augustine. Lactantius regarded Hermes Trismegistus as one of the most important heathen prophets who lived prior to Pythagoras and Plato and prophesied Christianity.[20] Although Augustine condemned the Hermetic doctrine, he also held the opinion that Hermes was a seer of heathen antiquity "long before wise men and prophets came to the fore in Greece" and that he lived not much later than Moses.[21] These assessments had weight when Hermeticism was rediscovered in the Renaissance, because for the intellectuals of that time old age meant nearness to the sources of wisdom. When Cosimo de' Medici brought the Hermetic scriptures to Florence in 1460, he directed Marsilio Ficino to immediately translate the *Corpus* into Latin and to postpone the translation of the works of Plato which he had collected. The Hermetic doctrine was considered to be a *prisca theologia* (such was the term Ficino used in the introduction to his translation), a primordial and venerable theology and Ficino called Hermes Trismegistus the "first author of theology," from whom Orpheus, Pythagoras, and finally also Plato had derived their wisdom.[22] Ficino's translation of the *Corpus Hermeticum* was published in 1471 under the title *Pimander* (actually the title of the first book only),

---

20. Lucius Caecilius Firmianus Lactantius, *Divinarum institutionum libri VII. De ira Dei liber I . . .* (Basileae, Andreas Cratandrus, 1532), *Div. Inst.* 1, 6; *De ira Dei* 11.

21. Aurelius Augustinus, *De Civitate Dei libri XXII*, ed. Bernardus Dombart and Alfonsus Kalb (Stuttgart, B. G. Teubner, 1981), 2:315.

22. Marsilio Ficino, *Opera Omnia* (Basilea: Officina Henricpetrina, 1576), 1836. See also Frances A. Yates, *Giordano Bruno and the Hermetic Tradition* (Chicago: University of Chicago Press, 1964), 12–17.

and from then on it enjoyed a continuous reception. By the end of the sixteenth century, it had gone through sixteen editions. Johann Albert Fabricius's *Bibliotheca Graeca* lists more than thirty editions from Ficino's translation of 1471 until the first translation into German of 1706. Most were in Latin, but there were also editions of the original Greek text and translations into other languages.

Ficino's characterization of the Hermetic doctrine as a *prisca theologia* was of great consequence; up to the eighteenth century it was accepted by many scholars, especially by those who were attracted by Hermeticism. Although the philologist Casaubon had proven as early as 1614 that the *Corpus Hermeticum* could not have been written before the beginning of Christianity, his findings did not dispel the conviction that in its essence the *Corpus* contained old Egyptian wisdom. Scholars of great, even international, reputation maintained this conviction.

The humanist Francesco Patrizi, editor of a collection of Hermetic writings, also published a major philosophical work influenced by Hermeticism, *Nova de universis philosophia* in 1591, before Casaubon's critique. He dedicated it to Pope Gregory XIV and even tried to have the traditional Aristotelian philosophy, legitimized by the Catholic Church, replaced by it. When in 1678 Ralph Cudworth, the intellectual doyen of the Cambridge Platonists, published his monumental work *The True Intellectual System of the Universe*, he could no longer ignore Casaubon's critique. His work set standards for the scholarly assessment of the Hermetic scriptures throughout the following century. In their essence, Cudworth contended, the Hermetic texts were genuine "because, though they had been all forged by Christians never so much, yet being divulged in those ancient times, they must needs have something of the truth in them." And he concluded: "That there was anciently, amongst the Egyptians, such a man as *Thot*, *Theut*, or *Taut*, who, together with letters, was the first inventor of arts and sciences, as arithmetic, geometry . . . and of hieroglyphick learning, (therefore called by the Greeks *Hermes* and by the Latins *Mercurius*) cannot reasonably be denied."[23] Johann Albert Fabricius, whom his biographer called, even more than a century after his death, "one of the greatest polyhistors of the last century," dealt with the Hermetic scriptures in his multivolumed

23. Ralph Cudworth, *The True Intellectual System of the Universe* (London: Printed for Richard Royston, 1678), 1.4.18.

Bibliotheca Graeca of 1708 in the first volume, dedicated to authors *"qui ante homerum fuisse feruntur."*[24] The orientalist Jablonski, last but not least, depicted the old Egyptian religion in his *Pantheon Aegyptiorum* of 1752 by making use of the Hermetic scriptures.[25]

I have followed this line of transmission and influence in some detail because it also leads directly to Herder. Herder knew the works of the scholars mentioned above who were so familiar with Hermeticism and repeatedly quotes them in his book *Älteste Urkunde des Menschengeschlechts* of 1774, along with upright Hermeticists like Johann Georg Wachter and Johann Heinrich Ursin. In his library Herder had numerous Hermetic scriptures and works of authors who were inclined to Hermeticism—for example, an edition of the *Corpus Hermeticum* edited by Roselius in 1630, a *Fama mystica hermetica*, several works by Ursin, the complete works of Ficino and of both Picos della Mirandola, Campanella's *Philosophia universalis*, all theosophical works of Jakob Böhme, Colberg's *Platonisch-Hermetisches Christentum*, and the famous histories of heretics by Arnold and Mosheim. It is conspicuous how many heterodox or outright heretical works Herder's library contained. At any rate, it is certain that Herder had a very good knowledge of Hermeticism. As early as 1765 there are allusions to Hermetic thoughts in Herder's writings and sermons.

Before I approach the question of how Herder was influenced by Hermetic thoughts, I have to briefly outline the main characteristics of Hermeticism. This can best be done by following the excellent account Ernest Lee Tuveson has given of the gist of the Hermetic doctrine.[26] In its classical form Hermeticism can be characterized as a religious worldview which holds a middle position between the Judeo-Christian and the pantheist conception of God and the world. With both of them Hermeticism has points of contact, as well as sharp contrasts. According to the Judeo-Christian belief, God is an extramundane being who created the world as an artifact. Although the human being as the *imago dei* shares certain attributes with God, the gap between God and the world is nonetheless absolute. It can only be bridged through revelations

---

24. *Allgemeine Encyclopädie der Wissenschaften und Künste*, ed. J. S. Ersch and J. G. Gruber, vol. 40, part 2 (Leipzig: Johann Friedrich Gleditsch, [after 1842]), 69; *Ioannis Alberti Fabricii Bibliotheca Graeca . . .* (Hamburg: Carolus Ernestus Bohn, 1708), 1:1, 46–80.

25. Paul Ernst Jablonski, *Pantheon Aegyptiorum . . .* (Frankfurt: Academische Buchhaudlung Sander, 1752), 2:55, 105–6.

26. Ernest Lee Tuveson, *The Avatars of Thrice Great Hermes: An Approach to Romanticism* (London: Associated University Presses, 1982).

by the transcendent God, on whom human beings have no influence. In contrast, pantheism in its purest form, considers the whole cosmos to be divine and conceives of God as the totality of all being. The latter position is not very satisfying intellectually, for as Tuveson pointed out, "it actually amounts to saying nothing. If everything is God, it would be as meaningful to say nothing is God."[27] On the other hand, the Judeo-Christian conception is difficult to bear for many, because it means that the human beings are subjugated to the judgment of the transcendent God and can hope only for his mercy.

Hermeticism, in contrast, does not conceive of the world as an artifact created by God, but as a living organism in which God manifests himself as the body of the divine spirit, as it were, from which this spirit is distinct nonetheless. The human being cannot see the divine spirit, only his bodily manifestation in the world. This conception has been coined "panentheistic" by the German philosopher Krause in order to distinguish it from plain pantheism. It is a very attractive conception because it avoids making God identical with some animal or material object; while it opens a path to salvation which leads humans to God. Moreover, the *Corpus Hermeticum* holds that the world is contained within God's thoughts and is permeated by them. The thoughts of the humans are similar to God's for they can comprehend everything too. Hermes Trismegistus is instructed by the god Nous: "You are not hindered by anything to regard yourself as being immortal, as having knowledge of everything, of the arts, the sciences, morals, and of all animals. . . . Imagine that you are everywhere at the same time, on the earth, in the sea, in the sky; that you never were born, that you are still an embryo, that you are young, old, dead, and beyond death." The god Nous calls upon Hermes to comprehend everything, "the times, the places, the things, the qualities, the quantities,—then you comprehend God." And to comprehend God means to become equal to God.[28] According to the Hermetic conviction, there is not only a likeness between human nature and God, in the Judeo-Christian sense of the *imago dei*, but also an analogous relationship between macrocosm and microcosm, between the divine spirit with his manifestations and the human mind with its thoughts, with its imagination. Although this con-

---

27. Ibid., 4.
28. *Corpus Hermeticum*, book 11; quoted from *Hermès Trismégiste*, trans. Louis Menard, (Paris: Guy Trédaniel, 1983), 78–79.

viction is not compatible with Christian belief—it also makes the saving function of Christ superfluous—many Christian philosophers and theologians tried again and again to reconcile Hermeticism with Christian belief, from Ficino, Pico della Mirandola, and Campanella, to Humanists like Patrizi, to the Christian Platonists Cudworth and More, Protestant theologians like Ursin, up to Herder.

The scriptures of the *Corpus Hermeticum* present their doctrine in a mythological imagery which is similar to the Gnostic one. But whereas Gnosis depicts a dualistic image of God and the world, the Hermetic one is analogous; it depicts the cosmos as a process of polar forces. The Hermeticist does not need to escape from the world in order to save himself; he wants to gain knowledge of the world in order to expand his own self, and utilize this knowledge to penetrate into the self of God. Hermeticism is a positive Gnosis, as it were, devoted to the world.

Hermeticism considers the cosmos (in modern terminology, "nature") to be a living organism and therefore views processes, which we understand as merely physical, in analogy to organic and even psychic ones. Metal, for instance, can grow in the earth according to this view. There is sympathy between substances of the same kind, but antipathy between heterogeneous substances. This perception, along with the challenge to know God's manifestation in the cosmos, fostered the development of alchemical and magic practices. They revived in the Renaissance and were still exercised in the eighteenth century, particularly in medicine. Usually Hermetic magic and alchemy had nothing to do with occult sorcery, but were attempts to discover the divine in nature through the laws of nature. Therefore, the Hermeticists could discard the mythological fundamentalism of the tradition without abandoning the essence of the Hermetic doctrine. Without major difficulties they could proceed from the medieval worldview to the Newtonian one. With their inclination to think in analogies between macrocosm and microcosm, and in the polar categories of attraction and repulsion, concentration and expansion, they even found themselves confirmed by the discoveries of the modern natural sciences. In the eighteenth century Hermeticism presented itself as religious worldview, which had the advantage that it did not need to resist the modern scientific image of the world, as the Christian churches did. This was the context in which Herder encountered Hermeticism.

The way Herder adopted the Hermetic tradition can best be seen in his book *Älteste Urkunde des Menschengeschlechts* (1774). At first view this work appears to be a new exegesis of the Book of Genesis, directed against fundamentalist as well as rationalistic interpretations of the Bible. Herder interprets the history of creation symbolically. He does not separate image and fact, but assumes a symbolical meaning which comprises fact and meaning *within* the image of language. He understands the myth of creation as a historical document from the childhood of humankind, whose sensual mode of expression was in accordance with the way of thinking in oriental antiquity. And sensuality, in Herder's opinion, does not contradict truth; images do not exclude abstract theories.

This was an important new methodological development. Of equal importance, however, were the materials to which Herder applied his method. After a first chapter on the Book of Genesis, Herder describes what he calls the "Holy sciences of the Egyptians" and what he derives from the *Corpus Hermeticum* and from the modern sources mentioned above. He concludes with a chapter on Greek philosophy, Gnosis, Cabala, and Zoroastrianism. On the face of it, Herder's consideration of religions and philosophies with similar symbolical expositions to those in the Book of Genesis appears to be an attempt to prove the great antiquity and truth of the latter. In fact, however, this line of argument relativizes the uniqueness of the biblical document. Nevertheless, I think this was not contrary to Herder's intentions. With his theory of symbolic meaning and the respective interpretations, Herder construes a primordial revelatory truth, a *prisca theologia*, which in the Hermetic religion found an expression of equal rank and antiquity to that in the Mosaic religion. Moreover, Herder's assessment was in line with a long tradition. Already Ficino, in his commentary to *Pimander*, had pointed out many parallels between the Book of Genesis and the Hermetic cosmogony. Above all, these parallels were also emphasized by the Protestant theologian and Hermeticist Johann Heinrich Ursin (1608–1667), to whom Herder referred frequently and of whose book *De Zoroastre bactriano, Hermete Trismegisto, etc.* he even had two copies in his library.

What did Herder's version of the *prisca theologia*, which he deduced from the Book of Genesis as well as from the Hermetic tradition, look like? Herder interprets the six days of Creation and the Sabbath as a "great and significant *allegory* of God," with light, created on the first day, as the highest and most meaningful symbol.[29] The light is "the first beginning of creation, the oldest symbol and image of God, primordial image of all beauty, power, splendor, and goodness." The symbolic quality of the light is so significant because this symbol refers to spiritual as well as sensual and material phenomena, to nature as well as morality. Beyond that, the divine "Be light!" (as Herder translates, "*Sei Licht!*") is a symbol not only for the "stream of divinity and creativity through the whole of nature," but also for God's activity in history.[30] Herder constructs a network of analogies with correlations between polarities, and he sees the whole of creation with its relations between God, world, and human beings, between nature and history, comprehended by this network.

There is an even more concise symbol for the totality of creation which Herder finds in the Hermetic tradition in the "holy hieroglyph of Hermes." This "hieroglyph" (fig. 8) is indeed a very old symbol for the cosmos; it can be found among the most ancient petroglyphs. Herder could not abstain from charging it with some Hermetic magic of numbers and letters. However, what matters ultimately is the quintessential meaning of the "primordial symbol of Hermes," as Herder calls it: "One holy symbol: primordial image of creation, from which everything originated." This quintessential meaning is the Hermetic analogy between macrocosm and microcosm, the *aurea catena*, the golden chain of Hermeticism which embraces everything: "One in All! and All in One! one universe of formation [*Bildung*]! seed-corn out of which everything was to unfold, down the eternities!" The human being is, in Herder's words, "a magnificent chord of seven tones," "the image of the Whole in the shape and appearance [*Bildung*] of man: the great universe in the hieroglyph of the small!" He is "the image of God in all his powers, uses and attractions; at the same time he is the symbol and quintessence of the entire visible and invisible world."[31]

In *Älteste Urkunde des Menschengeschlechts* Herder disclosed the "genetic source" for his adaptation of Hermeticism. The religious and philosophical consequences of this adaptation he had already drawn before. In two essays written in 1769 (he was 25 years old then) he had laid down the general ideas of Hermetic

29. Johann Gottfried Herder, *Sämmtliche Werke*, ed. Bernhard Suphan (Berlin: Weidmannsche Buchhandlung, 1877–1913), 6:278.
30. Ibid., 222, 267, 449.
31. Ibid., 320–22, 340, 351, 365, 403.

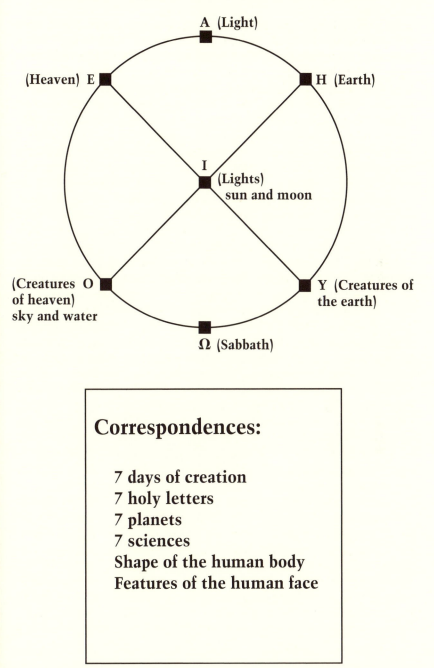

Figure 8. Holy Hieroglyph of Hermes.

panentheism. First, he presented the conception of the world as a manifestation of the divine spirit: "The power of God is omnipotent; he exerts his power over the universe which is his body: the body of his thoughts." Second, he made the analogy between human beings and God: God "is the idea, the power of the world: I am below him, like the earth is below the sun, but I have my own moon, too; my own sphere: I am a God in my world." His third principle was that everything is held together by the *aurea catena:* "I am real in the chain with God, just as I am in the chain with the worm on whom I tread with my feet."[32] In contrast to the worm, however, the human being can draw near to God and strive for perfection on the strength of his cognition, because the thoughts of human beings are, as parts of God's manifestation in the world, parts of God's thoughts and therefore an active power analogous to God's creative power. In Herder's words, the human being "is a part of God's thoughts; a part of God's thoughts are his thoughts." This means that with his thoughts the human being has power over the universe like God: "I aspire to have an idea of the universe; . . . as a result a world of bodies takes shape." The expansion of thoughts is a process of perfection: "In its formation [*Bildung*] everything must be explained by the thoughts which strive to reach the universe and are therefore perfect." This process of perfection is equivalent to approximation, even assimilation, to God, for the universe is nothing else than the body of God's thoughts: "The human being gravitates towards everything, even towards God." The term *gravitation* indicates that Herder had also adopted the Hermetic principle of thinking in polarities. In accordance with this principle, he interprets not only creation and the formation of all beings, but also the inner structure of the comprehensive whole of the universe: "just as planets in the universe have formed themselves through the powers of attraction and repulsion: in the same way our soul has formed the body: and in the same way God has formed the world." "There is attraction and repulsion between us and everything which exists on earth."[33]

As early as 1769 Herder had also applied his method of thinking in analogies and polarities to the historical world, to the formation and development of nations. When he first read Montesquieu

---

32. Johann Gottfried Herder, "Grundsätze der Philosophie," *Euphorion* 54 (1960): 288.
33. Herder, *Sämmtliche Werke* 32:229; "Grundsätze der Philosophie," 229–31.

he noted: "Just as our soul fills the body: God fills the world: and a monarch fills his kingdom." He criticized Montesquieu's *L'esprit des lois* for not offering "metaphysics of the formation of nations." In Herder's opinion Montesquieu's notion of laws remained on the surface of institutions and could not grasp the inner laws of the living organism of nations. These inner laws, which penetrate the life of nations in all its dimensions, Herder found again in the principle of polarities, "in the laws of attraction and repulsion, which are natural to the character of a nation, which have originally formed this nation and maintained it in the same way as those laws have formed and maintained the body."[34] In his *Ideen zur Philosophie der Geschichte der Menschheit* (1784), Herder proceeded from the principle that the laws of history follow the "great analogy of nature" and that "the thoughts which God had revealed actively in his works every day" manifest themselves in history just as in nature. Therefore—and this is decisive—the laws can be discovered.[35]

In other writings of his middle period, Herder applies the principle of polarities, again on the strength of analogies, to human interrelationships. He uses this principle as a psychological instrument of cognition, as it were. Regarding attraction and repulsion of the bodies, Herder observes: "the great magnetism of nature, which attracts and repels" has "analogy with the human being." "In my opinion no psychology is possible which is not, with each step, a firm physiology." Again we can detect a typical characteristic of Hermeticism: Hermetic thinking tries to avoid dualism in the sense of radical antagonism between good and evil. Both powers are necessary; both sustain life: "Whoever cannot repel, cannot attract; both powers are but one pulsation of the soul." Another polarity, which Herder also uses very often in his psychological considerations, the polarity of concentration or contraction and expansion, makes this even more obvious. Herder translates this polarity as presumption and love, self-reliance and empathy. "Self-reliance and empathy (again: expansion and contraction) are the two expressions of the elasticity of our will." It does not escape Herder that presumption and self-reliance, if emphasized too much, can destroy humanity; therefore, this pole must form a field of tension with the opposite pole, but within this tension it is necessary: "Self-reliance is only to be the *con-*

34. Ibid., 4:467, 466, 469.
35. Ibid., 13:9.

ditio sine qua non, the clod which keeps us in our place, not object, but means. But a necessary means: because it is and it remains true that we love our neighbor only as we love ourselves. . . . The degree of the depth of our self-reliance is also the degree of our empathy with others." Once again Herder formulates the great credo of Hermeticism: "Look at the whole of nature, consider the great analogy of creation. . . . In short, follow nature!"[36]

In one of his last works, *Hermes und Poemander*, written one year before his death Herder recapitulates his Hermetic worldview. This work imitates the dialogues between Hermes and Pimander in the *Corpus Hermeticum*; it is inserted into a treatise on the development of sciences in the seventeenth and eighteenth centuries, and it comments upon the new scientific discoveries in the symbolic language of the Hermetic myth. The astronomical discoveries of Kepler and Newton and the mechanics and optics of the latter are, in Herder's eyes, corroborations of the Hermetic worldview, particularly the principle of polarities. Attraction and repulsion, concentration and expansion were, in Herder's words, "from ancient time the generating as well as sustaining central causes of the system of the universe; each age, each school applied its own terms and forms to the Whole. Newton's system defined the terms and forms most appropriate for his time with relations and numbers, without thereby explaining them."[37] In Herder's opinion, Newton used the instruments of modern sciences to describe the same truth which ancient Hermeticism had expressed already in the symbolic language of myth, and the mystery of this truth itself could not be explained in either form.

Herder takes the same view with respect to the scientific theories on the quality of light. Here, however, Herder does not follow Newton's hypothesis that space is a vacuum, but holds to the older conception that space is filled with aether. It is not clear whether Herder was unaware or just kept silent about the fact that the *young* Newton had also subscribed to the aether hypothesis. Richard Westfall has shown that Newton, in his *Hypothesis Explaining the Properties of Light* (1675), presented this conception as a Hermetic cosmogony in the language of science.[38] Herder's view is almost identical with this conception. In his opinion space is

36. Ibid., 8:169–70, 47, 180, 15:325, 8:199–201.
37. Ibid., 23:522.
38. Richard S. Westfall, "Newton and the Hermetic Tradition," in *Science, Medicine and Society in the Renaissance*, ed. Allen G. Debus (New York: Science History Publications, 1972), 2:183–98.

not a vacuum, but filled with a "subtle, highly elastic aether" which can condense and vaporize.[39] Light does not emanate *from* the sun, but is produced through condensation of the aether *around* the sun. Newton even put forward the hypothesis that aether, in its different degrees of condensation, is the substance of all bodies, and that it produces, by means of perpetual condensation and vaporization, the cycle of becoming and vanishing. This sounded like the adoption of a central proposition of the *Corpus Hermeticum*, that the energies of the world are "composition and decomposition," and that nothing in the world gets lost.[40] In Newton's early theory aether assumed the role of a divine creative *quinta essencia*.

Herder ascribes the same role to light, through which, "all life is sustained, perhaps also produced and propagated," although "the light as such . . . remains invisible for us." With this conception it is easy for Herder to draw again analogies to God, to creation, and to human beings: God's thoughts are invisible, like light as such, but they can be detected in the visible universe in which they are embodied; and this can be done by virtue of the instrument which is analogous to God's creativity, by virtue of "the most noble part of us that thinks, *our* light." With this sentence Herder refers back to his symbolical interpretation of light in *Älteste Urkunde des Menschengeschlechts*. In the dialogue *Hermes und Poemander* he comments through the mouth of Pimander upon the scientific discoveries of his time: "Pursue this golden chain of creation; it is an eternal becoming. Light is the silent agent of the ubiquitous deity which produces and always renews." "In the same way the light in yourself, your thoughts; it is always in a state of becoming." Finally, Herder puts in the mouth of Hermes the central conviction of modern Hermeticism: "I see that the most recent discoveries lead back to the most ancient philosophy, though the latter was shrouded in legends."[41]

The Hermetic worldview enabled Herder to be a modern, enlightened intellectual and to adopt the discoveries of modern sciences without being hindered by orthodox Christian belief. Nonetheless, this worldview enabled him to consider himself as a faithful Christian because the Christian faith can be amalgamated with key ingredients of Hermeticism. The Hermetic worldview

39. Herder, *Sämmtliche Werke* 23:536.
40. *Corpus Hermeticum*, book 11; quoted from *Hermès Trismégiste*, 71.
41. Herder, *Sämmtliche Werke* 23:528–35.

makes it possible to strive for godlike perfection by virtue of one's own power of cognition and still remain the child of the transcendent God. Hermeticism also makes it possible to explore the laws of nature and still look upon nature not as dead matter, but as a living organism whose laws even apply to history. Finally, Hermeticism makes it possible to comprehend these laws symbolically and to understand ancient myths and the discoveries of modern sciences alike as equivalent expressions of the same truth, of a *philosophia perennis.*

Herder's Hermetic worldview contributed to a new conception of nature and human nature: of nature as a living, even animated organism, in which the divine is embodied, and of the human being not only as creature and part of nature, but also as godlike creator. So far it has not been sufficiently appreciated that this conception of Hermeticism influenced the new German anthropology and philosophy of nature of the late eighteenth century, and gave new impulses to the search for a universal science.

A MYTHOLOGY OF REASON
The Persistence of
Pseudo-Science in the Modern World

David Walsh

It is surely one of the oddest features of our odd civilization that so much irrationality is tolerated alongside such scrupulously rational self-discipline. We are a putatively scientific civilization, yet the criteria of science seem to apply to only a very small segment of contemporary life. Once we are beyond the confines of professional science, the rules of evidence and logic no longer apply. Sometimes the nonrational prejudices even infect the debates among scientists themselves. All sides, of course, continue to invoke the authority of scientific method, but its selective application gives the lie to the claims of objectivity. The paradox is best recognized, perhaps, in the contradiction between the indisputable preeminence of scientific authority and the paucity of occasions when its influence is socially decisive. Being a scientific society does not mean that scientific analysis always carries the day. What it means is that all public discourse must assume the language of science. It must become pseudo-science.

The persistence of pseudo-science in this sense is not surprising, although given our scientific dispositions, we are not normally comfortable with admitting the situation. Indeed, there is frequently such a tendency to deny or downplay the pseudo-scientific that it may be well to provide some examples, before examining the historical sources in more detail. The difficulty is that we have all too often accepted the claims of scientific authority at face value, without subjecting the assertions to the scrutiny of critical and empirical verification. They have become the taken-for-granted parameters of our world, and the discovery of their lack of substance is always an astonishing event.

The most spectacular recent example has been the demise of the ideological movements, especially the disintegration of Communism. What is surprising in this case is not that Communism has collapsed, but that it survived this long. Here is a movement that dominated twentieth-century politics, that was dressed in all the garb of a scientific theory, and that seemed to have an appeal well nigh irresistible. Yet by all the standards of empirical evidence it did not work as an economic or political system. We are told now of the "failure of Communism" as if this were a sufficient explanation of its current precipitous decline. But the system has been a failure for over seventy years and still managed to survive. That is what needs to be explained, and when it is, then we will have some context for understanding contemporary events.

The most pervasive and effective forms of pseudo-science are those that form the penumbra of science itself. The leading example is positivism or scientism, the belief that the methodology of the natural sciences is capable of answering all questions and is therefore the only valid form of knowledge. What is intriguing about this suggestion is not the groundless nature of the assertion itself. Most astonishing is the extent to which it is persisted in even when it yields no fruitful results and when subsequent reflection reveals its inherent irrationality. The social sciences have diligently emulated the natural sciences for over two hundred years (not much younger than the natural sciences themselves) and arrived at almost nothing in the form of laws, theories, or generalizations.[1] Nor is the explanation difficult to discover. The study of man and society is not the same as the study of planets and electrons because the human reality is largely known through our own participation in it. There is no objective, external viewpoint. Science is itself an activity within this human reality and ultimately escapes encapsulation within its own explanations.

Related to scientism is the equally dominant set of expectations concerning the application of science to remedy the defects of the human condition. Technology is the term that conjures up this Promethean drive that lies at the core of our civilization. In part, of course, the expectations are fully justified. Technology has transformed our lives. Our successes in harnessing the energies of nature, of providing material abundance, and of removing much of the suffering of human life are too obvious to need elaboration. Generally not so well recognized is the halo of virtually unlimited expectations that has formed the background for such tangible achievements.[2]

1. For a good overview of the problems, see Alasdair MacIntyre, "The Character of Generalization in the Social Sciences and their Lack of Predictive Power," in *After Virtue* (Notre Dame: University of Notre Dame Press, 1984), 88–108.

2. An empirical examination of the actual achievements of modern technology, in contrast to the promises and claims made for it, has been provided by David

We have become accustomed to the idea that all problems are technical and are amenable to a technical solution. If a cure or an answer has not so far been found, it is not because none is available, but only because not enough time and effort have been expended on the search. There are no inherent limits to our capacity to solve problems. Reality is a plastic medium that is infinitely malleable in our hands, so long as we work hard enough at unlocking its secrets. Through the scientific method the vast transformative powers of nature may be attained and placed in the service of man. Bacon's dream of employing science for "the relief of man's estate" seems more realizable every day. Eventually it will become possible for humanity to dominate reality as a whole and live in a state where all problems have been removed.

This is the dream of a totally controlled environment, which extends to the dreamer too. More and more human nature itself has become the object of technical manipulation, with only the faintest ripples of awareness that this may not lead toward the perfection of human happiness. Such concerns are readily dismissed because of the deep-rooted faith that technological control of man and his world will necessarily lead toward human fulfillment. If the conditions of human existence improve, then human nature itself is bound to undergo a moral and spiritual advance. Besides, even if it does not, there are further technical solutions. It is only a matter of employing the right therapies and techniques in order to ensure more altruistic, more adventurous, or more moral human beings. The problem is never one of the limits of the approach itself.[3]

What is pseudo-scientific about these expectations is not merely that they have no basis in fact, but that they are based on a faith that survives even in the face of overwhelming contrary evidence. If one applies the criteria of science to the extra-scientific faith of science, the irrationality quickly becomes clear. All of the evidence is that reality is only partly amenable to our control. We

---

Ehrenfeld, *The Arrogance of Humanism* (New York: Oxford University Press, 1978). He presents a factual account of "the wide and widening discrepancy between the world-pervasive faith in reason and human power and the living reality of the human condition" (xii).

3. There is a vast contemporary literature on these problems, and I can only suggest some of the more relevant discussions here: Leon Kass, *Toward A More Natural Science* (New York: Free Press, 1984), especially "The New Biology: What Price 'Relieving Man's Estate'?"; Hans Jonas, *The Imperative of Responsibility* (Chicago: University of Chicago Press, 1978); George Parkin Grant, *Technology and Justice* (Notre Dame: University of Notre Dame Press, 1986).

may be able to solve certain problems, but there is always a cost, very often in the form of unintended consequences. More aggressive methods of cultivation in Africa, for example, have had the unintended effect of expanding the deserts and increasing the likelihood of drought. Even antibiotics have led to the emergence of resistant strains of bacteria. And as soon as those problems have been solved, another set will surely appear on the horizon. Reality seems peculiarly intractable to anything approaching real human control. We cannot effectively plan for all the eventualities in a modern power plant, let alone approach anything like the ability to create new "worlds" in space or anywhere else. This applies doubly to human beings themselves. Despite the dazzling array of techniques and the marvelous material advances, it does not appear that we possess the means of making ourselves better or happier.

What then is involved in the persistence of such beliefs? They are all forms of illegitimate extrapolation, from success within a fairly narrow range to the anticipation of reality as a whole. Without empirical foundation, they derive their strength from the faith in man's power to penetrate and dominate reality that coincided with the Scientific Revolution itself. The Renaissance, we have come to realize, was not merely about the rebirth of classical learning and humanism. It was marked by a widespread explosion of magico-mystical movements that emphasized man's role as a semidivine being and ruler of the material world. Neoplatonism, Hermeticism, Cabalism, alchemy and other forms of "ancient theology" assumed such prominence that they came to displace the traditional Judeo-Christian understanding of man and the world. Modern science and technology was only the most pragmatically successful strand of this complex of interrelated movements. It shared with them the conviction that man is a magus, capable of comprehending all reality and perfecting it through his power.

However, science separated from these occult forms of magic and by its success have thoroughly discredited them. Modern science and technology has achieved through physical operations what the Renaissance magi thought could also be accomplished through magical operations. The necessity of distinguishing itself from its magico-mystical contemporaries is particularly evident in Bacon's opposition to magic, especially in light of his own obvious connections to such movements. Indeed, the differences had so frequently been emphasized that it has not always been easy for historians to acquire a sense of the continuities between the successful branch and its disreputable relatives. But why then did the success of the rational experimental method not also lead to the demise of the magico-mystical worldview from which it had separated? That is the question I would like to address.

My hypothesis is that the pseudo-scientific penumbra did not disappear because it continued (and continues) to play an indispensable role in the self-understanding of modern civilization. The Hermetic and alchemical symbolisms may have no value as scientific theories, but they do considerable service as forms of civil theology. Even when shorn of their overtly theological heritage and in their most militantly secular formulations, they provide the constitutive public myth of our technological civilization. They give expression to the Promethean aspirations that have been the driving force of its achievements. When one thinks of the world-conquering energies our civilization has unleashed, whether the domination of space or time or biology or society, one is struck by the lack of congruence with the dispassionately rational methods employed. In search of an explanation we must look to some more passionately encompassing sources of inspiration.

This essay is an attempt to explore those extra-scientific motivations, which ultimately unite the scientific and pseudo-scientific in a common modern civilization. To do so, it will be necessary to return to the sources where the motivations are most explicit, before the contrast with science itself succeeds in discrediting them and they begin to lead a more implicit, fragmented, and subterranean existence. Even more important, however, is to identify the thinkers at every stage who sought a comprehensive elaboration of the modern worldview. They are the ones whose own self-articulation reveals the motivations most clearly. Invariably this takes the form of a transformation of the traditional constructions of philosophy and Christianity. As a consequence it provides the fullest insight into the changes taking place. By contrast with the traditional perspectives it replaces, the novelty and nature of the new public philosophy can be most adequately revealed.

The first great flowering of the new outlook, as we have indicated, was the Hermetic-Cabalist philosophy of the Renaissance. To appreciate what occurred during this epoch it is important to look beyond the moderate Christian humanist center, represented by men like Erasmus and Thomas More. The dramatic nature of what was occurring is best revealed by some of those who, until recently, were regarded as on the fringes of the social and cultural spectrum. But historians have now discovered the importance of extremists like Giordano Bruno or Robert Fludd for an understanding of the broad cultural upheavals taking place. Very often it is the extremists who give expression to what others only carry at the back of their minds. They are the ones who reveal the inner logic of the newly emerging positions and therefore expose their nature most fully to the light of day. Moreover, it is only after reading them that we become aware of the resonances of sympathy that may exist in such more familiar figures as Shakespeare or Bacon. This, so far as I can see, has been the revolution that has occurred among intellectual historians of the Renaissance in recent years.[4]

There is more to the Scientific Revolution, they have shown, than meets the eye. Beyond the turn to nature and the discovery of the mathematical-experimental method, there lies a profound shift of spiritual orientation by modern man. The empirical investigation of nature received its impetus from the conviction of Neoplatonic Hermeticism that reality is a hierarchy of occult or hidden sympathies uniting the whole and ultimately emanating from the divine One. Nature itself becomes the way by which man can apprehend the revelation of God and ascend toward his own original divine condition. Now whether this precise conception was influential for all the early modern scientists is not the central issue. The essential thing is that the Hermetic construction expresses the motivating background for the work of the empirical and mathematical investigators of nature, a motivation that can still be discerned behind the meticulous investigations of our own science too. Marsilio Ficino, the guiding force behind the Neoplatonic Academy of Florence, has put it best. In the introduction to his translation of the *Corpus Hermeticum*, he gives expression to his desire that the Divine Mind "may glow into our mind and we may contemplate the order of all things as they exist in God."[5] It remains a continuing expectation of modern science that the laborious and incremental study of phenomena will

4. The work of Frances Yates, D. P. Walker, Eugenio Garin, Gershom Scholem, and their successors form the core of this revision in Renaissance scholarship. An extensive bibliography is provided in Stephen A. McKnight, *Sacralizing the Secular: The Renaissance Origins of Modernity* (Baton Rouge: Louisiana State University Press, 1989).

5. Quoted in Eric Voegelin, "Response to Professor Altizer's 'A New History and a new but Ancient God?'," in Ellis Sandoz, ed., *Eric Voegelin's Thought: A Critical Appraisal* (Durham: Duke University Press, 1982), 193.

eventually yield a profound spiritual illumination of the order of the whole.[6]

To attain that goal, however, Ficino and his successors knew that it was necessary for man to ascend to the divine perspective on the world. Man must become capable of seeing everything as God sees it. The techniques of Hermetic magic, sympathetic manipulation of the harmonies that unite the cosmos, were merely a means toward the goal of the divinization of man. Then, as the fully realized divine being, man could assume his rightful position as ruler of the material world. "Universal providence is proper to God who is the universal cause. Therefore man who universally provides for all things living and not living is a certain god." Ficino identifies the divinity of man with his capacity to imitate God in ruling over all things, including the power of "transmuting the species of things by command, which work is indeed called a miracle." He asserts the aspiration toward divinity as the essence of man and as the essence of Christianity: "The entire striving of our soul is that it become God. Such striving is no less natural to men than the effort to flight is to birds."[7]

A dramatically new note was sounded in the writings of this scholar priest. The older aspiration for mystical union with God was still there, but now shorn of any concern about the temptations of pride and excess. The Renaissance Hermeticists display no hesitation in proclaiming their goal of "becoming God," not merely becoming united with God. This lack of caution becomes even clearer in the members of the younger generation like Pico della Mirandola. Pico is notable for his absorption of the Jewish Cabala into the Neoplatonic Hermeticism of Florence and thereby into the Western intellectual mainstream. The Cabala is a parallel symbolism to Hermeticism, in the sense of an effort to follow the path by which all things emanate from and return to God. It differs from Hermeticism principally in its setting within a clearly transcendent understanding of God, and so provides an important

6. Fritjof Capra's, *The Tao of Physics* (New York: Bantam Books, 1977) is only one recent example. One could also point to the intense public interest in questions of cosmology, as evidenced by the best-seller status of Stephen Hawking's *A Brief History of Time* (Toronto: Bantam Books, 1988). But it is a dimension that has attracted the attention of the greatest scientists of the century, such as Heisenberg and Einstein.

7. Ficino, *Theologia Platonica* (1482); quoted in Charles Trinkaus, *In Our Image and Likeness: Humanity and Divinity in Italian Humanist Thought*, 2 vols. (Chicago: University of Chicago Press, 1970), 2:483, 486, 487.

illustration of the way in which the new emanationist theology can be reconciled with the traditional revelations of Judaism and Christianity. Pico exemplifies the new air of self-confidence as man assumes increasingly more of the divine creative role in the order of things. The address of God to Adam as imagined in *The Oration on the Dignity of Man* perfectly captures the conviction:

> The nature of all other creatures is defined and restricted within laws which We have laid down; you, by contrast, impeded by no such restrictions, may, by your own free will, to whose custody We have assigned you, trace for yourself the lineaments of your own nature. I have placed you at the very center of the world, so that from that vantage point you may with greater ease glance round about you on all that the world contains. We have made you a creature neither of heaven nor of earth, neither mortal nor immortal, in order that you may, as the free and proud shaper of your own being, fashion yourself into the form you may prefer.[8]

The man who has unlocked the divine mysteries of creation has assumed a quite different role within it. Frances Yates identifies the nature of the revolution well when she explains:

> What has changed is Man, now no longer only the pious spectator of God's wonders in creation, and the worshipper of God himself above creation, but Man the operator, man who seeks to draw power from the divine and natural order. . . . To use the terminology now so familiar, it may be said that by Magia man has learned to use the chain linking earth to heaven, and by Cabala he has learned to manipulate the higher chain linking the celestial world, through the angels, to the divine Name.[9]

This is a change that is broader and more decisive than the discoveries of science themselves. Indeed, the new scientific developments were initially located within this context of the wider spiritual revolution of Hermeticism.[10] Excitement was generated not so much by the advance of new theories of motion and of planetary orbits, as by the confirmation they provided of the spiritual truth of man's capacity to penetrate the divine mysteries of creation and become the active participant in its transformation.

8. Giovanni Pico della Mirandola, *Oration on the Dignity of Man*, trans. A.R. Caponigri (Chicago: Regnery Gateway, 1956), 7.
9. Frances Yates, *Giordano Bruno and the Hermetic Tradition* (Chicago: University of Chicago Press, 1964), 144–45.
10. This is how Giordano Bruno, for example, saw the significance of the Copernican Revolution, that it represented the return to an Egyptian heliocentric religion. See Yates, *Giordano Bruno*.

Giordano Bruno best represents the activist phase of Renaissance Hermeticism. The expansion of man's knowledge to include the creative powers of God meant that man had become "the equal of God." By his capacity to comprehend all things, ranging freely over the whole of creation and exploring all without limit, the bounds of human finitude had been transcended.[11] Bruno was among the first to take seriously the consequences of this new situation. If man had ascended to the divine creative level, it meant that he now possessed the means of bringing nature to perfection. This inspiration launched Bruno on the path of a messianic reformer, appealing successively to whatever monarchs would listen to be guided toward the Hermetic transformation of the world and society. It is no accident that the writing of utopias coincided with the appearance of these esoteric religious movements.[12]

Bruno's grandiose schemes for cosmic and political transformation were rivaled by such famous contemporaries as Thomas Campanella's *City of the Sun*. This was a fully Hermetic utopia, complete with a talismanic organization of the city to draw down the beneficent heavenly influences and ward off their harmful alternatives. It is a classic of utopian literature. All that separates it from the later secular evocations of the genre is that the faith in man's powers of natural magic is fully explicit. Otherwise, the description as summarized by Yates could apply to any number of successors. Under the government of their priest-king

the people of the City lived in brotherly love, having all things in common; they were intelligent and well-educated, the children beginning at an early age to learn all about the world and all arts and sciences from the pictures on the walls. They encouraged scientific invention, all inventions being used in the service of the community to improve

11. "Unless you make yourself equal to God, you cannot understand God: for the like is not intelligible save to the like. Make yourself grow to a greatness beyond measure, by a bound free yourself from the body; raise yourself above all time, become Eternity; then you will understand God. Believe that nothing is impossible for you, think yourself immortal and capable of understanding all arts, all sciences, the nature of every living being. Mount higher than the highest height; descend lower than the lowest depth. Draw into yourself all sensations of everything created, fire and water, dry and moist, imagining that you are not yet born, in the maternal womb, adolescent, old, dead, beyond death. If you embrace in your thought all things at once, times, places, substances, qualities, quantities, you may understand God" (quoted in Yates, *Giordano Bruno*, 198).

12. Thomas More coined the term with the publication of his *Utopia* (literally "no-place") in 1516. Moreover, there is a strong connection between More and the Neoplatonic Academy in Florence, which he had earlier visited on his travels. See Yates, *Giordano Bruno*, chap. 10.

the general well-being. They were healthy and well skilled in medicine. And they were virtuous. In this City, the virtues had conquered the vices, for the names of its magistrates were Liberality, Magnanimity, Chastity, Fortitude, Justice. . . . Hence among the Solarians, there was no robbery, murder, incest, adultery, no malignity or malevolence of any kind.[13]

The picture was so appealing that it, not too surprisingly, proved a source of attraction for the actual monarchs themselves. Bruno received the attentions of the Elizabethan court, as well as Henry II of France and Henry of Navarre, before eventually falling foul of the Italian Inquisition. Campanella, after languishing in prison for much of his life, was released under the influence of the Spanish court, performed interesting astrological service for Pope Urban VIII and ended his career by providing the title for the leading French monarch of the seventeenth century—Louis XIV who would be known as *Le Roi Soleil.* The monarchs of the new nation-states were, moreover, not slow to recognize the value of the Hermetic symbolism in the formation of a civil theology. Elizabeth I encouraged the depiction of herself as Astrea, the virgin queen who draws the heavenly justice down to earth in a new golden age. The ballets and masques of the French court had as their purpose the talismanic attempt to draw Jovian order down to transfigure the vicissitudes and conflicts of France. Rudolf II of Bohemia surrounded himself with a legendary constellation of scientists and magi. And Frederick and Elizabeth of the Palatine could evoke such expectations of an imminent Hermetic reformation that it became the basis for the legendary "Rosicrucian Enlightenment."[14]

There was much about the new occult philosophy to recommend it to the emerging monarchs and the new nation-states. In a public arena evacuated of spiritual authority, especially as a result of the breakup of the universal Church, it was left to the monarchs themselves to shape the civil theology. A spiritual symbolism derived from a pristine "ancient theology," free of the dogmatic contentiousness of late medieval Christianity, would encourage

13. Tommaso Campanella, *La Città del Sole: Dialogo Poetico,* trans. Daniel J. Donno (Berkeley: University of California Press, 1981); quoted in Yates, *Giordano Bruno,* 369.

14. Yates, *Giordano Bruno; Astraea: The Imperial Theme in the Sixteenth Century* (London: Routledge and Kegan Paul, 1975); *The Occult Philosophy in the Elizabethan Age* (Boston: Routledge and Kegan Paul, 1979); *The Rosicrucian Enlightenment* (Boston: Routledge and Kegan Paul, 1972). R. J. W. Evans, *Rudolf II and His World* (Oxford: Clarendon Press, 1973).

the essential political virtue of toleration.[15] At the same time, the focus on building a great civilizational order of scientific, cultural, and social progress coincided exactly with the aspirations of the new national communities themselves. And, not to be underestimated within this symbolism, is the flattering role reserved for the monarch who mediates harmony and abundance of order to his or her realm. Hermetic philosophy could provide the umbrella under which was sheltered a nondogmatic evangelical Christianity, a dedication to science and philanthropy, and a broad expectation of the progress of the human race. In short, it encouraged all the themes we recognize as constituting our modern world.

What only gradually became apparent was the extent to which the occult philosophy came into conflict with Christianity. There were undertones of rivalry from the start, and by the end of the sixteenth century, a reaction against Hermeticism had begun.[16] But the nature and extent of the conflict only becomes apparent in the thinkers who struggle toward a genuine synthesis of the two, the assembly of esoteric symbolisms loosely denoted by Hermeticism and the revealed transcendent theology of Christianity. The effort at synthesis was a comparatively late development, but it is of profound theoretical significance. For it is in the struggle to integrate the two symbolisms that the situation is revealed most clearly. We can see the nature of the changes taking place in the adjustments that Hermeticism requires of Christianity when they are brought into coincidence. For the new occult philosophy to work, the old Christian philosophy must be redirected. The individual with the theoretical genius to effect their reconciliation

---

15. D. P. Walker, *The Ancient Theology: Studies in Christian Platonism from the Fifteenth to the Eighteenth Centuries* (Ithaca, N.Y.: Cornell University Press, 1972). A parallel search for a politically unifying ancient theology was carried on by Jean Bodin; he sought it within a purified form of Judaism. See Paul Lawrence Rose, *Bodin and the Great God of Nature: The Moral and Religious Universe of a Judaiser* (Geneva: Droz, 1980).

16. D. P. Walker summarizes the tension thus: "Natural, non-demonic magic is an obvious threat to religion, since it claims to produce the same effect without any supernatural agent; its logical consequent is atheism or deism. Demonic or angelic magic avoids this danger, but is more evidently unacceptable to a Christian because it is a rival religion" (*Spiritual and Demonic Magic from Ficino to Campanella* [London: Warburg Institute, University of London, 1958], 83). Frances Yates discusses the transformation of the Magus figure that occurs in Marlowe's *Doctor Faustus*, where his power is derived not from nature but from his pact with the devil. Of course, the reaction is most evident in the burning of Giordano Bruno at the stake in 1601 and the witch crazes that followed in the seventeenth century.

and, thereby, become the transmitter of the new symbolism to the modern world was Jakob Böhme.

This assessment of Böhme's significance has the support of no less perspicuous an authority than Hegel. He proclaimed Böhme "the first German philosopher" and the first to seriously take up the core modern intellectual challenge that had arrived at its culmination in Hegel's own System. This judgment, which was shared by many of the romantics and idealists, ought to be given considerable credence in light of Hegel's own pivotal role within the self-understanding of modernity. Böhme provided for him the most profound insight into the modification Christianity must undergo if it was to be reconciled with the spirit of the age. In his hands the nature of that spirit is most dramatically illuminated by virtue of its effect on the traditional Christian formulations. He shows the extent to which the earlier Christian definitions of man and God, creation and redemption, must be transformed to accommodate the new roles of the divine and human within history. Above all, it is Böhme who gives expression to the new conception of the process of reality that enables man to become the co-creator in the divine work of creation and redemption, once he has penetrated to the perspective of the mind of God.

The crucial shift is from the idea of all reality as moving toward God to the idea of God himself as part of the movement of reality as well. The shift of man's focus from a fulfillment beyond this world to a state of perfection within it is a distinctive feature of the civilization that begins with the Renaissance. But the theoretical expression of this change does not occur until the process of reality as a whole is seen to participate in the same reorientation. The human shift toward intramundane fulfillment is confirmed when it is understood to be part of the larger process of reality, including the reality of divine Being. Jakob Böhme is the thinker who elaborates the modern *Weltanschauung* into its theological consequences. Within his speculative reconstruction of reality, all of the separate dimensions of human knowledge, power, and prospects for self-realization come together.[17]

Böhme is the one who grapples most profoundly with the tension between the expansion of man's power and the constraints imposed by the Judeo-Christian symbolism. They can come to be

17. A fuller account of Böhme's significance can be found in David Walsh, *The Mysticism of Innerworldly Fulfillment: A Study of Jacob Boehme* (Gainesville: University Presses of Florida, 1983).

regarded as compatible only if the traditional understanding of God is revised. Man's creative partnership with God does not become a rivalry and is indeed legitimized if it forms part of the divine way with the world. The theological justification of man's new transformative powers is the distinctive achievement of the shoemaker-mystic from Silesia. This was a large part of the task Böhme had set for himself. He struggled to understand the mystery of reality, why there is evil as well as good, and how God can be present in the infinite space of the universe. Above all, he wanted to know how assurance of salvation through Christ was continuous with the recovery of man's original divine powers of creation.

The breakthrough came when Böhme penetrated the inner divine process. He realized that the struggle between good and evil, light and dark, expansion and contraction, which he beheld in all things, had its origin within the Godhead itself. This was his "glimpse into the center" (*Zentralschau*) in which he beheld the being of all beings (*das Wesen aller Wesen*). In this mystical intuition, in which he "saw more in a quarter of an hour than if he had gone to school for many years," Böhme claimed to have penetrated into the innermost birth of the Godhead. "In this light my spirit saw directly through all things and recognized God in all creatures, in plants as well as grass, who he is and how he is and what his will is. Suddenly my will to describe the being of God also grew with great force in this light."[18] The conflict between opposing principles which he saw in all things, Böhme now understood as a necessary process of opposition that had its source in the divine essence itself. Everything became clear once he had traced the ultimate foundation within the being of God. His theosophic speculation on the unfolding divine process constituted and exemplified the new understanding of God within the modern world.

At the core of his construction was Böhme's discovery that conflict and opposition were necessary to the self-revelation of God. It was an extrapolation from what is required for the self-realization of man to what is required for the self-realization of God. "No thing can be revealed to itself without opposition [*Wiederwärtigkeit*]. For if there is nothing that opposes it then it always goes out of itself and never returns to itself again. If it does not

---

18. Jakob Böhme, *Morgenröthe im Aufgang* (1613), in *Sämtliche Schriften*, ed. Will-Erich Peuckert (Stuttgart: F. Frommanns Verlag, 1955–1961), vol. 1, chap. 19, paragraph 13.

return into itself, as into that from which it originated, then it knows nothing of its origin [*Urstand*]."[19] Self-consciousness and self-awareness is dependent on this contrast between the self and that which is outside the self. Without differentiation there would hardly even be a self of which to be conscious. Correlatively, the more intense the conflict between inner and outer, the more complete the awareness of self. For full self-knowledge, therefore, all that is present in the self must be expressed and projected outside the self in order that the "I" may most completely apprehend that which it is and that which it is not. The more profound the conflict between the self and the not-self, the more fully all that is contained within the self is called forth. This is the process of self-expression and self-realization.[20]

Böhme's genius consisted in the expansion of this insight into the revelatory process of God. Where previously the self-expression of God had been necessary for his revelation to us, Böhme insisted that it was also necessary for the revelation of God to himself. Before the process of divine self-unfolding has occurred (that is in the nontemporal sense of "before"), God is a dark unconscious abyss. Böhme coined the term *Ungrund* to denote the divine Being in this phase: "One cannot say of God that he is this or that, evil or good, that he contains distinctions within himself. For he is himself nature-less, as well as affect-less and creature-less. He has no inclination to anything, since there is nothing before him to which he could incline himself, neither evil nor good. He is in himself the *Ungrund*. . . . He is the Nothing and the All."[21]

As such, God is a dark inchoate will for self-revelation, but before any self-knowledge can occur he must generate an "other" that is different from himself. This eventually becomes the inner trinitarian process of God, and strictly speaking, God is not even a person until the generation of Christ. Before that it is a pre-per-

---

19. Böhme, *Von Göttlicher Beschaulichkeit*, in *Sämtliche Schriften*, vol.6, chap. 1, paragraph 8.

20. The experience is most readily identified with artistic creation in which the artist does not properly know the work until it is created and is even at times surprised by what has come forth in the struggle for expression. We do not know what we contain until it has been objectified outside of ourselves. The same may be said of the development of the person in general. Self-realization involves a process of going outside ourselves; it is through expressing ourselves that we come to know ourselves.

21. Böhme, *Von der Gnaden Wahl*, in *Sämtliche Schriften*, vol.6, chap. 1, paragraph 3.

sonal process of the self-generating *Ungrund*. However, the process does not reach its conclusion with the emergence of the divine Trinity or its intra-divine phase. Ultimately the creation of heaven and earth, angels and men, with their successive falls, and the divine response of redemption and restoration must all be worked through before the process is complete. All of the possibilities must be brought forth and all of the conflicts overcome if the revelation of divine Being to itself is finally to be achieved.

This is what makes Böhme one of the great sources, if not the greatest, for the later modern speculation on the dialectical process of reality.[22]

> The reader should know that in Yes and No stand all things, whether divine, devilish, earthly or whatever it may be called. The One, as the Yes is a pure power and life, and is the truth of God or God himself. He would be unknown in himself and there would be neither joy nor exaltation nor sensibility therein, without the No. The No is a counterstroke of the Yes or the truth, so that the truth may be revealed and be something, and that there may be a *Contrarium*, wherein the eternal love may be active, feeling, willing and such as can be loved.[23]

He provides the theological confirmation for the modern shift of expectations away from a world-transcendent telos, toward a culmination to be attained within this world. Moreover, he also provides the theoretical mechanism that explains how the present imperfect state of affairs may eventually reach a perfect transformation of existence. The dialectical overcoming of opposition permits the full acknowledgement of the present imperfections and justifies the faith in its eventual transfiguration. Innerworldly fulfillment is not a mere aspiration, nor is it dependent on the uncertain determination of the human will. It is a *telos* that is inherent to the process of reality itself, which reaches up to its roots in divine Being.

Within that process the new role of man likewise receives its

22. No doubt an important source is also the Neoplatonic speculation on the unfolding or emanationist process from the divine One and the eventual return of all things to this primordial unity. This is certainly an insight that Hegel could have derived from Plotinus and especially Proclus, two thinkers with whom he was quite familiar. But he would not have derived the peculiarly dialectical quality of the movement from these sources. They stress the dynamic aspect but not the struggle with opposites that reaches back into the divine nature itself. This is the Böhmean contribution.

23. Böhme, *Betrachtung Göttlicher Offenbarung*, in *Sämtliche Schriften*, vol.9, chap. 3, paragraph 2.

confirmation. Man as a participant in all the levels of being is a microcosm, the point at which the unity of creation is mirrored back to God in its most self-conscious form. This was the original role of Adam, and it is now to be recovered more profoundly by Christ and those who are united with his spirit. Just as at the beginning,

> the hidden divine man could go into and contemplate all things. The outer man was indeed in the outer [world] but as Lord over the outer; it was under him and did not tame him. He could have broken rocks without difficulty, the tincture of the earth was entirely known to him, and he would have found all the wonders of the earth. For to that end was he created in the outer, so that he should reveal in figures and introduce into action, what he had seen in the eternal Wisdom; for he had the virgin Wisdom within him.[24]

Of considerable importance too is the new understanding of evil that is implied by the dialectical symbolism. It is a necessary phase in the unfolding of God's self-revelation, without which the divine redemptive Love would never have been called forth. "For if there were no evil then good would not be known." In a certain sense, evil is no longer so radically and irretrievably evil. But above all is the new conception of God as an *ens manifestativum sui*, a being whose essence is to reveal itself. This God who begins as barely conscious *Ungrund* is deficient without the entire unfolding of world-history. Created reality is necessary "in order that God might have an image or likeness in an essence, where he might no longer need to contemplate himself in a mirror but experience himself in an essence."[25]

The significance and value of this construction is demonstrated by its resurgence within the era of scientific rationalism known as the Enlightenment. At the point where the triumph of science and the scientific method seems complete, there is a veritable explosion of interest in the occult, the mystical and magical, and perhaps most of all in the theosophic speculations of Jakob Böhme.[26] The Enlightenment began as a movement for the popularization and expansion of scientific knowledge. Its heroes were

24. Böhme, *Von der Menschwerdung Jesu Christi*, in *Sämtliche Schriften*, vol. 4, part 1, chap. 4, paragraph 7.

25. Ibid., chap. 10, paragraph 5.

26. "In a certain sense one can refer to the philosophy of German Idealism as a Boehme-Renaissance, when Boehme was discovered at the same time by Schelling, Hegel, Franz von Baader, Tieck, Novalis and many others" (Ernst Benz, *Adam der Mythus vom Urmenschen* [Munich: Barth, 1955]), 23.

Newton and Locke and the members of the Royal Society. But right at the apogee of the spirit of rationalism something snaps. Reason and science alone are shown not to be enough. Throughout Western civilization a new consensus begins to take shape concerning the need to go beyond the perspectives afforded by a parsimonious empirical methodology. What is lacking in modern science is the visionary comprehension of the whole of which it is a part.[27] Man cannot live by facts alone; nor by the cold light of reason. The need for an appropriately modern spiritual symbolism was so widely recognized, that the quest for it may be taken as the hallmark of the new age of Romanticism.

Science itself lacked the rhetoric with which to express its own penumbra of visionary expectations. The Enlightenment faith in progress and the incremental benefits of the rational experimental method seemed a rather thin foundation for the limitless aspirations of perfection. What was needed was a means of demonstrating the transition between the two. How would the progressive expansion of reason and the accelerating decline of superstition lead to the transformation of human nature? This was a question that became even more urgent after the debacle of absolute reason and freedom in the French Revolution. It set in motion a vast panorama of new religious experiments, mainly outside of the boundaries of traditional ecclesiastical formulations. The emergence of Masonry and other secret esoteric societies in the latter part of the eighteenth century is well known. But it is essential to place this phenomenon within the context of the broad range of efforts by poets, philosophers and statesmen at articulating a new public religion, a *theologia civilis*.[28] It would have to perform the same

27. Goethe exemplifies this new outlook perfectly through his own efforts to bridge the worlds of science and art. "Who would study and describe the living, starts / By driving the spirit out of the parts; / In the palm of his hand he holds all the sections, / Lacks nothing except the spirit's connections" (*Faust: Part One*, lines 1936–39). On Goethe's interest in Hermeticism, see Rolf Zimmerman, *Das Weltbild des jungen Goethe: Studien zur Hermetischen Tradition des deutschen 18. Jahrhunderts* (Munich: Fisk, 1969); and on the broader situation, Antoine Faivre and Rolf Zimmerman, eds., *Epochen der Naturmystik: Hermetische Tradition im wissenschaftlichen Fortschritt* (Berlin: Erich Schmidt Velag, 1979).

28. Eric Voegelin, *From Enlightenment to Revolution*, ed. John Hallowell (Durham, N.C.: Duke University Press, 1975); James Billington, *Fire in the Minds of Men* (New York: Basic Books, 1980), and his earlier *The Icon and the Axe* (New York: Vintage Books, 1970); August Viatte, *Les sources occultes du romantisme 1770–1820* (1928; reprint, Paris: H. Champion, 1965); Ernst Benz, *Les sources mystiques de la philosophie romantique allemande* (Paris: J. Vrin, 1968); M. H. Abrams, *Natural Supernaturalism* (New York: Norton, 1971); Antoine Faivre, *L'ésoterisme au XVIIIe siècle en France et en Allemagne* (Paris: Seghers, 1973).

existential role as Christianity, and remain fully supportive of the Promethean humanist spirit of the age.

The pseudo-science that appeared to have been jettisoned by the more successful branch of natural science now returned with a vengeance. The nineteenth century is the great century of pseudo-science. It is the century of megalomaniacal schemes of human perfection, which are only approached by the grotesque efforts at implementation in the twentieth century. Reason and science continue to be invoked, but their authority is usurped by apocalyptic visions of the transfiguration of reality on a global scale. Often the contrast between the language of science and the irrationality of the content is quite striking. One may recall August Comte's juxtaposition of Positivism (the scientific method) with his Religion of Humanity.[29] Or there is the equally striking incongruity between Marx's scientific materialism and the utter unwillingness to consider contrary or qualifying evidence. In the same way we may view the rise of racist ideologies, nationalism, Darwinism, Freudianism and so on. Theories that begin from a core of empirical insight are pushed beyond the bounds of reason and fact and are persisted in despite the abundance of countervailing evidence.

We begin to realize that science does not exist as a self-contained entity, but as part of a whole understanding of man and his place within reality. Science is surrounded by a penumbra of expectations from which it is separate, but which it is not always able to resist. In the nineteenth century we observe the phenomenon of the penumbra overshadowing the rational core. The thinker who provides the greatest insight into the event is Hegel, because he is the one who undertook their reconciliation most self-consciously. He set out to create a new "mythology of reason," in which the rationality of the Enlightenment would be united with the symbolic power of faith.[30] Yet he was profoundly aware that

---

29. Many of Comte's followers, including J. S. Mill, thought that the incongruity between the two poles of Comte's thought was so great that it could only be explained in terms of a nervous breakdown. This of course is without foundation. See Voegelin, *From Enlightenment to Revolution*, chaps. 6 and 7.

30. In 1796 Hegel declared, "We must have a new mythology, but this mythology must be in the service of the Ideas, it must be a mythology of Reason. Until we express the Ideas aesthetically, i.e. mythologically, they have no interest for the *people*, and conversely until mythology is rational the philosopher must be ashamed of it. Thus in the end enlightened and unenlightened must clasp hands, mythology must become philosophical in order to make the people rational, and philosophy must become mythological in order to make the philosophers sensible [*sinnlich*]." *Hegel's Development Toward the Sunlight: 1770–1801*, trans. H. S. Harris (Oxford: Clarendon Press, 1972), 511–12.

one could not be reduced to the other. If rationality was to be subsumed into a mystical unity, then it would lose its critical autonomy; if the depth of faith were to be narrowed to a rational comprehension, then it would no longer be faith in a divine whole. The former had been the error of romanticism, the latter had been the failing of rationalism. This was why, in Hegel's view, their syntheses of autonomous freedom and universal nature had successively unraveled.

What Hegel set out to do was to integrate the rationality of modern science with the penumbra of larger spiritual expectations which have also been an abiding feature of the modern world. It is perhaps the most impressive attempt at reconciling science with pseudo-science. The turning point in his enterprise came when he shifted the search from a reconciliation within human consciousness to the quest for a reconciliation within the divine self-consciousness. Instead of talking about man, Hegel began to talk about Spirit, *Geist*. He struggled to develop a way of articulating the process by which the difference between human and divine, finite and infinite, is overcome without being annihilated. It must be a process in which unity is achieved without sacrificing what is essential to either pole. And it must be a process or movement, since the consummation has not yet been reached but will eventually be realized.

The breakthrough occurred when Hegel discovered the dialectic. It was possible for finite human reason to preserve its independence and be integrated with the whole if finite humanity was a moment to be overcome within the self-reconciliation of absolute Spirit. Moreover, since there is no divine Spirit outside of this process of self-revelation, the reconciliation occurs within the apprehension of the necessity for the process that remains transparent to human consciousness. Man's reason is not submerged in an emotional mystery, the "night in which all cows are black" which was the undifferentiated absorption that Hegel complained of in the romantics. The reconciliation occurs through the rational apprehension of the necessity for finiteness as the self-expression or other of the infinite. At the same time, it is not an integration that occurs simply within the human mind, the mind of Hegel or any other. The reconciliation occurs within the self-unfolding of absolute Spirit, for which human consciousness has become the vehicle. This is why Hegel insists that he is not presenting his ideas about God, but "the self-contemplation of the divine."[31]

31. Charles Taylor, *Hegel* (Cambridge: Cambridge University Press, 1975).

Now whether Hegel developed his notion of dialectic independently or was more or less influenced by other sources is a difficult question for scholarship to explore. A plausible case can be made that it was his reading of Jakob Böhme during the early years at Jena that decisively shaped his construction. I have presented that case elsewhere and do not wish to insist on it here.[32] What can be stated certainly, however, is that Hegel found powerful confirmation of his dialectical understanding of God within Böhme's theosophic speculation. Indeed, the argument can be made that the conception of a dialectically self-unfolding Godhead is to be found nowhere articulated as forcefully as it is within the Silesian mystic. Hegel himself is the best guide to what is most essential in the theosophic construction.

The genius of Böhme, as it was also the genius of Hegel, was to grasp the negative as a necessary moment in the divine. In the *Lectures on the History of Philosophy* Hegel devotes an extensive chapter to Böhme as, along with Francis Bacon, one of the two great fountainheads of the modern world.

> He is called the *philosophus teutonicus,* and in fact through him philosophy first entered Germany with its characteristic nature. . . . In the idea of God to apprehend the negative, to comprehend God as absolute identity—this is the struggle that he had to endure; it had a frightful appearance because Böhme was so far behind in conceptual development. On the one hand there is the completely rough and barbaric representation; on the other hand one recognizes the deep German disposition (*Gemüt*) that associates with the innermost and therein exercises its might, its power.[33]

Böhme had understood the self-centering separation of the "I" from God not simply as evil, but as the necessity which generates a separate reality outside of divine Being. As such, the self-centering force is itself a moment or a dimension of God. It is the negative, the wrath of God. This highest achievement of representational Christianity, Hegel identified with the speculative dialectic

32. David Walsh, "The Historical Dialectic of Spirit: Jacob Boehme's Influence on Hegel," in *History and System: Hegel's Philosophy of History,* ed. Robert Perkins (Albany: State University of New York Press, 1984), 15–35.

33. Hegel, *Vorlesungen: Ausgewählte Nachschriften und Manuskripte Bd. 9,* in *Vorlesungen über die Geschichte der Philosophie,* Teil 4, ed. Pierre Garniron and Walter Jaeschke (Hamburg: Felix Meiner, 1986), 80. See also the letter of gratitude to his former student, van Ghert, for sending Hegel an edition of Böhme's collected works in *Hegel: The Letters,* trans. Clark Butler and Christiane Seiler (Bloomington: Indiana University Press, 1984), 573–74.

of Böhme.[34] It is an achievement that is now superseded, of course, within the conceptual dialectic of Hegel's System. The conscious immanent reconciliation of all oppositions and differences is the logical culmination of the self-unfolding divinity of Böhme. Neither man nor God exists as a separate entity any longer within Hegel's conception; all have reality to the extent that they are moments with the self-negating and self-overcoming of Spirit.

I have argued elsewhere that this constitutes the "essential ambiguity" of Hegel's thought.[35] Everything works so long as one does not question the underlying assertion that everything must be immanent to the dialectical process itself. One cannot talk of God or man apart from the movement of their dialectical self-realization. They do not exist apart from the process. Nor can one ask whose consciousness it is in which Spirit becomes self-conscious. Realities in depth apart from the dialectical process cannot be acknowledged.[36] To that extent, Hegel's construction, despite its enormous rational coherence, is rooted in an irrational construction of reality. He insists on identifying the dialectical process of consciousness with the process of reality as a whole. It was an impossible project and its futility is best reflected in the history of philosophy after Hegel. It is largely the history of the disintegration of the Hegelian synthesis and the successive attempts to create an alternative or to live with the consequences of nihilism.[37]

The real significance of Böhme and Hegel as preeminent theoreticians of the modern worldview has been to provide the outline that all such articulations must follow. This is the conception of reality as a moving dialectical process. Reality is a fluid medi-

34. Hegel depicts Böhme's conception of God as the highest achievement of Christianity: "Picture-thinking takes the other aspect, evil, to be a happening alien to the divine Being; to grasp it in the divine Being itself as *the wrath of God*, this demands from picture-thinking, struggling against its limitations, its supreme and most strenuous effort, an effort which, since it lacks the Notion, remains fruitless." (*Phenomenology of Spirit*, trans. A.V. Miller [Oxford: Clarendon Press, 1977], 470).

35. David Walsh, "The Essential Ambiguity of Hegel's Political Thought," *Modern Age*, forthcoming. See also Voegelin, "On Hegel: A Study in Sorcery," *Studium Generale* 24 (1971): 335–68.

36. This is in many ways the essence of two of the most forceful critiques of Hegel, from Marx and Kierkegaard. The one points to Hegel's neglect of the concrete social and economic reality, the other objects to the absence of the existential subject with all of its concrete uniqueness.

37. Karl Löwith, *From Hegel to Nietzsche*, trans. David E. Green (New York: Holt, Rinehart and Winston, 1967).

um in which progress and transformation can occur, especially when it is manipulated by those who possess the knowledge of its inner laws. Even science is seduced by this expectation, as the talk of biological engineering and behavioral conditioning indicates. We are surprised by the discovery that natures are not infinitely malleable, that species have a fixity that at some point resists transformation, and that the behavior of organisms cannot be molded beyond instinctual limits. But it has been in the social and political world that the influence of this belief has been strongest. The philosophy of history behind the various ideological movements has been based on a view of reality as moving toward the ultimate perfection of human nature and society. Crucial to this conception has been the conviction that it is reality as a whole that is on the way toward a culmination. It is not simply wishful thinking or dependent on mere human effort.

This is the conviction that Marx received from Hegel. It is what made it possible for him to believe that a proletarian revolution is capable of "transforming men on a mass scale." It is what supports his confidence that the world can be changed, and not merely interpreted. It is the basis for his own claim to possess the secret that "unlocks the riddle of history," that a transformation in the economic conditions of existence will bring about a transformation in the totality of the human condition.[38] It is what enables Marx to declare with such supreme assurance that socialist man will no longer even ask the question of who created the world.

> But since for the socialist man the *entire so-called history of the world* is nothing but the begetting of man through human labor, nothing but the coming-to-be of nature for man, he has the visible, irrefutable proof of his *birth* through himself, of his *process* of *coming-to-be.* Since the *real existence* of man and nature has become practical, sensuous and perceptible—since man has become for man as the being of

38. "This communism . . . is the *genuine* resolution of the conflict between man and nature and between man and man—the true resolution of the strife between existence and essence, between objectification and self-confirmation, between freedom and necessity, between the individual and the species. Communism is the riddle of history solved, and it knows itself to be this solution" (*The Marx-Engels Reader*, ed. Robert Tucker [New York: Norton, 1978], 84). Or there is the following: "Both for the production on a mass scale of this communist consciousness, and for the success of the cause itself, the alteration of men on a mass scale is necessary, an alteration which can only take place in a practical movement, a *revolution*; this revolution is necessary, therefore, not only because the *ruling* class cannot be overthrown in any other way, but also because the class *overthrowing* it can only in a revolution succeed in ridding itself of all the muck of ages and become fitted to found society anew" (193).

nature, and nature for man as the being of man—the question about an *alien* being, about a being above nature and man—a question which implies the admission of the inessentiality of nature and of man—has become impossible in practice. *Atheism*, as the denial of this inessentiality has no longer any meaning.[39]

Atheism cannot become even a possibility for the man who possesses the Promethean self-confidence of being his own "supreme divinity." Man creates his own nature. The theme of man as magus, as co-creator with God, as the shaper of his own being and the god of the material world, has reached its conclusion in Marx's evocation of the socialist secular messiah.[40]

The pivot on which the entire edifice depends, however, is the depiction of reality as the kind of process which man, a part, may learn to manipulate and direct toward its culmination. This in turn depends on the removal of a transcendent creator and his absorption into the moving process itself. The creative and transformative divine powers must become part of the reality that can be operated on by the saving man or the saving party. This has been the effect of the process which began in the Renaissance of the expansion of man's knowledge and power toward the divine pole. It has meant, as Böhme and Hegel realized and developed, the correlative increasing involvement of God in the world of created reality. Man cannot penetrate the workings of God and become a participant in the primordial divine powers unless the movement of God toward man and the world has become a necessity. There can be no expansion of man's power without a corresponding diminution of God's power.

Nietzsche represents the end point of this development. He is the one who formulated most clearly the intimate connection between the death of God and the divinization of man. Nietzsche stripped away the veil of idealism to reveal the will to power behind it, especially the most unlimited expression of it in the will to become God: "But let me reveal my heart entirely to you, my friends: *if* there were gods how could I endure not being a god. *Hence* there are no gods."[41] Nietzsche or his Zarathustra is willing

---

39. Ibid., 92.
40. The Promethean theme in Marx is declared in the famous preface to his doctoral dissertation. A good recent study of this dimension of Marx, although without much on the Hermetic background, is provided by Leonard P. Wessell, *Prometheus Bound: The Mythic Structure of Karl Marx's Scientific Thinking* (Baton Rouge: Louisiana State University Press, 1984).
41. Friedrich Wilhelm Nietzsche, *Thus Spoke Zarathustra*, trans. Walter Kauf-

to admit the murder of God for otherwise there is no way for man's will to power to reign supreme over reality. The process that begins with the drawing together of God and man in the Renaissance, which reaches its most complete formulation in Hegel, ends when the man-god replaces the God-man. What is interesting is that this rivalry and its consequence were foreseen at the very beginning. In an illuminating document from the thirteenth century, two Cabalists confront the logical consequence of the death of God implied by their magical practices. It is so extraordinary that the account is worthy of quotation in full.

> The prophet Jeremiah busied himself alone with the *Book Yetsirah*. Then a heavenly voice went forth and said: Take a companion. He went to his son Sira, and they studied the book for three years. Afterward they set about combining the alphabets in accordance with the Kabbalistic principles of combination, grouping, and word formation, and a man was created to them, on whose forehead stood the letters YHWH *Elohim Emeth* [God is truth]. But this newly created man had a knife in his hand, with which he erased the *aleph* from *emeth;* there remained: *meth.* Then Jeremiah rent his garments [because of the blasphemy: God is dead, now implied in the inscription] and said: Why have you erased the *aleph* from *emeth?* He replied: I will tell you a parable. An architect built many houses, cities, and squares, but no one could copy his art and compete with him in knowledge and skill until two men persuaded him. Then he taught them the secret of his art, and they know how to do everything in the right way. When they had learned his secret and his abilities, they began to anger him with words. Finally, they broke with him and became architects like him, except that what he charged a thaler for, they did for six groats. When people noticed this, they ceased to honor the artist and came to them and honored them and gave them commissions when they required to have something built. So God has made you in His image and in His shape and form. But now that you have created a man like Him, people will say: There is no God in the world beside these two! Then Jeremiah said: What solution is there? He said: Write the alphabets backward on the earth you have strewn with intense concentration. Only do not meditate in the sense of building up, but the other way around. So they did, and the man became dust and ashes before their eyes. Then Jeremiah said: Truly, one should study these things only in order to know the power and omnipotence of the Creator of this world, but not in order really to practice them.[42]

mann (Harmondsworth: Penguin, 1966), 86. Dostoevsky is the other great diagnostician of the modern world, and he confirms Nietzsche's analysis of the conflict as a confrontation between the "God-man" and the "man-god." See David Walsh, *After Ideology: Recovering the Spiritual Foundations of Freedom* (San Francisco: Harper Collins, 1990), chap. 3
42. Quoted in Gershom Scholem, *On the Kabbalah and Its Symbolism*, trans.

The great difference is that the later secular Prometheans do not shrink from the consequences of their actions. Indeed they persist in them even when their futility has become transparent. This too is a feature of the mythology of reason that forms the symbolic worldview of our civilization. The pseudo-scientific fixities endure even in the face of overwhelming contrary evidence, as the modern ideological movements have abundantly revealed. With Nietzsche, Marx, Comte, and the other great ideological thinkers we have arrived at the core of what sustains the irrational, pseudo-scientific component of modernity. It is the desire to become God by eclipsing the true God. When expressed with this starkness, the revolt against God is exposed as an impossible project. But this does not quite capture the obsessive power of the idea. For it is an idea that modern human beings have declared themselves willing to persist in "even if I were wrong."[43] We begin to realize that our scientific culture is a rational fragment that is surrounded, not only by a circle of irrationality, but by a ring of unmitigated anti-rationality.

Reflection naturally turns to the prospects for remedying such a disastrous rejection of reason. The great benefit of tracing the path of the irrational in the modern mythology is that we have acquired a sense of what it is that makes rational openness possible. If science and reason are threatened by the persistence of pseudo-science, then the fault lies not in science or reason but in the larger worldview of which their operation is a part. Science is not a self-contained entity, functioning in rarified isolation from the rest of human life. It had its origin within a specific historical context, shaped by a certain understanding of man's relationship to reality and its divine source. Modern science became successful the more it was able to distance itself from the exaggerated and grandiose expectations that were also a possibility within that worldview. The authority and validity of science is, in turn, jeopardized to the extent that those unbalancing expectations become

---

Ralph Mannheim (New York: Shocken Books, 1965), 180–81.

43. "We deny God as God. If one were to *prove* this God of the Christians to us, we should be even less able to believe in him" (Nietzsche, *The Anti-Christ* in *The Portable Nietzsche*, ed. Walter Kaufmann [New York: Viking, 1968], 627). Or there is the famous passage from Ivan Karamazov which captures the sentiment of revolt perfectly: "I don't want [divine] harmony. From love for humanity I don't want it. I would rather be left with the unavenged suffering. I would rather remain with my unavenged suffering and unsatisfied indignation, *even if I were wrong*" (*Brothers Karamazov*, trans. Constance Garnett [New York: Modern Library, 1950], 291).

more pervasive. If we are convinced of our ability to achieve the transfiguration of human nature, then we construct reality as the kind of process that leads toward that conclusion and science is powerless to resist the fatality.

The only possibility for a restoration of reason lies in the recovery of a mythology that promotes empirical openness. Agnosticism is not a viable option because a whole society cannot live that way. Sooner or later the vacuum is filled by more powerful spiritual visions. The essential thing is to make contact with a spirituality of maximum openness to reality. This would be one in which man is not presumed or pressured into an exaggerated messianic role of which he has never been capable. Nor must there be any premature imposition of a pattern on the movement of reality that insists that at some point its meaning has been definitively fixed for all time. Above all, there must be no obstacle to the process of inquiry, no prohibition of questions. There must be an acceptance of a horizon of mystery within which humanity lives and explores reality. Man must acknowledge that he is not God, and that the origin and end of his existence lies beyond himself. He must be sufficiently assured of the meaning of the mysterious process in which he participates, so that he is no longer compelled to search obsessively for a means by which he can dominate the whole. Released from this Sisyphean project, man will again be free to contemplate his world. There must be, in other words, a horizon of spiritual openness that is not too far different from that which prevailed in the West at the time when modern science first began its career.

EPISTEMOLOGICAL AND POLITICAL IMPLICATIONS OF THE SCIENTIFIC REVOLUTION

Wilbur Applebaum

The preceding essays in this volume have addressed particular issues in the transformation of our understanding of the relations among the natural sciences, the occult sciences, and the sacred in the early modern period. It is my task to examine some issues connected with them, on the one hand in the development of natural philosophy into science as it is more or less understood today, and on the other, to explore how they may be perceived in the larger cultural context of the emergence of modernity.

Efforts to define the modern world or modernity began long ago and have continued ever since. Among the most influential attempts were those by Marx and Weber, who tried to come to grips with the unique character and history of Western Europe, which from the sixteenth to the eighteenth centuries was transformed "so as to lay the social, economic, scientific, political, ideological and ethical foundations for the rationalist, democratic, individualistic, technological industrialized society in which we now live."[1] For Marx the modern era was defined by a substantive change in the means of production and the rise of a new class. Max Weber, standing Marx on his head, ascribed the unique character of European civilization and its economic style to rationalization and a restless energy promoted by particular religious norms.

However one wishes to define modernity, there must clearly be in it a place for what we today call science and what was once called natural philosophy. Several hundred years ago, profound changes took place in the content, style, and explanatory modes of natural philosophy, and these changes, generally known as the Scientific Revolution, occurred in the context of a culture in which were reflected shifts in the aims of natural knowledge, its

---

1. Lawrence Stone, *The Past and the Present Revisited*, rev. ed. (London: Routledge and Kegan Paul, 1987), xi.

possibilities and limits, ideas of the knowledge most worth having, and the means of acquiring it.

A sphere of inquiry once the province of a minute segment of that tiny portion of humanity that occupied itself with intellectual concerns has come to engage the efforts of a substantial number of individuals. The consequences of what these individuals think and do have become a most significant part of our means of livelihood and of the ways we live, conduct our affairs, and think; science has transformed and continues to transform the world. Its ability to do so is woven into the fabric of the modern world and developed along with it, and has therefore found increasing recognition as an important subject of historical investigation.

The Scientific Revolution and Its Interpreters

Histories of science have long been written, but their content, form, and underlying premises have changed with time. In the early days of the genre, self-contained histories of individual sciences describing progressive achievements within the field or biographies of famous scientists listing their accomplishments were the dominant forms. The influence of the Enlightenment, with its emphasis on the growth of science and technology as the embodiment of progress, shaped the positivistic strain so influential in the historiography of science in the nineteenth century and the first half of the twentieth. Positivist historians tended to interpret the history of science as an autonomous development, the story of how we threaded our way in the study of nature past the Swamp of Ignorance, Error, and Superstition through the gradual accumulation of established Facts to the Truth. An early example is William Whewell's three-volume *History of the Inductive Sciences* (1837). Whewell's work typified an aspect of the continuing close relationship between history of science and philosophy, which saw in the history of scientific thought raw material for the exploration of epistemological problems. Meanwhile, a variation on a theme of Comte found expression in several histories written in terms of a warfare between science and religion. The volumes of Lecky, Draper, and White exemplify this historiographical tradition.[2]

2. W. E. H. Lecky, *History of the Rise and Influence of the Spirit of Rationalism in Europe*, 2 vols. (New York: D. Appleton, 1866); John William Draper, *History of the Conflict Between Religion and Science* (New York: D. Appleton, 1874); Andrew D. White, *A History of the Warfare of Science with Theology in Christendom*, 2 vols. (New York: D. Appleton, 1900).

C. S. Peirce, redressing the balance against an excessive empiricism, added a new dimension to traditional epistemological concerns by expressing an interest not only in the justification of claims to knowledge, but also in the problem of how our knowledge grows through the creation of new theories. In the twentieth century several philosophers took up the challenge and rejected positivism, including the idea of an antagonism between science and religion. Cassirer, Burtt, Bachelard and Koyré showed that scientific concepts could be influenced by extra-scientific ideas, even metaphysical and religious ones.[3] This approach coincided with and received reinforcement from the emerging history of ideas movement. Problems of the birth, development, and reception of theories were now investigated in a significant departure from the positivist assumptions that new theories were introduced when new facts invalidated the old one, and that new truths when presented to the world were manifest, or ought to have been. The development of scientific theories, particularly during the seventeenth century, received their most illuminating and influential expression in the works of Alexandre Koyré. Since the 1950s, the era and the historiographic style were adopted by many in the growing cadre of professionally trained historians of science.

Science had by now also come under the scrutiny of the sociologists. The late nineteenth-century theorists and modern founders of their discipline saw science as an important component of modern culture, shaped by and in turn helping to shape society. The sociology of science has been influenced to a great degree by two nineteenth-century extensions of the Enlightenment debate over whether "the world governs opinion" or "opinion governs the world." The stimulus of Marx on the one hand and Weber and Durkheim on the other has produced a literature which has had a measurable impact on the writing of history of science. In the 1930s the Marxist Boris Hessen attempted an analysis of Newton's achievement in terms of the class structure of his time, and Robert Merton extended Weber's thesis of the influence of Puritanism on capitalism to the development of science. Edgar Zilsel

3. Ernst Cassirer, *The Individual and the Cosmos in Renaissance Philosophy*, trans. Mario Domandi (1927; reprint, Philadelphia: University of Pennsylvania Press, 1963); Edwin A. Burtt, *The Metaphysical Foundations of Modern Physical Science* (Garden City, N.Y.: Doubleday, 1925); Gaston Bachelard, *The New Scientific Spirit*, trans. Arthur Goldhammer (1934; reprint, Boston: Beacon Press, 1984); Alexandre Koyré, *Études Galiléennes*, 3 parts (1935–1939), reprinted in 1 vol. (Paris: Hermann, 1966).

advanced the thesis in the 1940s that the Scientific Revolution owed its characteristics and accomplishments to the needs of an emerging bourgeoisie expressed through a union of scholar and craftsman which produced new attitudes toward the acquisition of knowledge.[4] Both Marxist and non-Marxist traditions of the social analysis of science have since been refined and extended to diverse areas.

In recent years historians of science have continued to borrow themes and categories of analysis from a number of disciplines. From sociology have come the concepts of scientific community, the social roles and status of scientists, norms of scientific behavior and science as ideology. There have been borrowings from anthropology, employing concepts of scientific culture and field work, "thick description" and "deep structure." Semiotics and linguistic analysis have also recently been applied to the history of science. (The past few years have seen a continuing and vigorous debate among historians, philosophers, and sociologists of science over the uniqueness of science as a human endeavor. For those who deny its uniqueness, theory choice is a matter of taste, an exercise in power, or an expression of ideology; for those who affirm the uniqueness of its problem-solving core, it is a matter, to some extent at least, of rational, extra-rhetorical argument and persuasion.) A distinct trend, however, points to "a growing inclination among historians to take science down from its traditional pedestal and treat it as mere ideological property, intrinsically no different from any other kind of knowledge—religious, political or social."[5]

4. Boris Hessen, "The Social and Economic Roots of Newton's 'Principia,'" *Science at the Crossroads: Papers Presented to the International Congress of the History of Science and Technology Held in London from June 29th to July 3rd, 1931 by the Delegates of the U.S.S.R.* (London: Kniga, 1931); Robert K. Merton, "Science, Technology and Society in Seventeenth-Century England," *Osiris* 4 (1938): 360–632; Edgar Zilsel, "The Sociological Roots of Science," *American Journal of Sociology* 47 (1941–1942): 544–62; "The Origin of Gilbert's Scientific Method," *Journal of the History of Ideas* 2 (1941): 1–32; "The Genesis of the Concept of Scientific Progress," *Journal of the History of Ideas,* 6 (1945): 325–49. A. R. Hall, rejecting Zilsel's thesis, holds that the roles of scholar and craftsman were complementary but the dominant, "active" role was that of the scholar. The craftsman's role was "passive, to provide some of the raw material with which the transformation was effected" (The Scholar and Craftsman in the Scientific Revolution," in *Critical Problems in the History of Science,* ed. Marshall Clagett [Madison: University of Wisconsin Press, 1959], 2–23). A review of the reception of the Zilsel thesis is provided by Edward T. Layton, Jr., "Technology as Knowledge," *Technology and Culture* 15 (1974): 35–39.

5. David C. Lindberg and Ronald L. Numbers, eds., *God and Nature: Historical Essays on the Encounter between Christianity and Science,* (Berkeley: University of California Press, 1986), 9. Representative examples of these borrowings from

These new ways of examining science and its history have resulted in what appear to be two distinct kinds of problem areas: one called "internal," dealing with the history of scientific ideas *per se;* the other "external," concerned with the relations of science to society. Thomas Kuhn has offered the opinion that "putting the two together is perhaps the greatest challenge now faced by the profession" and has expressed the conviction that their union would prove fruitful. There has been a distinct reluctance, however, by many historians of science to depart from internal history, although the number writing external history has been growing. The editor of *Isis* recently commented that "few historians of science succeed in relating ideas to social and institutional contexts; many are unwilling to try. Most articles still fall unambiguously into one or another category."[6]

One reason for the persistence of internal history may be a fear of dealing with knowledge and explanation that is merely probable, plausible, or even only possible, rather than with the more rigorous determinations attainable in investigating the development of scientific ideas in great men by what may be called the Watergate hearings method of inquiry: What did he know and when did he know it? Lynn White ascribes to internal historians a perception of science as immaculate conception and notes that "history of science in terms of the developing internal tradition of scientific problems and solutions . . . offers unrivalled clarity of definition . . . but absolute clarity may not be the sole virtue in the writing of history. Many prospects are at their best when somewhat clouded." On the other hand, A. R. Hall, among others, is convinced that the history of science should be analyzed and written as an autonomous intellectual exercise.[7]

other disciplines are Robert S. Westman, "The Astronomer's Role in the Sixteenth Century: A Preliminary Study," *History of Science* 17 (1980): 105–47; Yehuda Elkana, "A Programmatic Attempt at an Anthropology of Knowledge," in *Science and Culture: Anthropological and Historical Studies of the Sciences,* ed. Everett Mendelsohn and Yehuda Elkana (Dordrecht: D. Reidel, 1981), 1–76; Fernand Hallyn, *La structure poétique du monde: Copernic, Kepler* (Paris: Editions du Seuil, 1987); Alistair C. Crombie, "Designed in the Mind: Western Visions of Science, Nature and Humankind," *History of Science* 26 (1988): 1–12.

6. Thomas S. Kuhn, "The History of Science," in *The Essential Tension: Selected Studies in Scientific Tradition and Change* (Chicago: University of Chicago Press, 1977), 110, 120; "Mathematical versus Experimental Traditions in the Development of Physical Science," in *Essential Tension,* 32–35; Charles Rosenberg, "Woods or Trees? Ideas and Actors in the History of Science," *Isis* 59 (1988): 565.

7. Lynn White, "Pumps and Pendula: Galileo and Technology," in *Galileo Re-*

Some of the difficulties in creating a union of the two types of history have been addressed by Kuhn. Despite his desire to see them joined, he asserts the unimportance of the intellectual milieu for an understanding of the Copernican theory and suggests that in the development of scientific ideas the "technical core" of a research tradition is overwhelmingly important compared to the "extrascientific" climate: "Except in the rudimentary stages of the development of a field, the ambient intellectual milieu reacts on the theoretical structure of a science only to the extent that it can be made relevant to the concrete technical problems with which the practitioners of that field engage." Likewise, "when a science has become thoroughly technical, its role as a force in intellectual history becomes relatively insignificant."[8]

Michel Foucault abandons all efforts to unite cognitive developments with their social matrices as ineffectual or magical "in the absence of a theory of scientific change and epistemological causality." Instead, he opts for a phenomenological "theory of discursive practice." In light of these debates over content and context, a recent work on the Scientific Revolution speaks of the fracturing of the discipline and the lack of a unifying theme. This point has

---

appraised, ed. Carlo L. Golino (Berkeley: University of California Press, 1966), 98. Internalist history of science was long ago criticized by Marxists, beginning with Engels, who complained that the history of the sciences was being written "as if they had fallen from the skies" (Letter to H. Starkenburg, 25 January 1894, in Karl Marx and Frederick Engels, *Selected Correspondence*, trans. and ed. Dona Torr [New York: International Publishers, 1942], 517). A. R. Hall, "Science, Technology and Utopia in the Seventeenth Century," in *Science and Society, 1600–1900*, ed. Peter Mathias (Cambridge: Cambridge University Press, 1972), 33–53; *Ballistics in the Seventeenth Century: A Study in the Relations of Science and War with Reference Principally to England* (Cambridge: Cambridge University Press, 1952); "Scholar and Craftsman"; "Merton Revisited, or Science and Society in the Seventeenth Century," *History of Science* 2 (1970): 1–16. See also the stimulating analysis and defense of Hall's point of view in Zev Bechler, "The Essence and Soul of Seventeenth-Century Scientific Revolution," *Science in Context* 1 (1987): 87–101.

8. Thomas S. Kuhn, "The Relations between History and History of Science," in *Essential Tension*, 137–38. Yet the influence of the "intellectual milieu" on the development of the Copernican theory is what Kuhn attempted to show in his work on Copernicus, *The Copernican Revolution: Planetary Astronomy in the Development of Western Thought* (Cambridge, Mass.: Harvard University Press, 1961). The parallels Kuhn pointed to in that work between ideas in contemporary society and the specific theories of Copernicus, however, were essentially a program for investigation rather than an explanation. On the problem of "parallels" or "correspondences" between contemporaneous "mentalities" and scientific ideas, see Gideon Freudenthal, *Atom and Individual in the Age of Newton: On the Genesis of the Mechanistic World View* (Dordecht: D. Keidel, 1986), 209; and Wilbur Applebaum, review of *La structure poétique du monde*, *Isis* 80 (1989): 527.

also been made in a recent editorial in *Isis:* "Sometimes one wonders whether the history of science is a coherent discipline or just a collection of scholars suggested by the accidents of history and the accretion of a common historiography." Whether such a unifying theme emerges or not, with varying degrees of success, the search for satisfying explanations in terms of a union between scientific ideas and the social milieux in which they live, grow and die, persists.[9]

Until recently, the primary locus of such efforts has been the seventeenth century, since it contained within it the great names who collectively have been assigned the key role in fathering what we take to be the essential characteristics of modern science: Galileo, Kepler, Bacon, Descartes, Harvey, Pascal, Boyle, Huygens, Newton, and Leibniz (with a deep bow to the previous century in the persons of Copernicus and Vesalius). Their achievements were characterized by Butterfield, echoing Whitehead, as "the real origin both of the modern world and of the modern mentality." Newton came to be seen as "the concluding figure in a basic intellectual transformation." Burtt and Koyré focused their attention on this period and helped spread the name and the concepts associated with the Scientific Revolution. For them, the time gave birth to a profound shift in perspective concerning traditional subjects of scientific inquiry, with a new role for mathematics. Kuhn's *Structure of Scientific Revolutions* came out of this tradition. Its attempt to provide a model for revolutions within the sciences has been influential in philosophy of science; less so in the history of science, except to reinforce the concept of scientific change as revolutionary.[10]

9. Michel Foucault, *The Order of Things: An Archaeology of the Human Sciences* (1966; reprint, New York: Vintage, 1973), xiii–xiv; David C. Lindberg and Robert S. Westman, eds., *Reappraisals of the Scientific Revolution* (Cambridge: Cambridge University Press, 1990), xi; Rosenberg, "Woods or Trees?" 570. A recent effort at a unified approach is by David Hull, for example, who, addressing the development of cladistics, asks, "What is the relative importance in science of reason, argument, and evidence on the one hand, and power, prestige and influence on the other?" (*Science as a Process: An Evolutionary Account of the Social and Conceptual Development of Science* [Chicago: University of Chicago Press, 1988], xi). Freudenthal's *Atom and Individual* is an interesting and sophisticated analysis of the social determinants of Newton's natural philosophy, particularly his theories of matter and space.

10. Herbert Butterfield, *The Origins of Modern Science, 1300–1800,* rev. ed. (New York: Free Press, 1965), viii; Alfred N. Whitehead, *Science and the Modern World* (New York: Free Press, 1925), 2 (The echo extends to a comparison of the Scientific Revolution with Christianity); David C. Lindberg, "Conceptions of the Scientific Revolution from Bacon to Butterfield: A Preliminary Sketch," in *Re-*

At the same time, the pioneering work of Duhem, followed by that of a number of medievalists, considerably broadened our knowledge of the achievements of the Middle Ages in natural philosophy and in a resulting transformation of Aristotelianism, which it is alleged paved the way for the revolutionary changes associated with the seventeenth century. Some historians, rejecting the concept of revolution altogether, see the creation of modern science as an evolutionary process; others continue to insist on the revolutionary character of the events of the early modern period.[11] The evolutionists focus on continuity and gradualism, the revolutionists on tempo and discontinuity. Still others question the usefulness of the evolution-revolution dichotomy altogether, seeing it as having been confined to an internalist approach which misses the significance of the social factors playing so important a part in the changes in content and methodology of the sciences.

It will probably prove as difficult to get rid of the term *Scientific Revolution* as it has been of the term *Renaissance*, which despite continuing demonstrations of its inadequacy or inappropriateness, continues to provide a useful context of time, place, and circumstances for multifarious investigations. One of the arguments of this paper is that Scientific Revolution is an expression both useful and appropriate as a characterization of natural philosophy in the seventeenth century, for it was only then that its long-established and traditional foundations were decisively and rather rapidly overthrown and new goals proclaimed for its cultivation.

Natural Philosophy and the Culture of the Renaissance

The pursuit of natural philosophy has always been accompanied by its justification. For the Greeks philosophy was self-justifying, of the essence of being human. "All men by nature desire to

appraisals of the Scientific Revolution 25, n. 67; Thomas S. Kuhn, *The Structure of Scientific Revolutions* (Chicago: University of Chicago Press, 1962)

11. Representative examples include Pierre Duhem, *Etudes sur Léonard de Vinci: ceux qu'il a lus et ceux qui l'ont lu* (Paris: A. Hermann, 1906); Marshall Clagett, *The Science of Mechanics in the Middle Ages* (Madison: University of Wisconsin Press, 1959); Alistair C. Crombie, *Robert Grosseteste and the Origins of Experimental Science, 1100–1700* (Oxford: Oxford University Press, 1953); John H. Randall, Jr., *The School of Padua and the Emergence of Modern Science* (Padua: Editrice Antenore, 1961). That Butterfield and Crombie want to have it both ways is shown by John Krige, *Science, Revolution and Discontinuity* (Brighton: Harvester Press, 1980), 15–16.

know," Aristotle tells us again and again. Medieval Christendom concurred, but thought the desire something to be mistrusted. Natural philosophy might be justified, however, as promoting the greater glory of God. Acknowledging the worth of the earlier justifications, Francis Bacon's "the relief of man's estate" was offered as an object of social choice. By linking the advancement of material life and learning, he thereby gave to the progress of knowledge a political aspect. In his marvelously rich and evocative prose, the Lord Chancellor reflected profound changes in attitude toward knowledge, its possibilities, its worth, and the means of acquiring it that had been building for a century and a half and would come to dominate the sciences and the larger culture.

Scholars have long noted that several generations before Bacon there had emerged in Europe a new attitude toward the relation of man to God and his universe, characterized by a newfound sense of human dignity and a corresponding self-assertiveness. In the course of the Renaissance, the idea of a world created for the good became the world created for man, who, in the image of God, was perceived as creative. Ficino, Alberti, and Pico della Mirandola were instrumental in the creation of a "metaphysics of man the creator," whose creativity was most evident in the arts and technology. Well before Bacon, in the prophetic tradition of the approach of a Golden Age, some scholars emphasized that ordinary men can contribute to the growth of knowledge and the benefit of mankind.[12]

The philosophers and theologians of the earlier era had operated with a firm conviction of the existence of natural limits on the acquisition of knowledge. However much we learn is as nothing to the wisdom and omniscience of God and the complexity of his creation. This mental framework had determined the shape of natural philosophy. The medieval belief, for example, in the inaccessibility of the true motions of the planets—out of theological conviction as well as for practical reasons stemming from the nature of astronomy—was precisely what would be challenged by Copernicus, Kepler, and their followers. Kepler explained that if he were to eliminate his proposed physical causes for the motions

12. Eugenio Garin, *Science and Civic Life in the Italian Renaissance*, trans. Peter Munz (Garden City, N.Y.: Doubleday, 1969), 4–5; Charles Webster, *From Paracelsus to Newton: Magic and the Making of Modern Science* (Cambridge: Cambridge University Press, 1982), 61–62; Piyo M. Rattansi, "The Social Interpretation of Science in the Seventeenth Century," in *Science and Society, 1600–1900*, ed. Peter Mathias (Cambridge: Cambridge University Press, 1972), 12.

of the planets, relying on the traditional "will of God" to explain them would be to abandon natural philosophy. A new outlook concerning the possibilities for human knowledge existed for a time side by side with a firm belief in its limits, a belief shared by the leaders of the Reformation. Osiander's notorious preface to Copernicus's *De revolutionibus* has been interpreted in terms of a characteristic Reformation fideism. As part of his general position that "the realism of truth [is] an exclusive attribute of the realm of theology," Osiander also changed the title of Copernicus's manuscript to hide its implication of terrestrial motion, inserted his anonymous preface, and deleted Copernicus's Proemium. Luther affirmed that "no reason can grasp or understand even the natural works of God's creation." Kepler made a representative challenge to this limitation on human capabilities in the form of the idea that man, made in the image of God, can construct successful hypotheses and thus engage in mimetic creation or re-creation of the divine act. Galileo, reflecting the new outlook, asked "Who indeed will set bounds to human ingenuity?" Thomas Hobbes wrote of the philosophers "imitating the creation."[13]

How and under what circumstances did this new conviction concerning the possibility for knowledge arise? Various explanations have been offered. Some look to an evolution within medieval philosophy or theology whereby one of two different aspects of God—God the redeemer and God the creator—became dominant. They had been expressed respectively in terms of the limitations on man's ability to attain the truth and in the belief in a world created for our sake, in which God had given us the power to know the ways in which His created world truly worked.[14] The

13. For examples of the medieval attitude, see Mary S. Kelly, "Celestial Motors 1543-1632," (Ph.D. diss., University of Oklahoma, 1964), 20–21. Johannes Kepler, *Gesammelte Werke*, ed. Walther von Dyck et al. (Munich: C. Beck, 1937-), 14:372, 419. Hans Blumenberg, *The Genesis of the Copernican World*, trans. Robert M. Wallace (1975; reprint, Cambridge, Mass.: MIT Press, 1987), 293–294, 316–17. Blumenberg also goes on to suggest that a similar belief within the Catholic Church underlay the papal reaction to the publication of Galileo's *Dialogo* in 1632. (*Genesis*, 422). For Galileo, see *Discoveries and Opinions of Galileo*, trans. Stillman Drake (Garden City, N.Y.: Doubleday, 1957), 187. See also Richard S. Westfall, "The Rise of Science and the Decline of Orthodox Christianity: A Study of Kepler, Descartes and Newton," in *God and Nature*, 220, 224. Thomas Hobbes, *De corpore*, in *The English Works of Thomas Hobbes of Malmesbury*, ed. William Molesworth, 11 vols. (London: J. Bohn, 1839-1845), 1:xiii.
14. This analysis is presented in Jürgen Hübner, *Die Theologie Johannes Keplers zwischen Orthodoxie und Wissenschaft* (Tübingen: Mohr, 1975); Blumenberg, *Genesis*; Gerald Galgan, *The Logic of Modernity* (New York: New York University Press, 1982); M. B. Foster, "The Christian Doctrine of Creation and

latter conception came to be associated with the belief that man participates in the divine through his self-creative nature and that as a consequence he developed a greater attentiveness to the world around him.

On the other hand, appear those who see the source of the new attitudes toward knowledge in the changes in economy, social structure, institutions, and the texture of life which were transforming Europe in the late Middle Ages and the Renaissance. In the vibrant urban centers, first of Italy, then of northern Europe, were men who for themselves had experienced the adventure, allurements, and possibilities of enterprise, possession, power, and pleasure and wished to continue to engage them. The contrast with time, economy, and society in the Middle Ages is a sharp one. The medieval economy had been "dominated by agrarian rhythms, free of haste, careless of exactitude, unconcerned with productivity—and [existed] in a society created in the image of that economy, *sober and modest*, without enormous appetites, undemanding and incapable of quantitative efforts."[15] Has not Le Goff described here the very antithesis of the modern age?

Wallerstein, following Braudel, sees the period from 1450 to 1640 as one in which a wholly new world-economy was born in Europe with capitalist forms of production, which, coupled with unique political institutions, led to the growth of a widening and dynamic market economy. Life in a society in which classes for whom commerce and utility were important and in which machines

---

the Rise of Modern Science," in *Creation: The Impact of an Idea*, eds. Daniel O'Conner and Francis Oakley (New York: Charles Scribner's Sons, 1969), 49. Edward Grant sees the sources of the change in the condemnation of the Aristotelian propositions at Paris in 1277 ("Science and Theology in the Middle Ages," in *God and Nature*, 55–59). A good summary of the argument and the extension of it to the thesis of the pivotal role of William of Ockham in creating the possibility for a new natural philosophy in the seventeenth century is provided by Richard Olson, *Science Deified and Science Defied: The Historical Significance of Science in Western Culture* (Berkeley: University of California Press, 1982), 199–206. The extension to the seventeenth century of theological change as a factor in the Scientific Revolution is discussed in Eugene M. Klaaren, *Religious Origins of Modern Science: Belief in Creation in Seventeenth-Century Thought* (Michigan: Eerdmans, 1977).

15. For the social changes associated with the Renaissance, see Rattansi, "Social Interpretation," 6–7; Garin, *Science and Civic Life*, x (Garin asserts that humanism was born out of the experience of civic life "and affected the various fields of knowledge from that angle."); Jacques Le Goff, "Labor Time in the 'Crisis' of the Fourteenth Century: From Medieval Time to Modern Time," in *Time, Work and Culture in the Middle Ages*, trans. Arthur Goldhammer (Chicago: University of Chicago Press, 1980), 44.

were increasingly significant, had its effect on those outside the universities who speculated about nature and knowledge.[16]

The humanist movement did much to bring the concerns and disputational styles of the Schoolmen into discredit. Two distinct humanist styles emerged, one centered on the rapidly growing number of schools, serving as an instrument of elite consolidation, differentiation, and control; the other aiming at scholarly critical clarification. Having at first rejected formal philosophy, some humanists began to see merit in ancient philosophers other than Aristotle and were much impressed by the new knowledge, particularly from the voyages of exploration and the development of the crafts.[17]

Those engaged in commerce and the arts, shopkeepers and artisans, were also led to new ways of thinking, different from those associated with the learned, whether Schoolmen or humanists. The technical literature of the sixteenth century praises cooperation and openness in the acquisition of knowledge and expresses conviction concerning the possibility of its perfection, themes which would later be taken up by Bacon.[18]

The progressive broadening of commercial activity and widening of the political arena beyond the Church and its affairs, beyond kings and nobles, beyond aristocrat and burgher to the politics of the modern nation-state helped promote a perception of the relationship between knowledge and power. Thus were born the intelligence networks of the Florentine bankers and the Fuggers, the practices of diplomacy and the spy system of the republic of Venice. Bacon would urge that "as secretaries and spials of

16. Immanuel Wallerstein, "Three Paths of National Development in Sixteenth-Century Europe," in *The Capitalist World-Economy* (Cambridge: University of Cambridge Press, 1979), 37. See also Carlo Cipolla, *Clocks and Culture, 1300–1700* (1967; reprint, New York: W. W. Norton, 1978), 32–36.

17. Anthony Grafton and Lisa Jardine, *From Humanism to the Humanities: Education and the Liberal Arts in Fifteenth-and Sixteenth-Century Europe* (Cambridge: Harvard University Press, 1986), 61;. Barbara Shapiro, *Probability and Certainty in Seventeenth-Century England: A Study of the Relationships between Natural Science, Religion, History, Law and Literature* (Princeton: Princeton University Press, 1983), 7; Dorothy Koenigsberger, *Renaissance Man and Creative Thinking: A History of Concepts of Harmony, 1400–1700* (Atlantic Highlands, N.J.: Humanities Press, 1979), 207. For growing disappointment in the universities with the usefulness of logic for either theology or natural philosophy, see Mark A. Smith, "Knowing Things Inside Out: The Scientific Revolution from a Medieval Perspective," *American Historical Review* 95 (1990): 737.

18. Paolo Rossi, *Philosophy, Technology and the Arts in the Early Modern Era*, ed. Benjamin Nelson, trans. Salvatore Attanasio (New York: Harper and Row, 1970), ix.

princes bring in bills for intelligence, so you must allow the spials and intelligencers of nature to bring in their bills, or else you shall be ill advertised."[19]

It was both the seductions of the temporal world and the perceived barrenness of academic learning that, on the wider political stage of the Renaissance, promoted action and a new praise of action. The man of *virtù* (the etymological ancestor of the *virtuoso*) is the man of action, possessing daring, boldness, initiative, and competitiveness. He possesses "active intellectual power," acting with foresight and in control "of what he did and what he made." The *vita activa* rather than the *vita contemplativa* came to be judged not only the proper life for men, but the means to a surer knowledge. Crombie asserts that "The conception of the *virtuoso*, the rational artist aiming at reasoned and examined control alike of his own thoughts, intentions, and actions, and of his surroundings, seems to me to be of the essence of the European morality, meaning both habits and ethics out of which the European scientific movement was generated and engineered." St. Thomas, in the earlier era, had proclaimed the *vita contemplativa* the preferred life. A characteristic feature of Renaissance humanism, whether expressed in literature, the arts, or magic, is the pursuit of knowledge for the sake of acting in the world as well as for its own sake. Guarino Guarini of Verona (1374–1460), an outstanding humanist scholar and teacher, often proclaimed the importance of humanist education at his famous school as preparation for the *vita activa*. Although this was propaganda, contradicted by curriculum and classroom practice, it reveals the importance attached to the new ideal.[20] That civilians rather than clerics were now increasingly in the service of princes and their bureaucracies must have helped promote this outlook.

It is in this context that some scholars as well as craftsmen exhibited not only a new respect for technology, but linked it to a

19. On the importance of intelligence for the great merchant capitalists, see Fernand Braudel, *The Wheels of Commerce*, vol. 2, *Civilization and Capitalism*, trans. Siân Reynolds (New York: Harper and Row, 1984), 408–11. Francis Bacon, *Advancement of Learning*, in *Seventeenth-Century Rationalism: Bacon and Descartes* eds. Norman F. Cantor and Peter L. Klein, (Waltham, Mass.: Blaisdell, 1969), 68.

20. Alistair C. Crombie, "Historical Commitments of European Science," *Annali del' instituto e museo di stori della scienza di Firenze* 7 (1982): 40–41. Hannah Arendt points out that for the Greeks the *vita activa* was the life of concern with public affairs—a life of cares—and represented a striving for immortality (*The Human Condition* [Garden City, N.Y.: Doubleday, 1959], 290). On Guarino, Grafton, and Jardine, see *From Humanism to Humanities*, 1–3.

new conception of the nature of knowing. The Renaissance view-point, in Burckhardt's pregnant phrase, of "the state as a work of art," reflects the new importance of technique in human affairs and in perception of the world. Leonardo expressed the new significance of *homo faber* by asserting that the measure of a man is his ability to transform the created object into a concept. For Leonardo, the mind is a mediator, which, with the aid of mathematics, leads to the enlargement of knowledge through the transforming work of the hands. Further, without physical action, moral or spiritual action is sterile, useless.[21]

The new social conditions in the Italian city-states promoted the rise within the artisan class of a group of craftsmen with greater technical training and superior technique—the artist-engineers like Brunelleschi and Leonardo—who were acquainted with the social elites and who were fascinated by machines and their possibilities. Numerous works describing machines and devices were published in the fifteenth and sixteenth centuries, many by men who had been to the university and who associated with craftsmen. Moreover, the social changes about them led the artists to a new respect for the mimetic ideal. The phrase "imitator of nature" was commonly applied in praise of Renaissance painters.[22] Hamlet's advice to the players "to hold the mirror up to nature" reflects this ideal in another artistic context.

A new attitude toward "mathematical practitioners" was shown by the learned: "He . . . is a proud man if he contemn expert artisans, or any sensible industrious practitioner, however unlettered in schools or unlettered in books." Thus wrote Gabriel Harvey at the end of the sixteenth century. Observation, operations, and experience were emphasized by Palissy, Vives, Rabelais, and many others. For Leonardo, experience meant both observation and experiment, for which instruments were necessary aids. Technology and the arts appear to have been the seedbed from which experimental science sprang. Makers and shapers were praised and con-

21. Jacob Burckhardt, *The Civilization of the Renaissance in Italy*, trans. S. G. C. Middlemore, 2 vols. (1860; reprint, New York: Harper and Row, 1958), part 1; Garin, *Science and Civic Life*, 63–64.

22. Cipolla, *Clocks and Culture*, 23–4. Hiram Haydn views this new respect for technology as connected with "a radical anti-intellectualism" (*The Counter-Renaissance* [1950; reprint, New York: Grove Press, 1960]), xv. Michael Baxandall, *Painting and Experience in Fifteenth-Century Italy: A Primer in the Social History of Pictorial Style*, 2d ed. (Oxford: Oxford University Press, 1988), 118, 121. See also William Leiss, *The Domination of Nature* (New York: George Braziller, 1972), 35.

trasted with those who display mere book learning, possessors of sterile knowledge. Theory and practice, talking and doing, were constantly juxtaposed in attacks on the Schoolmen. The Peripatetics were talkers; the new philosophy of the seventeenth century would proclaim itself the philosophy of doers, the accomplishers of deeds. The Florentine Platonists saw only slight differences between the power inherent in the work of craftsmen and the powers of sympathy and antipathy, Cabalistic lore and the various virtues and correspondences known to the magus. Both had their sources and sanction in the divine. Paracelsus consistently emphasized experience over talk and saw the divine in the human capacity to perfect the arts. Bacon would insist that "whether or not anything can be known was to be settled not by arguing but by trying."[23]

The tradition of knowing by making (*verum factum*), as so much else in the sixteenth century, had roots in classical antiquity. The new conditions of life in the Renaissance and the breakdown of the Aristotelian distinction between formal and artificial constructions promoted a widespread rejection of the concept of the baseness of the manual arts. The traditional conception of the role of reason in natural philosophy was replaced by the idea of knowledge as constructed through the hands of a knowledgeable inquirer.[24] The *vita activa* of the classical world had been changed from the idea of involvement in public life to acting by fabricating and thus exhibits a change from the medieval search for essence via contemplation to the study of process and technique inherent in fabrication. For Copernicus and Kepler, the astronomer must overcome the traditional constraints on his scope of operations and become an *artifex*, fashioning a true likeness of the universe. Kepler commissioned a cosmological model, the true mathemat-

---

23. Harvey is quoted by Robert Mandrou, *From Humanism to Science, 1480–1700*, trans. Brian Pearce (1973; reprint, Harmondsworth: Penguin Books, 1978), 150–51. Paolo Rossi, *Philosophy, Technology and the Arts*, 7; and *Francis Bacon: From Magic to Science*, trans. Sacha Rabinovitch (Chicago: University of Chicago Press, 1968), 1–8. For a contemporary example, see John Webster's advice to English youth in *Academiarum examen* (London: Giles Calvert, 1654), 106. On Paracelsus, see Rattansi, "Social Interpretation," 9; Webster, *Paracelsus to Newton*, 52–56. A similar theme may be found in Giordano Bruno. Olson, *Science Deified*, 27. Bacon, *The New Organon and Related Writings*, ed. Fulton H. Anderson (Indianapolis: Bobbs-Merrill, 1960), i, 78.

24. The *verum factum* tradition is treated in great detail in various fields and at different times in Antonio Pérez-Ramos, *Francis Bacon's Idea of Science and the Maker's Knowledge Tradition* (Oxford: Oxford University Press, 1988). See also Rossi, *Philosophy, Technology and the Arts*, ix–xi. Rossi also points to political aspects of the denigration of labor and the arts prior to the Renaissance (13–15).

ical structure of the universe given material form. And as artists, both astronomers sought harmony in their constructions.

The Turning Point

What then of the Scientific Revolution, if indeed there was one? Some historians, notably medievalists, locate a turning point in natural philosophy in a medieval modification of ancient ideas, beginning in the thirteenth or fourteenth centuries. We have recently been asked to drop *world views* and *revolutions* and to see *Scientific Revolution* as a metaphor for shifting relations of the cultures of university and court. The seventeenth century, however, constituted a revolutionary break with medieval conceptions about the cosmos, about the fundamental principles within specific sciences, and about the nature of man. It was revolutionary in a qualitative sense, in its tempo, and in the creation of the institutions within which the new ideas were born and were promulgated. Bacon, Descartes, and Newton held up the discovery of laws of nature as a goal of natural philosophy. The world as a hierarchically structured organism was superseded by a system of equal elements in a mechanical model in both social theory (as in Hobbes, for example) and in natural philosophy.[25]

In the seventeenth century belief in magic and witchcraft declined, after having substantially increased during the previous century. Natural magic, Hermeticism, and the alchemical tradition had represented a program, the chief components of which were an emphatic empiricism and the existence of anthropomorphic, spiritual, and hidden powers in the universe. The ethico-religious foundation of the tradition is reflected in the role assigned the spiritual condition of the magus or alchemist as a factor in his efficacy. The mechanical philosophy of the seventeenth century

25. For the Scientific Revolution as a metaphor, see Westman, "Astronomer's Role." For an enumeration of differences between the science of the seventeenth century and earlier science, see Paolo Rossi, "Hermeticism, Rationality and the Scientific Revolution," in *Reason, Experiment and Mysticism in the Scientific Revolution*, ed. Maria L. Righini Bonelli and William R. Shea (London: Science History Publications, 1975), 249–51. The origin of the modern concept of scientific law has roots in the late Middle Ages and the Renaissance. It appears in the mathematical sciences and reflects a shift from prescription to description. The common belief that its origins lay in the metaphor of legislation by God or nature seems untrue; see Jane E. Ruby, "The Origins of Scientific Law," *Journal of the History of Ideas* 47 (1986): 341–60. On social theory and natural philosophy, see Freudenthal, *Atom and Individual*, 165–66.

purged the study of nature of its spiritual and moral dimension, expressed, among other ways, in the concept of scientific law, while retaining the empirical. It substituted matter and motion for the occult and magical powers of nature, macrocosm-microcosm correspondences, and the doctrine of signatures, and it transformed simple empiricism into analysis by disassembly and the use of mathematics. The contribution of the mechanical philosophy to the falling off of belief in witchcraft, however, has been questioned. It has been suggested that, to the contrary, the decline in magic and belief in the existence of witches paved the way for the victory of the mechanical philosophy. In any event, the magical tradition of the pursuit of arcana persisted for a time along with the new conception of the proper means to acquire knowledge.[26] With respect to those means the seventeenth century saw a decisive replacement of the old *organon* and the creation of a new one profoundly different from that taught for centuries in the schools. The new methodology had its source in the technological developments of the earlier period.

Bacon had not been the first to cite printing, the compass, and gunpowder as signaling advances over the ancients and as possessing greater worth than all the disputations of the Peripatetics. It was the invention of the mechanical clock, however, that helped shape an outlook that would exert an important influence on the character of natural philosophy. The fascination of the late medieval period and the Renaissance with clocks and automata reflected a delight in the power of machines and the control of nature. The

26. Brian Easlea, *Witch Hunting, Magic, and the New Philosophy: An Introduction to the Debates of the Scientific Revolution, 1450–1750* (Brighton, Sussex: Harvester Press, 1980), 1. For the social factors responsible for the earlier increase in witch-hunting, see Stone, *Past and Present Revisited*, 186–87. Simon Schaffer shows how the Mechanical Philosophers of Restoration England created a space within their philosophy for nonmaterial spirit ("Godly Men and Mechanical Philosophers: Souls and Spirits in Restoration Natural Philosophy," *Science in Context* 1 (1987): 55–85. Zev Bechler asserts that seventeenth-century mechanism included a role for nonmaterial entities in its very formulation). ("Essence and Soul of Scientific Revolution," 87–101). The articles by Schaffer and Bechler address the Mechanical Philosophy as explanation; neither deals with its important effect on scientific practice. A change in attitude by the clergy, doctors, and lawyers and in the standards of proof has been offered as explanation for the drop in prosecutions for witchcraft in the early modern period. Stone, *Past and Present*, 191–92; Easlea, *Witch Hunting*, 196–97; Shapiro, *Probability and Certainty*, 197. On the pursuit of arcana and natural philosophy side by side, see Hall, "Science, Technology and Utopia," 51; Webster, *Paracelsus to Newton*, 11; Patrick Curry, *Prophecy and Power: Astrology in Early Modern England* (Princeton: Princeton University Press, 1989).

clock provided political, theological, and metaphysical meta-
phors. St. Bonaventure had seen inventors of machines as imitating the Divine Artisan. Henry of Monantheuil, in a preface to a
book on mechanics published in 1599, wrote of God as a mechanic.
He would be echoed by Descartes, who referred to God as "the
greatest Artificer." Similar language may be found in Boyle and
Newton and throughout the seventeenth century. "People started
to formulate their idea of the universe on the model of the clock
and to conceive of the three essential systems within which mankind exists—the cosmos, the state and the body—as being clock
mechanisms." Clocks and automata were at first seen as a kind of
magic—mechanical, mathematical, or natural magic. In the course
of time, cause and effect came to be identified and related to the
moving parts and their functions. There were frequent references
to learning how a clock works by taking it apart. The use of cut-
away or exploded views of machines became common. Descartes
and Gassendi referred to disassembly as a means of learning about
a mechanism and Hobbes indicated that was his method in the
study of civil government.[27]

The machine analogy and the vague yearnings of the Renais-

27. Preceding Bacon on the importance of technology were Bodin, Cardan, Le
Roy, and Campanella, for example; see J. B. Bury, *The Idea of Progress: An Inquiry
into its Origin and Growth* (1932; reprint, New York: Dover Publications, 1955),
40–41, 54 n. 1. On the clock and its implications, see Otto Mayr, *Authority, Liberty and Automatic Machinery in Early Modern Europe* (Baltimore: Johns Hopkins University Press, 1986), xvii. Analogies of inventions and works of art
with the divine Creation considered as a machine were common in the sixteenth
and seventeenth centuries. See Rattansi, "Social Interpretation," 8–9; Francis C.
Haber, "The Clock as Intellectual Artifact," *The Clockwork Universe: German
Clocks and Automata, 1550–1650*, ed. Klaus Maurice and Otto Mayr, trans.
H. Bartlett Wells (New York: Neale Watson Academic Publications, 1980), 13.
While the image of God as artisan may have had its origin in Plato's *Timaeus*,
the Platonic Demiurge did not fashion machines as they were known in the late
Middle Ages and the Renaissance. See also Mayr, *Authority, Liberty and Machinery*, 213 n. 8; and Rossi, "Hermeticism, Rationality, and the Scientific Revolution," 251–53. Descartes, *Principles of Philosophy*, trans. Valentine R. Miller and
Reese P. Miller (Dordrecht: D. Reidel, 1983), part 4, chaps. 204, 286. The quotation on the clock metaphor is from Maurice and Mayr, *Clockwork Universe*, 8. According to Mayr, it was the "quintessential symbol of authority." Its regularity
led it to be compared to the prince who guides the community, in contrast to the
political and social turmoil of the later Middle Ages and the wars of religion
(*Authority*, xvii–xviii, 42–45). On clocks as magical, see Mayr, *Authority*, 26. Descartes, *Principles of Philosophy*, part 4, chap. 204. For Gassendi, see Rossi, "Hermeticism, Rationality, and the Scientific Revolution," 252. For Hobbes, see *De
cive, English Works*, 4:xiv. On the role of machine illustration in promoting the
new style of thinking, see Samuel Y. Edgerton, Jr., "The Renaissance Development of Scientific Illustration," *Science and the Arts in the Renaissance*, ed. John
W. Shirley and F. David Hoeniger (Washington, D.C.: Folger Library, 1985), 168–97.

sance, resting on the conviction that practice and mathematics are the twin keys to the creation of a new technique for unlocking the secrets of nature, were given concrete form in the first four decades of the seventeenth century. For here were clustered a series of intellectual events which together constituted a revolutionary turn in the very fiber of natural philosophy. Within the span of little more than half a lifetime, the chief authorities of ancient physics (in the Aristotelian sense of the science of motion or of change) and their prime axioms were overthrown. Motion came to be studied not in the abstract or as a metaphysical or meta-mathematical concept, but with an attention to the details of the motions of planets, of the blood, of projectiles and falling bodies, which challenged Ptolemy, Galen, and Aristotle at the foundation of their thought. And these studies by Kepler, Harvey, and Galileo were conducted by the application of specific techniques to specific types of motion—the techniques of disassembly, by the slowing down, as it were, of planets, of blood, and of falling bodies: Kepler, by dividing the planetary path into 360 segments to study the minutely changing relationship of planetary velocity to distance from the sun; Harvey, by observing the hearts of dying and cold-blooded animals to determine the sequences of movement in heart, valves and blood; and Galileo, by rolling balls down inclined planes to observe the paths of projectiles and the relation of time to distance in free fall. Moreover, this dissection and reconstitution of motion was accomplished by attention to the insistence of the previous century on experience and mathematics as necessary to the process of discovery.

It is no wonder, then, that those *anni mirabiles* of the early seventeenth century saw the multiplication both of a cluster of new techniques to ease calculation and of instruments to enlarge the senses. Both were new tools for the natural philosopher, now become a theorizing craftsman, an artisan for the production of knowledge. The telescope, thermometer, microscope, barometer, mechanical calculator, pendulum clock, logarithms, slide rule, decimal system, telescopic micrometer, and the instruments from which they evolved were invented or began to be used more extensively. They reflected a new respect for measurement, precision, and detail, which were significant aspects of the mechanical and experimental philosophies and the mathematical sciences. After the precise observations of Tycho Brahe, there was a great growth in recorded astronomical observation, and in the same four decades astronomers compared their observations with tables constructed on the basis of four different worldsystems to help them determine which was the true one. Stevin, Kepler, and Galileo were themselves inventors of importance during this period. The tradition continued after them with Huygens, Hooke, and Newton. Thus in those decades were nature and motion restricted to locomotion and to be understood now by analogy with a machine rather than an organism or a soul.

In place of the old dichotomy between heaven and earth, the new philosophy created a new one: *res extensa* and *res cogitans*, knower and known, subject and object, fact and value, man and nature. In time, Cartesian systematic doubt, while wedded to an effort to find a means for certainty in a universe intelligible in terms of matter and motion, would contribute to the belief not only that all is knowable and possible, but also to the eventual abandonment of certainty as a goal of natural philosophy. In the search for certainty, however, the model of mathematical demonstration was ever present. Together with the insistence on the unalterable character of the laws of nature, mathematics helped establish for natural philosophy the criterion of prediction as a standard for scientific theory.

The New *Organon*

The Renaissance saw both the growth of skepticism and a continued search for certain knowledge. For the ancients demonstrable certainty about the physical world was attainable by logic applied to first principles; the certainties of mathematical demonstration could not tell us anything about the natures of the entities for which mathematical description was employed. The pronounced effort during the Renaissance at a "restoration" of mathematics represented, among other things, a search for certainty as a usable substitute for an Aristotelian syllogistic under skeptical attack. Following an earlier call by Regiomontanus, Antonio Maurolico noted in 1528 that of the areas of concern to philosophy, "only mathematics enjoys a certainty of demonstration that precludes skepticism." Galileo, Kepler, and Descartes were seekers after certainty in science through the use of mathematics, increasingly seen as the "language of nature."[28] In the

28. For Maurolico, see Paul L. Rose, *The Italian Renaissance of Mathematics: Studies on Humanists and Mathematicians from Petrarch to Galileo* (Geneva: Druz, 1975), 97, 101, 161, 177–78. "There is no certainty in sciences where one of the mathematical sciences cannot be applied, or are not in relation with these

course of the seventeenth century, mathematical description of natural phenomena, rather than logical demonstration from the first principles, slowly made its way against a skepticism with respect to the possibility of knowledge of true causes.

The role of the "mixed sciences" in the newly important technologies—gunnery, fortification, cartography, navigation, surveying, and architecture—had given mathematics a new significance. According to Ramus, technological supremacy, and therefore economic and military supremacy, depended on knowledge of mathematics. John Dee's preface to the first English translation of Euclid was a paean to applied science. By the early part of the seventeenth century, the "mathematical practitioners"—instrument-makers with their specialized craft subdivisions or producers of textbooks, ephemerides, and almanacs—had become firmly established in a number of European centers. By the second half of the century, the mathematical sciences encompassed sophisticated mathematical techniques as well as a considerable number of practical applications.[29]

---

mathematics" (*The Notebooks of Leonardo da Vinci*, ed. Jean P. Richter [1883; reprint, New York: Dover Publications, 1970], 2:289). Christopher Wren's inaugural lecture as Gresham Professor of Mathematics in 1657 made the same point; see *The Life and Works of Sir Christopher Wren: From the Parentalia*, ed. Christopher Wren (his son) (London: privately printed, 1903), 25. In the case of Leonardo and Wren, the certainty of mathematics was invoked for its utility in physics, illustrating the change that had taken place since the fifteenth century. For mathematics as the "language of nature," see Burtt, *Metaphysical Foundations*, 66. Alistair C. Crombie holds that Galileo owed his search for certainty to his Aristotelian training ("The Sources of Galileo's Early Natural Philosophy," in *Reason, Experiment and Mysticism*, 158–59). The position of Burtt, Cassirer, Whitehead, and Koyré that there was a metaphysical core based on the mathematical properties of bodies shared by the proponents of the new philosophy is challenged by Gary Hatfield in "Metaphysics and the New Science," in *Reappraisals of the Scientific Revolution*, 93, 94, 117.

29. Aristotle defined "mixed sciences" as "mathematical objects qua physical" (*Physics* 193b, 31–32). For Ramus, see Alex F. Keller, "Mathematicians, Mechanics and Experimental Machines in Northern Italy in the Sixteenth Century," in *The Emergence of Science in Western Europe*, ed. Maurice Crosland (London: MacMillan, 1975) 16. Braudel points to the importance of mathematics "in long-distance trade from the fourteenth through the seventeenth centuries" (*Wheels of Commerce*, 409). John Dee, *The Mathematicall Praeface to the Elements of Geometrie of Euclid of Megara* (1570; reprint, New York: Science History Publications, 1975). Charles Webster, *The Great Instauration: Science, Medicine and Reform, 1626–1660* (New York: Holmes and Meier, 1975), 349, describes the English scene. J. A. Bennett, "The Mechanics' Philosophy and the Mechanical Philosophy," *History of Science* 24 (1986): 1–28, attacks the position that the Mechanical Philosophy was a construction of the natural philosophers and had little to do with the growth of the mathematical crafts. A similar position on the importance of the "mixed sciences" for Galileo, Descartes, Hobbes, "and many

The forms and styles of literature and expression likewise reflected a useful attribute of mathematics. The language of natural philosophy in the course of the seventeenth century became, in imitation of the function of mathematical symbolism, more denotative, economical, and rigorous. Thomas Sprat, propagandizing for the Royal Society, held up "mathematical plainness" as a model for the language of science. The century saw a number of efforts to create universal and "real" languages which would severely limit ambiguity. Bacon and Hobbes had earlier explored the relation between words and their referents with a similar aim. Descartes's earliest writings show a concern with finding such a language to express scientific knowledge. To be sure, such studies were not new. Aristotle and the nominalists of the fourteenth century had also been concerned to eliminate ambiguity from language. In the sixteenth century, however, discourse employing reasoning by analogy and the discernment of symbols and patterns of resemblances and sympathies had become common. The alchemists, Hermeticists, and magicians were excoriated by Bacon and others for obscurity of language, ambiguity, and mysticism. In the occult sciences little distinction was made between words and their referents; the manipulation of the former could affect the latter. The new philosophy distinguished sharply between them. The language characteristic of the occult sciences and of late medieval and Renaissance worldviews would begin to be replaced in the early seventeenth century by a discourse employing analysis, mechanical causality and logical relation. Clarity of language was sought not only in natural philosophy, but also in history, law, religion, and literature. According to Sprat, the Royal Society desired "to separate the knowledge of *Nature*, from the colours of *Rhetorick*, the devices of *Fancy*, or the delightful deceit of *Fables.*"[30]

---

others" is taken by Peter Machamer, in "Galileo and the Causes," *New Perspective of Galileo*, ed. Robert E. Butts and Joseph C. Pitt (Dordrecht: D. Reidel, 1978), 163. The seventeenth century saw a substantial increase in university posts in mathematics and astronomy; see John Gascoigne, "A Reappraisal of the Role of Universities in the Scientific Revolution," in *Reappraisals of the Scientific Revolution*, 220.

30. Thomas Sprat, *History of the Royal Society*, ed. Jackson I. Cope and Harold W. Jones (St. Louis: Washington University Press, 1958), 113. Comenius tried to create such a universal language; see Sprat, *History*, 65. The best-known example is John Wilkin's *Essay Towards a Real Character and a Philosophical Language* (London: S. Gellibrand, 1668), which Robert Hook praised as "perfectly free from all manner of ambiguity" (*Lectiones Cutlerianae* [London: John Martin, 1676], 31). Descartes eventually became skeptical of the possibility of a strictly denota-

With the increasing importance of experiment, however, and of hypotheses in the new sense of conjecture about the physical world, the advocates of the new philosophy came to doubt that the certainty once thought to be a chief objective of inquiry in natural philosophy was attainable. The doubts of the philosophers were shared by historians, theologians, and lawyers. A hierarchy from certainty by means of mathematical or logical demonstration through "moral certainty," a concept borrowed from religion, to varying degrees of probability came to be accepted in the course of the seventeenth century. Religion contributed through the acute Protestant sense of fallibility. Law, as well as theology and natural philosophy, was affected by changing notions of what was acceptable as evidence in reaching a verdict. Galileo had affirmed that some physical propositions can only be judged with respect to their plausibility or probability, while "there are other propositions of which we have (or may confidently expect) positive assurance through experiments, long observation, and rigorous demon-

---

tive language. To overcome what he saw as resistance to the new science, he turned to the rhetorical style of *Le Monde;* see Sylvie Romanowski, "Descartes: From Science to Discourse," in *Science, Language and the Perspective Mind: Studies in Literature and Thought from Campanella to Boyle.* Yale French Studies, no. 49 (New Haven: Yale University Press, 1973), 96–109. M. M. Slaughter, *Universal Languages and Scientific Taxonomy in the Seventeenth Century* (Cambridge: Cambridge University Press, 1982), 127–29. Slaughter sees the efforts to create taxonomic structures for languages in the seventeenth century as arising from the "information explosion" of the early modern period and a reflection of a persisting Aristotelian essentialism (vii). On the nominalists, see Amos Funkenstein, *Theology and the Scientific Imagination from the Middle Ages to the Seventeenth Century* (Princeton: Princeton University Press, 1986), 35. For attacks on Hermetic language, see Webster, *Great Instauration*, 384–85; Robert Boyle, *The Sceptical Chymist* (1661; reprint, London: J. M. Dent and Sons, 1964), 114; Giorgius Agricola, *De re metallica*, trans. Herbert C. Hoover and Lou H. Hoover (1556; reprint, New York: Dover Publications, 1950), xxviii. Brian Vickers, "Analogy versus Identity: The Rejection of Occult Symbolism," in *Occult and Scientific Mentalities in the Renaissance*, ed. Brian Vickers (Cambridge: Cambridge University Press, 1984), 95ff. See also the valuable article by William B. Ashworth, Jr., "Natural History and the Emblematic Worldview," in *Reappraisals of the Scientific Revolution*, 303–32, which examines the shift in discourse in the midseventeenth century in natural history and, despite Foucault, offers some interesting conjectures as to its causes. Timothy J. Reiss, *The Discourse of Modernism* (Ithaca: Cornell University Press, 1982), 13, 49, 52. Reiss uses the terms "patterning" and "analytico-referential" for the two styles. See also Shapiro, *Probability and Certainty*, chap. 7; and Sybille Krämer-Friedrich, "The 'Universal Thinking Machine,' or on the Genesis of Schematized Reasoning in the Seventeenth Century," in *Scientific Knowledge Socialized*, ed. Imre Hronszky et al. (Dordrecht: D. Reidel, 1988), 180. George Williamson sees a similar change in the later seventeenth century but casts it in terms of a classical debate between logic and rhetoric (*The Senecan Amble: A Study of Prose Form from Bacon to Collier* [Chicago: University of Chicago Press, 1951], 265–76). Sprat, *History and the Royal Society*, 62.

stration." Yet so firmly had "moral certainty" in some instances replaced the certainty of demonstration two generations later, that Boyle, despite the gas law bearing his name, even held that mathematics was inappropriate in experimental science.[31]

Boyle, attempting to lay down a canon for proper procedure in the experimental philosophy, consciously made a distinction between the determination of facts by experience or experiment and the establishment of causes and explanations. He also called for open laboratories and claimed that a multiplicity of reproduced experiments was more valuable than a single one in establishing a hypothesis, while pointing out that a single contrary result should be reported for its importance in invalidating one. In general, a spirit of pragmatism obtained with respect to knowledge gained through experiment on limited problems rather than through an adherence to a methodology based on metaphysical or general epistemological theories or theories about proper method.[32]

The manipulation of nature and the beginnings of a role for experimentation in science owe something to the intensified interest in magic in the fifteenth and sixteenth centuries.[33] But just as revelation and contemplation came to be seen as inadequate means of learning about nature, so the insights, rituals, and secret lore of the magus, his unique access to sources of hidden power, shared only with the adept, were eventually seen as inadequate in comparison with the mechanism, openness, consensus, and free com-

31. Shapiro, *Probability and Certainty*, 4, 61, 163, 269; Steven Shapin and Simon Schaffer, *Leviathan and the Air-Pump: Hobbes, Boyle and the Experimental Life* (Princeton: Princeton University Press, 1985), 107. Robert H. Kargon, "The Testimony of Nature: Boyle, Hooke and the Experimental Philosophy," *Albion* 3 (1971): 73–74; Rose-Mary Sargent, "Scientific Experiment and Legal Expertise in Seventeenth-Century England," *Studies in History and Philosophy of Science* 20 (1989): 19–45. Galileo, Letter to the Grand Duchess Christina, in *Discoveries and Opinions*, 197; Steven Shapin, "Robert Boyle and Mathematics: Reality, Representation, and Experimental Practice," *Science in Context* 2 (1988): 23–58.

32. Shapin and Schaffer, *Leviathan and the Air-Pump*, 51, 56–58. Descartes, Hobbes, and to an extent Hooke, had trouble accepting the distinction as appropriate to natural philosophy. John Flamsteed reported that, contrary to his inclination, he became convinced of Newton's findings in his color experiments by duplicating them (Francis Baily, ed., *An Account of the Rev'd John Flamsteed, the First Astronomer-Royal* . . . [London: Admiralty Office, 1835], 29). Ernan McMullin, "Empiricism and the Scientific Revolution," in *Art, Science and History in the Renaissance*, ed. Charles S. Singleton (Baltimore: Johns Hopkins University Press, 1967), 357.

33. Frances Yates is the chief exponent of the thesis of a relation between the magus as "operator" and the experimental philosophy; see *Giordano Bruno and the Hermetic Tradition* (Chicago: University of Chicago Press, 1984).

munication encouraged by the new philosophy. Bacon attacked the ideals and methods of magic and Hermeticism, as did his followers. Boyle, opposed to occultism and to the medieval tradition of thought experiments, advocated publicly witnessed and reproducible ones. The idea of "public knowledge," in contrast to earlier notions of nature's "secrets," access to which should be available only to the worthy, could only have arisen in the wake of the social changes of the sixteenth and seventeenth centuries: the rise of new classes for whom secrecy represented a bar to social advancement, the development of new technologies which promoted knowledge-sharing, and the creation of new institutions for the protection of intellectual property.[34]

Efforts at clear definition, precision of description, and the use of mathematics as a tool to solve specific problems rather than as a means to metaphysical insight distinguished the manipulations of the experimental philosopher from those of the magician. Though springing from a similar Renaissance context, the tradition eventually became distinct and separate.

The Scientific Revolution also required a reordering of the traditional hierarchy of sciences and their structures, and these changes began to make their way against the conservatism of the universities. John Dee, Robert Recorde, Ramus, and others had advocated a new educational emphasis on the quadrivium; there were numerous proposals for university reform. Chemistry became a scholarly discipline, in part due to Ramist influence. Philosophy and theology since the seventeenth century have been driven in large measure by scientific innovation.[35] The Scientific Revolution, in addition, had political as well as epistemological implications.

---

34. Rossi, *Bacon*, 10, 11, 23ff.; Webster, *Great Instauration*, 163. Collaboration and openness did find some advocates within the occult movement; see Webster, *Paracelsus to Newton*, 59. Kuhn, "Mathematical versus Experimental Traditions," 44–45; William Eamon, "From the Secrets of Nature to Public Knowledge," in *Reappraisals of the Scientific Revolution*, 333–65.
35. Peter French, *John Dee: The World of an Elizabethan Magus* (1972; reprint, New York: Dorset, 1989), 167. For chemistry in the university see Owen Hannaway, *The Chemists and the Word: The Didactic Origins of Chemistry* (Baltimore: Johns Hopkins University Press, 1975). On science and philosophy, see Arendt, *Human Condition*, 247. See also Engels's *Dialectics of Nature*, where scientific discoveries are presented as military campaigns, taking one theological redoubt after another (Karl Marx and Frederick Engels, *Collected Works* [New York: International Publishers, 1975–], 25:480).

Knowledge and Power

The idea of progress, which was not entirely absent in the ancient world, received an important shift of emphasis and connotation with Bacon. He expressed the Renaissance vision of man in charge of his fate in a striking rhetoric of man's dominion over nature. All the innovative natural philosophers of the early modern period shared the belief that knowledge equals power over nature. Descartes announced a search for a "practical philosophy" in the *Discourse on Method* which would allow men to "become masters and possessors of nature." Hobbes, in the *Leviathan*, put an inclination to seek "power after power" in the human breast.[36] The mechanical philosophy's externalization of the world promoted the consideration of it as an object of manipulation, that is, of the application of technique. In Bacon and in subsequent writers, dominion over nature included dominion over others and is reflected in Bacon's repeated use of sexual imagery. For Bacon, the pursuit of science had a masculine character; nature was feminine. The images suggesting masculinity, chastity, domination, penetration, torture, and rape were present not only in Bacon but throughout his age. The imagery and the reality behind it had biblical origins, and the biblical Eden likewise provided a framework for Bacon's link between knowledge and power. Man could return to Eden through active labor. This was a vision shared by Milton and the followers of Bacon, as well as the Paracelsians, and was particularly appealing to Puritans. The ideal of a return to Eden via new knowledge had to deal with the problem of the acquisition of knowledge as the cause of the Fall. Bacon solved this by linking the search for knowledge as praise of God and the improvement of man's material conditions of life—a dialectical return to Eden through the acquisition of knowledge and a restoration of man's original domination of nature. Although present during the Middle Ages, before the Renaissance, the idea of mastery over nature had been tinged with evil, guilt, and fear as a thing linked to the Devil and as opposed to the early Christian tradition of the rejection of worldliness. Bacon made the idea respectable by purging it of alchemical fantasies and Faustian diabolism.[37]

36. Rossi, *Philosophy, Technology and the Arts*, 103–9; Keith Thomas, *Man and the Natural World: A History of the Modern Sensibility* (New York: Pantheon Books, 1983), 29.
37. Easlea, *Witch Hunting*, 237 and chap. 5. Paterson suggests that Bacon's turn

For Bacon science was a collaborative and cumulative enterprise and therefore a social product with a social purpose requir-
ing organization. The disciples of Bacon and practitioners of the
new philosophy developed a corporate identity which sprang from
the epistemological or cognitive issues embedded in the new outlook and which was distinct from most of the masters of the occult
or the guild of university professors. The professors had earlier
been threatened by efforts to trespass guild boundaries. How else
to understand Osiander's warning against an interpretation of
Copernicus which could throw the liberal arts into confusion?[38]
Even worse, was not Galileo challenging the practitioners of the
"queen of sciences" and its guild when he said, in effect, that the
conclusions of the natural philosopher may compel the theologians to revise their interpretations of Scripture, but the latter
may not advise the philosopher to modify his truths? Galileo and
the Church both rejected the Doctrine of Two Truths, but the
thick wall which he attempted to set up between the two realms,
and whose boundaries would be set by the philosopher, would
crumble both through political pressure from the side of the theologians *and* the growth of knowledge.

Galileo's effort to create a public for the new science was only
partially successful, and in his day the creation of standards of
practice for the new philosophy had not yet taken place. This was

to power may be due in part to his desire for a science which by its activity could
enable scientists to rule society and religion rather than being ruled by them
(Timothy H. Paterson, "Bacon's Myth of Orpheus: Power as a Goal of Science in
Of the Wisdom of the Ancients," *Interpretation* 16 [1989]: 427, 443). The extent to
which this rhetoric of domination has been used not only to justify dominion over
human beings, but has also shaped the texture of science itself, has recently generated a substantial literature. Representative examples are Carolyn Merchant, *The
Death of Nature: Women, Ecology, and the Scientific Revolution* (San Francisco:
Harper and Row, 1980); and Morris Berman, *The Reenchantment of the World*
(Ithaca: Cornell University Press, 1981). Evelyn Keller holds that the gender metaphor has helped determine the values and goals of modern science (*Reflections on
Gender and Science* [New Haven: Yale University Press, 1985]). Such claims, however, merely show how male sexual anxiety and domination of women were expressed in a rhetoric that reached into natural philosophy as it did into other forms
of mental life and served to reinforce existing norms. Pointing to expressions of
the ideology of male superiority cannot explain very well what a gender-free natural philosophy would look like or how it would function, although there has been
some speculation on this topic. Webster, *Great Instauration*, 325–26, 335; Leiss,
The Domination of Nature, 53.

38. In 1549 Melanchthon made the same point as Osiander, condemning the
Copernican theory as an innovation bringing "confusion into the liberal arts,"
which in an additional sense "means asserting the claim to detach astronomy
from the propaedeutic bundle of school subjects to which it had belonged since
the Middle Ages, and to elevate it into a 'science'" (Blumenberg, *Genesis*, 328).

best done through organization, and the organizations of those interested in science had not yet attained the stability and support they were to begin to achieve in the second half of the century. The Royal Society defined the ways in which the new experimental science must be carried on: publicly, in an open manner and with rules governing the validation of its results and managing its disputes. The guild was to be the judge of the products of its members.[39]

Science conceived as public knowledge is automatically thrust into the political realm. The establishment of a new kind of scientific community, with new norms of behavior appropriate to the natural philosopher and criteria capable of promoting public confidence in its activities and their outcomes, took shape through unique forms of organization. As Hannah Arendt pointed out, "An organization, whether of scientists who have abjured politics or of politicians, is always a political institution; where men organize they intend to act and to acquire power." And, we may add, they begin by trying to associate themselves with it. The frontispiece of Sprat's *History of the Royal Society* shows either Bacon or the president of the Royal Society (it is not clear which) pointing to scientific instruments and to a gun.[40]

The *virtuosi* of the Royal Society sought to bring the world into natural philosophy and natural philosophy into the world. The charter of the society commits it to the pursuit of knowledge and the perfection of the arts, and its Baconian program was fervently expounded in its publications and in those of its members. Sprat vigorously called for a union of business and science, too long separated, but now coming together for the benefit of England and mankind. "We have reason to expect that this change will proceed farther, for the better: if our *Gentlemen* shall more condescend to engage in commerce, and to regard the *Philosophy of Nature.*" He then cited the founding of the Royal Company of Adventurers into Africa as though the "Twin-Sister" of the Royal Society.[41]

---

39. Shapin and Schaffer, *Leviathan and the Air-Pump*, 70–79. At issue between Boyle and Hobbes in the dispute described here was whether society does or should define what counts as knowledge. Hobbes's position was that science is political; the Royal Society claimed that it stood outside politics.

40. On scientific organization, see Crombie, "Historical Commitments," 47. Arendt, *Human Condition*, 267 n. 26. Earlier, Galileo had presented his telescope to the Venetian Senate as offering a military advantage.

41. Sprat, *History of the Royal Society*, 118–19, 397, 407. The mercantile and scientific organizations were founded at the same time and had overlapping memberships; see Webster, *From Paracelsus to Newton*, 63.

While the members of the Society were convinced that natural philosophy would eventually yield practical applications, they also saw the importance of the promise for rhetorical purposes. Boyle wrote that "if we seriously intend to convince the distrustful world of the real usefulness of Natural Philosophy, we must take some such course, as that *Milesian Thales* did" and prove its practicality. Christopher Wren advised the president of the society on the kind of experiments to perform before the king. They must be "luciferous in philosophy, and yet whose use and advantage is obvious without a lecture."[42] Whether the work of the scientific societies had practical results or not, they soon enough came to be seen as national ornaments and objects of national pride.

The mercantilist milieu of the seventeenth century as well as the new philosophy and its dynamic raised novelty and success in competition to the status of prime desiderata. Linked to the medieval conception of the constraints on knowledge had been a stricture on novelty as a denial of the virtue of humility. Melanchthon had chastised Copernicus for contradicting Revelation, "either from the love of novelty, or to make a display of ingenuity." The desire of Renaissance thinkers not to appear novel was part of the humanist tradition of seeking ratification for their opinions in ancient authors lest they be charged with "a mania for innovation."[43] John Donne complained that "Every man thinks he has got to be a phoenix." With the growth of the new philosophy came indeed, and with increasing momentum, a mania for innovation, at first to supply a market for prestige among the patrons. Although seventeenth-century scientists frequently tried to justify their activities as having value in economic markets, before this became the powerful reality it has become today there had begun to develop an extended marketplace of ideas through the medium of books, journals, and the meetings of scientific societies. The word *new* or *improvement* began to appear in the titles of many

42. Robert Boyle, *Some Considerations Touching the Usefulness of Natural Philosophy*, in *The Works of the Honourable Robert Boyle*, ed. Thomas Birch (London: A. Millar, 1744), 2:3. See also Michael Hunter, *Science and Society in Restoration England* (Cambridge: Cambridge University Press, 1981), 90. For Wren, see Thomas Birch, *History of the Royal Society of London* (London: A. Millar, 1756–1757), 1:288.
43. Melanchthon is quoted in Allen G. Debus, *Man and Nature in the Renaissance* (Cambridge: Cambridge University Press, 1978), 98. Blumenberg, *Genesis*, 235, 267.

works in the sixteenth and seventeenth centuries, and Hakewill defended novelty as having divine sanction.[44]

On a more mundane level, the political uses of the new philosophy were apparent before its economic promise could be realized. It rapidly became a tool of ideology, of justification, providing a source of rhetoric for or against the social order. Illustrations of the celestial spheres in astronomical works were used as propaganda for royal power. The Royal Society from its founding lent itself to the promotion of political and religious orthodoxy.[45] Sprat was anxious to ally the society with official ideology; throughout his *History* he inveighed against the Commonwealth as "that dismal age" and against "enthusiasm." While toleration for dissenters was affirmed, the superiority of the Anglican faith was professed. The argument from design was raised to new heights of importance and the groundwork laid for natural theology from Newton to Darwin. The increasing weight of the state would place greater demands on this new source of expertise. Since religion was then seen as an important pillar of the social order, threats to conventional religious beliefs were perceived as threats to the very fabric of society. The new philosophy's insistence on mechanism and on the unalterable and universal character of the laws of nature struck horror into the hearts of theologians concerned about the effect of these ideas on the doctrine of Providence. If God did not intervene in human affairs, if all nature could be explained by secondary causes, did that not excuse libertinism, if not worse—social disorder? To a France with the memory of the Fronde, an England remembering its revolution and all Europe having emerged from the wars of religion, some of the ideas proved threatening indeed. Thus were engendered debates on Providence and the nature of God and his created universe, with the varied

---

44. Webster, *Intellectual Revolution*, 2; Lynn Thorndike, "Newness and Craving for Novelty in Seventeenth-Century Science and Medicine," *Journal of the History of Ideas* 12 (1951): 584–98; I. B. Cohen, *Revolution in Science* (Cambridge: Harvard University Press, 1985), 80–81, 481–82; Marie B. Hall, in "The Spirit of Innovation in the Sixteenth Century," *The Nature of Scientific Discovery*, ed. Owen Gingerich (Washington, D.C.: Smithsonian Institution Press, 1975), 309–21.

45. Cohen, *Revolution*, 61–62. James R. Jacob and Margaret C. Jacob, "The Anglican Origins of Modern Science: The Metaphysical Foundations of the Whig Constitution," *Isis* 71 (1980): 251–67; Michael Hunter, "Crown, Public and the New Science," *Notes and Records of the Royal Society* 43 (1989): 110. Hunter asserts that "fashionable interest in the new philosophy crossed party lines" and was not "associated with any specific political viewpoint," challenging the interpretation of the Jacobs (115, n. 33).

responses of Descartes, Hobbes, More, Newton, Leibniz, Male-branche, and others, and the persistent attacks on atheism. To free themselves from the taint of atheism, the apologists for the new philosophy found things for God to do in an otherwise self-regulating universe or allowed for spirit in the operations of nature; above all, they insisted on the well-worn argument that the study of the Book of Nature brings one closer to God. The persistent belief in witchcraft among some members of the Royal Society was in part a self-defense against the charges of irreligion hurled against a mechanical philosophy which had tried to oust spirit from the world. Nor did those who disbelieved in witches care to contradict those who affirmed their existence.[46]

With teleology beginning to be relegated to the First Cause, the success of the Baconian program for the progress of knowledge through man's active working upon nature would play its part in the relativization of value and in its eventual exclusion from nature. Just as our knowledge of the universe is made, so would we come to see our moral standards. Revelation questioned with respect to our understanding of nature would be paralleled by perceptions of the inadequacy of revelation for the determination of right behavior and of justice. Through the ironic dialectic of history, what is becomes divorced from what ought to be, and we are in a universe divested of values, a world no longer created "for us."

Toward Modernity

In the year 1700 educated Europeans were convinced that they were living at the end of a century that had seen a remarkable growth of knowledge, far surpassing that achieved by a still-admired classical antiquity. In innumerable ways perceptions of the nature of the universe and how it functioned had changed profoundly in the previous hundred years. With new methods and a new outlook, natural philosophers, following the mandate of Salomon's House to seek "the knowledge of Causes, and secret motions of things; and the enlarging of the bounds of human Empire, to the effecting of all things possible," had learned much.

The rapid growth of knowledge and the wider application of mathematics and experimentation were accompanied by an in-

---

46. Robert Boyle, *Usefulness of Natural Philosophy,* in *Works,* 2:21, 51–52; Joseph Glanvill, *Philosophia pia* (London: James Collins, 1671), 17. See also note 26 above. Webster, *Paracelsus to Newton,* 99.

crease in the size of the scientific community, which in turn became a factor in the rapidity of scientific change and in the nature of scientific practice. As new growth sprouted from the trunk of natural philosophy, the philosophers were required to confine their investigations to successively narrower branches and twigs. When in the course of the nineteenth century, however, natural philosophers became scientists and science a profession, new fruit resulted from grafts between the old tree and wholly new flora: electrochemistry, thermodynamics, electrodynamics, biochemistry. These in turn continued the branching and hybridizing process. The world of living things was brought into the system and came to be studied with the new techniques of experimentation and the application of mathematics. The Great Chain of Being was raised on new, secular foundations.

Mechanics and construction became the key to understanding society. Laws of society were to be modeled on the laws of nature. The successes of the natural sciences led inevitably to the extension of what were perceived as their successful methods to the social realm. And so the *philosophes*, adopting Bacon's hope for "the effecting of all things possible," began to question what had not been questioned before. With the inclusion of mankind as an object of research and the continued erosion of belief in the limitations on knowledge were born the social sciences. At a later date the humanists too would take up what they conceived as the methods of empirical study in the sciences.[47] The bounds of the social order would be questioned, and with the reappearance of the word *democracy* in a new context and informed by new connotations, public knowledge, including the discoveries of science, came to be seen as a necessary precondition for the new forms of political life. Just as the new philosophy of the seventeenth century broadened the eligibility requirements for admission to the craft, as well as the accessibility to the public of the new knowledge produced by that craft, so now, as in ancient Athens, the "tinker and the cobbler" were to be admitted to "meddle about politics." The construction of constitutions represented the creation of a new "political technology."[48]

47. Joseph Ben-David, *The Scientist's Role in Society: A Comparative Study* (1971; reprint, Chicago: University of Chicago Press, 1984), 112.
48. "Political technology" is Daniel J. Boorstin's phrase on the framing of the U.S. Constitution (*The Republic of Technology: Reflections on our Future Community* [New York: Harper and Row, 1978], chap. 4. Shapin and Schaffer refer to Boyle's role in shaping the norms of scientific activity in the early Royal Society as

The reductionist mechanical model eventually proved inadequate in the natural as well as the social sciences. No longer useful as a picture of the universe, the machine has nevertheless deeply penetrated the way we perceive the world, ourselves and our manner of functioning in it. Instrumental thinking is ubiquitous; every problem, it is believed, can be addressed with the proper technique. Even if, as came to be learned, our attempts at the attainment of absolute truth can never be successful, at least a new criterion of practical success is at hand. Thus, the pursuit of knowledge of the world is reflected in the transformation of the disciplines on the model of technology, itself becoming a technology. Not so much Is it the truth? as Will it work? becomes the standard, yielding in the nineteenth and twentieth centuries instrumentalism, pragmatism, operationalism. Once again we are in the world of the knower become craftsman and possessor of technique.

In the seventeenth century God's providential care assured the existence of the universe for the philosopher or theologian concerned about the implications of an autonomous, self-regulating world. Science today has become an important means of controlling the ecological, economic, social and political forces threatening to disrupt the social—indeed the global—order. Science has been given over more and more to serving instrumental functions—that is, to the transformation of all aspects of life in accordance with the ideal of the rationalization of all processes from production to politics, the arts, and the conduct of everyday life.[49] The "technical fallacy," which sees knowledge primarily in its practical functions, leaving moral culture to take care of itself, or perceiving it as unimportant or irrelevant, has been addressed by a number of philosophers and social critics.[50]

---

the creation of a "social technology" (*Leviathan and the Air-Pump,* 78).

49. Willis H. Truitt, "Values in Science," in *Research in Philosophy and Technology,* ed. Paul T. Durbin (Greenwich, Conn.: JAI Press, 1978), 1:129. The neo-Marxist Frankfurt School asserts the transformation of the function of knowledge from an enlightening and liberating one to one of domination and the legitimation of the present social order; see Max Horkheimer and Theodor W. Adorno, *Dialectic of Enlightenment,* trans. John Cumming (1944; reprint, Boston: Seabury Press, 1973); Herbert Marcuse, *One-Dimensional Man: Studies in the Ideology of Advanced Industrial Society* (Boston: Beacon Press, 1964); Jürgen Habermas, *Theory and Practice,* trans. John Viertel (Boston: Beacon Press, 1973).

50. On the "technical fallacy," see, for example, Sheldon Wolin, "Hobbes and Political Theory," in *Science and Culture in the Western Tradition: Sources and Interpretations,* ed. John G. Burke et al. (Scottsdale, Ariz.: Gorsuch Searisbrick, 1987), 135; Arendt, *Human Condition,* 279. Disturbed by the domination of tech-

Science is now a source of power and a means to power and therefore closely linked to politics.

> It is certainly not without irony that those whom public opinion has persistently held to be the least practical members of society should have turned out to be the only ones left who still know how to act and how to act in concert. For their early organizations, which they founded in the seventeenth century for the conquest of nature and in which they developed their own moral standards and their own code of honor, have not only survived all vicissitudes of the modern age, but they have become one of the most potent power-generating groups in all history.[51]

In conflicts over troubling social and political issues, men have drawn their polemical weapons from armories either closest to hand or thought to contain the most decisive weapons. For the validation of its prejudices society now seeks the cachet conferred by science rather than theology.

In large part science owes its authority to its role in the economy. Economic life and the exigencies of the market have come to dominate scientific activity. Indeed, the practice of science may now be seen as a process of production. It is not only that scientific ideas can be converted into marketable material goods; knowledge itself, no matter how abstruse, is a commodity and subject to the forces of the market. The scientific "economy" possesses the incentives of competition and the disincentives of monopoly, an increasing division of labor and managerial complexity, the requirements of ever larger infusions of capital, falling rates of "profit," globalization, entrepreneurship, "marketing," and ever shorter times from conceptualization or discovery to the market, that is, the journal. The politics of the economy is paralleled by the politics of science.[52] In the modern era "expand or die" has become the rule for science as for economic life and for the state,

---

nique and a resulting alienation, some philosophers have sought in the "essence" of humanity a foundation for moral judgement.

51. Arendt, *Human Condition*, 296.

52. "Market conditions so shape or permeate all social relations that it may properly be called a market society, not merely a market economy" (C. B. Macpherson, *The Political Theory of Possessive Individualism* [Oxford: Oxford University Press, 1962], 48). Bruno Latour, in *Science in Action* (Cambridge: Harvard University Press, 1987), sees "technoscience" as an integral part of the culture. For him a scientific "fact" is something that has to be sold; someone has to be persuaded to buy through appropriate utilization of the power "network." Cognitive issues are irrelevant.

but this rule has its source in the dynamism of the culture of Western Europe in the time of Machiavelli. "All human affairs are in motion, and it is impossible to stand still; they must progress or decline, and where reason does not lead, necessity often drives."[53]

Echoing the judgment of Herbert Butterfield forty years before and of Whitehead earlier, Richard Westfall says that "the Scientific Revolution was the most important 'event' in Western history."[54] If what is meant is the change in modes of inquiry and types of explanation about natural phenomena from Copernicus to Newton, then it was but one of the children, albeit a most robust and domineering one, of that culture born with the Renaissance that we call modernity. The aspects of life and perception that we so characterize antedate the Scientific Revolution and were its nursery. And crucial to the making of that revolution was the role of the arts and of technique in the acquisition of knowledge, in the creation of its social character, and in the devalorization of the objects of knowing. We have been much called on of late to judge and evaluate what are seen as consequences of the modern ways of knowing and we will continue to be so called upon. For Bacon's faith in progress has been somewhat tempered, at least in those parts of the world that gave it birth.

At the heart of any inquiry about the relation of the Scientific Revolution to modernity is a historiographical problem: how to unite the cognitive issues involving the details of theory, experiment, argument, demonstration, and explanation with their unique social contexts. To some extent the fracturing of the culture and the hyperspecialization within the academic disciplines (itself a consequence of the Scientific Revolution) has militated against such studies. Peter Gay has proposed an approach to "the social history of ideas" which has relevance for and is a reproach to historians and philosophers of science:

> This kind of intellectual history is guided by a single, simple principle: ideas have many dimensions. They are expressed by individuals, but they are social products; they are conceived, elaborated, and modified amid a specific set of historical circumstances. They reflect events

53. Machiavelli, *Discorsi*, quoted in John H. Randall, Jr., *The Making of the Modern Mind*, rev. ed. (Boston: Houghton Mifflin, 1940), 198. Machiavelli, of course, also began to question the relationship of moral philosophy to the practice of politics.
54. Richard Westfall, "The Scientific Revolution: Teaching in the History of Science, Resources and Strategies," *Histories of Science Society Newsletter* 15 (1986): 1. Butterfield, *Origins of Modern Science*, 7.

like war or persecution, social realities like the class system, pressures exerted by prevailing styles of thought or literary fashions. Therefore the social historian of ideas cannot rest content with analyzing their formal logical structure.[55]

But this is only one side of the coin: since, as Whitehead told us, "ideas have consequences," the obverse considers in the same fashion "the history of science and its cultural influences."[56] So far few have tried to come to grips with that most difficult (though most absorbing) project, a mode of historical inquiry and explanation uniting cognitive issues in the practice of science with their intellectual, institutional, and material matrices. The Scylla and Charybdis between which such undertakings have had to steer are the neglect of specific research traditions within the sciences on the one hand, and on the other, a concentration solely on efforts to solve problems within those traditions. When a sufficient number of historical studies engaging in their totality the attempts of mankind to understand its universe have been conducted, we will have a better picture of the relation between modernity and the Scientific Revolution.

55. Peter Gay, *The Party of Humanity: Essays on the French Enlightenment* (1954; reprint, New York: W. W. Norton, 1971), x.
56. The subtitle of the journal *Isis*.

TOPICAL BIBLIOGRAPHY

Listed below are sources for further reading on the basic themes and issues examined in this study. The listings under each heading and subheading are obviously not exhaustive. Their purpose is to serve as a concise guide to texts and inter-pretations pertinent to the analysis developed in essays in this collection.

Early Modern Science and Its History

Early Histories

Bailly, Jean Sylvain. *Histoire de l'Astronomie Ancienne, depuis son originie, jusqu'à l'éstablissement de l'école d'Alexandrie.* Paris: Frères Dubure, 1775.
———. *Histoire de l'Astronomie Moderne, depuis la fondation de l'école d'Alexandrie, jusqu'à l'époque de MDCCXXX.* 3 vols. Paris: Les Frères de Bure, 1779–1782.
Boerhaave, Hermann. "Prolegomena, or the History of Chemistry." In *A New Method of Chemistry; Including the Theory and Practice of that Art: Laid down on Mechanical Principles, and Accommo-dated to the Uses of Life . . . ,* translated by P. Shaw and E. Chambers, 1–50. London: J. Osborn and T. Longman, 1727.
Burnet, Thomas. *The Sacred Theory of the Earth.* Reprint of the 2d English ed. of 1690–1691; Carbondale: Southern Illinois University Press, 1965.
Freind, John. *The History of Physick; From the Time of Galen, to the beginning of the Sixteenth Century.* 4th ed. 2 vols. London: M. Cooper, 1750.
Laplace, Pierre Simon de. "Precis de l'Histoire de l'Astronomie." In *Exposition du Système du Monde.* 3d ed. 2 vols. Paris: Courcier, 1808.
Montucla, Jean Étienne. *Histoire de Mathématique, dans laquelle on rend compte de leurs progès . . . jusqu'à nos jours; où l'on expose le tableau et le développement des principales découvertes . . . et les principaux traits de la vie des mathématiciens les plus célèbres.* 2 vols. Paris, 1758. Expanded to 4 vols. Completed and edited by J. J. Le Francais de Lalande. Paris: H. Agasse, 1799–1802.

Webster, John. *Academiarum Examen, or the Examination of Academies.* London: Giles Calvert, 1654.

Whewell, William. *History of the Inductive Sciences: From the Earliest to the Present Time.* 3d ed. 2 vols. New York: D. Appleton, 1873.

The Scientific Revolution and the Mechanical Philosophy

Blumenberg, Hans. *The Genesis of the Copernican World.* Translated by Robert M. Wallace. Cambridge: MIT Press, 1987.

Burtt, E. A. *The Metaphysical Foundations of Modern Physical Science.* Rev. ed. Garden City, N.Y.: Doubleday, 1954.

Butterfield, Herbert. *The Origins of Modern Science, 1300–1800.* New ed. New York: Macmillan, 1957.

Debus, Allen G. *Man and Nature in the Renaissance.* Cambridge: Cambridge University Press, 1978.

―――, ed. *Science and Education in the Seventeenth Century: The Webster-Ward Debate.* London: Macdonald, 1970.

Duhem, Pierre. *Le Système du Monde.* 10 vols. Paris: Hermann, 1913–1959.

Easlea, Brian. *Witch Hunting, Magic, and the New Philosophy: An Introduction to the Debates of the Scientific Revolution, 1450–1750.* Brighton: Harvester Press, 1980.

Hunter, Michael. "The Crown, the Public, and the New Science, 1689–1702." *Notes and Records of the Royal Society* 43 (1989): 99–116.

Koyré, Alexandre. *Études Galiléennes.* 3 parts. 1935–1939. Reprint. 1 vol. Paris: Hermann, 1966.

―――. *From the Closed World to the Infinite Universe.* New York: Harper, 1958.

Kubrin, David. *Providence and the Mechanical Philosophy.* Ph.D. diss., Cornell University, 1968.

Malville, J. McKim. *The Fermenting Universe: Myths of Eternal Change.* New York: Seabury Press, 1981.

Mandrou, Robert. *From Humanism to Science, 1480–1700.* Translated by Brian Pearce. Middlesex, Eng.: Penguin Books, 1978.

Pederson, Olaf. "Galileo and the Council of Trent: The Galileo Affair Revisited." *Journal for the History of Astronomy* 14, no. 39 (1983): 1–29.

Rose, Paul L. *The Italian Renaissance of Mathematics: Studies on Humanists and Mathematicians from Petrarch to Galileo.* Geneva: Droz, 1975.

Rossi, Paolo. *The Dark Abyss of Time: The History of the Earth and the History of Nations from Hooke to Vico.* Translated by Lydia G. Cochrane. Chicago: University of Chicago Press, 1984.

Shapin, Steven, and Simon Schaffer, eds. *Leviathan and the Air-Pump: Hobbes, Boyle and the Experimental Life*. Princeton: Princeton University Press, 1985.

Thackray, Arnold. *Atoms and Powers: An Essay on Newtonian Matter-Theory and the Development of Chemistry*. Cambridge: Harvard University Press, 1970.

Thorndike, Lynn. *A History of Magic and Experimental Science*. 8 vols. New York: Columbia University Press, 1923–1958.

Westfall, Richard S. *The Construction of Modern Science: Mechanisms and Mechanics*. Cambridge: Cambridge University Press, 1977.

Alchemy, Medicine, and the Chemical Philosophy

Berthelot, Marcellin Pierre Eugene. *Les orignies de l'alchimie*. 1885. Reprint. Paris: Librairie des Sciences et des Arts, 1938.

Debus, Allen G. "The Chemical Philosophers: Chemical Medicine from Paracelsus to van Helmont." *History of Science* 12 (1974): 235–259.

———. *The Chemical Philosophy: Paracelsian Science and Medicine in the Sixteenth and Seventeenth Centuries*. 2 vols. New York: Science History Publications, 1977.

———. "Chemistry and the Quest for a Material Spirit of Life in the Seventeenth Century," In *Spiritus: IV° Colloquio Internazionale del Lessico Intellettuale Europeo, Roma, 7–9 gennaio 1983*, edited by M. Rattori and M. Bianchi, 245–63. Rome, Edizioni dell'Atneo, 1984.

———. "Edward Jorden and the Fermentation of the Metals: An Iatrochemical Study of Terrestrial Phenomena." In *Toward a History of Geology: Proceedings of the New Hampshire Inter-Disciplinary Conference on the History of Geology, September 7–12, 1967*, edited by Cecil J. Schneer, 100–21. Cambridge: MIT Press, 1969.

———. "An Elizabethan History of Medical Chemistry." *Annals of Science* 18 (1962, published 1964): 1–29.

———. "Harvey and Fludd: The Irrational Factor in the Rational Science of the Seventeenth Century." *Journal of the History of Biology* 3 (1970): 81–105.

———. "Mathematics and Nature in the Chemical Texts of the Renaissance." *Ambix* 15 (1968): 1–28.

———. "Palissy, Plat and English Agricultural Chemistry in the Sixteenth and Seventeenth Centuries." *Archives Internationales d'Histoire des Sciences* 21 (1968): 67–88.

———. "The Pharmaceutical Revolution of the Renaissance." *Clio medica* 11 (1976): 307–17.

———. "Robert Fludd and the Circulation of the Blood." *Journal of the History of Medicine and Allied Sciences* 16 (1961): 374–93.

Klutz, M. *Die Rezepte in Oswald Crolls Basilica chymica (1609) und ihre Beziehungen zu Paracelsus.* Vol. 14. Braunschweig: Veröff. aus d. Pharmaziegesch. Seminar der Technischen Universität Braunschweig, 1974.

Pagel, Walter. *Jo. Bapt. Van Helmont: Einführung in die philosophische Medizin des Barock.* Berlin: Springer, 1930.

———. *Joan Baptista van Helmont: Reformer of Science and Medicine.* Cambridge: Cambridge University Press, 1982.

———. *Paracelsus: An Introduction to Philosophical Medicine in the Era of the Renaissance.* Basel: S. Karger, 1958.

Partington, J. R. *A History of Chemistry.* 2 vols. London: Macmillan, 1961.

Rattansi, P. M. "Some Evaluations of Reason in Sixteenth- and Seventeenth-Century Natural Philosophy." In *Changing Perspectives in the History of Science: Essays in Honour of Joseph Needham,* edited by Mikulás Teich and Robert Young, 148–66. London: Heinemann, 1973.

Schneider, Wolfgang. "Der Wandel des Arzneischatzes im 17. Jahrhundert und Paracelsus." *Sudhoffs Archiv für Geschichte der Medizin und der Naturwissenschaften* 45 (1961): 201–15.

Severinus, Petrus. *Idea medicinae philosophicae.* 1571. 3d ed. Hagae Comitis: 1660.

Sigerist, Henry. *A History of Medicine.* 2 vols. New York: Oxford University Press, 1955.

Taylor, F. Sherwood. "The Idea of the Quintessence." In *Science, Medicine, and History: Essays on the Evolution of Scientific Thought and Medical Practice Written in Honour of Charles Singer,* edited by E. Ashworth Underwood. 2 vols. 1:247–65. London: Oxford University Press, 1953.

Van Helmont, J. B. *Ortus medicinae. Id est, initia physicae inaudita. Progressus medicinae novus, in morborum ultionem, ad vitam longam.* Amsterdam: Ludovicus Elsevir, 1648. Reprint. Brussels: Culture et Civilisation, 1966.

Newton, Alchemy and Esoteric Knowledge

Dobbs, B. J. T. *The Foundations of Newton's Alchemy: or, "The Hunting of the Greene Lyon."* Cambridge: Cambridge University Press, 1975.

———. *The Janus Faces of Genius: The Role of Alchemy in Newton's Thought.* Cambridge: Cambridge University Press, forthcoming.

———. "Newton as Alchemist and Theologian." In *Upon the Shoulders of Giants: Newton and Halley, 1686–1986,* edited by Norman J. W. Thrower. Berkeley: University of California Press, forthcoming.

———. "Newton's Alchemy and his 'Active Principle' of Gravitation."

In *Newton's Scientific and Philosophical Legacy*, edited by P. B. Scheuer and G. Debrock. Dordrecht: Kluwer Academic Publishers, 1988.

McGuire, J. E., and P. M. Rattansi. "Newton and the 'Pipes of Pan.' " *Notes and Records of the Royal Society of London* 21 (1966): 108–43.

Webster, Charles. *From Paracelsus to Newton: Magic and the Making of Modern Science*. Cambridge: Cambridge University Press, 1982.

Westfall, Richard S. "Newton and the Hermetic Tradition." In *Science, Medicine and Society in the Renaissance: Essays to Honor Walter Pagel*, edited by Allen G. Debus, 2:183–98. New York: Science History Publications, 1972.

Issues in Historiography

Agassi, Joseph. *Towards an Historiography of Science*. 's-Gravenhage: Mouton, 1963.

Brieger, Gert H. "The History of Medicine and the History of Science." *Isis* 72 (1981): 537–40.

Butterfield, Herbert. "The History of Science and the Study of History." *Harvard Library Bulletin* 13 (1959): 329–47.

———. *The Whig Interpretation of History*. 1931. Reprint. New York: W. W. Norton, 1965.

Clagett, Marshall, ed. *Critical Problems in the History of Science: Proceedings of the Institute for the History of Science at the University of Wisconsin, September 1–11, 1957*. Madison: The University of Wisconsin Press, 1962.

Cohen, I. Bernard. "Some Recent Books on the History of Science." In *Roots of Scientific Thought: A Cultural Perspective*, edited by Philip P. Wiener and Aaron Noland. New York: Basic Books, 1957.

Conant, James B. "History in the Education of Scientists." *Harvard Library Bulletin* 14 (1960): 315–33.

Debus, Allen G. *Science and History: A Chemist's Appraisal*. Coimbra: Edição do Serviço de Documentação e Publicações da Universidade de Coimbra Subsidiado pela Fundação Calouste Gulbenkian, 1984.

Gutting, Gary, ed. *Paradigms and Revolutions: Appraisals and Applications of Thomas Kuhn's Philosophy of Science*. Notre Dame: University of Notre Dame Press, 1980.

Hall, A. Rupert. "On Whiggism." *History of Science* 21 (1983): 45–49.

Kragh, Helge. *An Introduction to the Historiography of Science*. Cambridge: Cambridge University Press, 1987.

Kuhn, Thomas S. "History of Science." In *International Encyclopedia of Social Sciences*, edited by David L. Sills, 75–83. New York: Crowell, Collier and Macmillan, 1968.

————. *The Structure of Scientific Revolutions.* Chicago: University of Chicago Press, 1962.

Merton, Robert K. "Science, Technology, and Society in Seventeenth-Century England." *Osiris* 4 (1938a): 360–632. Reprint. New York: H. Fertig, 1970.

Sarton, George. *Introduction to the History of Science.* 3 vols. in 5 parts. Baltimore: Williams and Wilkins for the Carnegie Institution of Washington, 1927–1947.

————. *Sarton on the History of Science: Essays by George Sarton.* Edited by Dorothy Stimson. Cambridge: Harvard University Press, 1962.

Teich, Mikuláš, and Robert Young, eds. *Changing Perspectives in the History of Science: Essays in Honour of Joseph Needham.* London: Heinemann, 1973.

Thackray, Arnold. "History of Science." In *A Guide to the Culture of Science, Technology, and Medicine,* edited by Paul T. Durbin. New York: Free Press, 1980.

Westman, Robert, and David Lindberg, eds. *Reappraisals of the Scientific Revolution.* Cambridge: Cambridge University Press, 1990.

Wilson, Leonard G. "Medical History Without Medicine." *Journal of the History of Medicine and Allied Sciences* 35 (1980): 5–7.

Wood, Paul. "Recent Trends in the History of Science: The Dehumanisation of History." *British Society for the History of Science Newsletter,* no. 3 (September, 1980): 19–20.

Recovery and Influence of the *Prisca Theologia*

Ancient Sources and Their Interpretation

Corpus Hermeticum, translated by A. D. Nock and A. J. Festugière. 4 vols. Paris: Société d'édition "Les Belles Lettres," 1954–1960. (Vols. 1 and 2 are the 2d ed.)

Elsas, C. *Neuplatonische und gnostische Weltablehnung in der Schule Plotins.* Berlin: de Gruyter, 1975.

Festugière, A. J. *La Révélation d'Hermès Trismégiste.* 4 vols. Paris: Librairie Lecoffre, 1949–1954. (Vol. 3 is the 3d ed.).

Fowden, Garth. *The Egyptian Hermes: A Historical Approach to the Late Pagan Mind.* Cambridge: Cambridge University Press, 1986.

Georgi, Dieter, and John Strugnell. *Concordance to the "Corpus Hermeticum": Tractate One: the "Poimandres".* Concordances to Patristic and Late Classical Texts, vol. 0. Cambridge, Mass.: Boston Theological Institute, 1971.

González Blanco, A. "Hermetism: A Bibliographical Approach." In

Aufstieg und Niedergang der romischen Welt, edited by Hildegard Temporini. Part 2, vol. 17, no. 4, 2240–81. Berlin: De Gruyter, 1984.

Grese, William C. *Corpus Hermeticum XIII and Early Christian Literature.* Leiden: Brill, 1979.

———. "The Hermetica and New Testament Research." *Biblical Research* 28 (1983): 37–54.

Gundel, H. "Poimandres." In *Paulys Real-Encyclopädie der Classischen Altertumswissenschaft.* New ed. Stuttgart-Waldsee: Alfred Druckenmüller Verlag, 1951.

Hermetica. Edited and translated by Walter Scott. 1924–1936. 4 vols. Reprint. London: Dawsons of Pall Mall, 1968.

Jonas, Hans. *The Gnostic Religion: The Message of the Alien God and the Beginnings of Christianity.* 2d ed. Boston: Beacon Press, 1963.

———. "Gnosticism." In *Encyclopedia of Philosophy.* New York: Macmillan, 1967.

Kerényi, Karl. *Hermes, Guide of Souls: The Mythologem of the Masculine Source of Life.* Translated by Murray Stein. Dallas: Spring Publications, 1986.

Scholer, David M. "Bibliographica Gnostica: Supplementum I." *Novum Testamentum* 13 (1971): 322–36.

Tröger, Karl-Wolfgang. "Die hermetische Gnosis." In *Gnosis und Neues Testament,* edited by Karl-Wolfgang Tröger, 97–119. Berlin: Evangelische Verlagsanstalt, 1973.

*Renaissance Neoplatonism and
the Recovery of Ancient Wisdom*

Blau, J. L. *The Christian Interpretation of the Cabala in the Renaissance.* Port Washington, N.Y.: Kennikat Press, 1944.

Copenhaver, Brian P. "Renaissance Magic and Neoplatonic Philosophy: 'Ennead' 4.3–5 in Ficino's 'De vita coelitus comparanda.'" In vol. 2 of *Marsilio Ficino e il ritorno di Platone,* edited by Gian Carlo Garfagnini. 2 vols. Florence: L. S. Olschki, 1986.

———. "Scholastic Philosophy and Renaissance Magic in the 'De vita' of Marsilio Ficino." *Renaissance Quarterly* 37 (Winter, 1984): 523–54.

Ficino, Marsilio. *Opera Omnia.* 2d ed. 4 vols. 1576. Reprint. Torino: Bottega d'Erasmo, 1959.

———. *"Platonic Theology,* III 2, XIII 2, XIV 304." Translated by J. L. Burroughs. *Journal of the History of Ideas* 5 (1944): 227–39.

———. *Théologie Platonicienne de l'immortalité des âmes.* Translation and commentary by Raymond Marcel. 3 vols. Paris: Société d'édition "Les Belles Lettres," 1964–1970.

———. *Three Books on Life: A Critical Edition and Translation with*

Introduction and Notes. Edited by Carol V. Kaske and John R. Clark. Medieval and Renaissance Texts and Studies, vol. 57. Binghamton, New York: Renaissance Society of America, 1989.

Gandillac, M. De. "Neoplatonism and Christian Thought in the Fifteenth Century (Nicholas of Cusa and Marsilio Ficini)." In *Neoplatonism and Christian Thought,* edited by D. O'Meara, 143–68. Albany: State University of New York Press, 1982.

Garin, Eugenio. *Astrology in the Renaissance: The Zodiac of Life.* Translated by Carolyn Jackson and June Allen. Translation revised by Clare Robertson in collaboration with author. London: Routledge and Kegan Paul, 1983.

————. *La Cultura filosofica del Rinascimento italiano: Ricerche e documenti.* Florence: Sansoni, 1961.

————. *Medioevo e Rinascimento.* 2d ed. Rome: Laterza, 1987.

————. *Science and Civic Life in the Italian Renaissance,* translated by Peter Munz. Garden City, N.Y.: Anchor Books, 1969.

————. *Testi umanistici su l'ermetismo.* Rome: Bocca, 1955.

Hersey, G. L. "Marsilio Ficino's Cosmic Temple." In *Collaboration in Italian Renaissance Art,* edited by W. Sheard and J. T. Paoletti, 91–98. New Haven: Yale University Press, 1978.

————. *Pythagorean Palaces: Magic and Architecture in the Italian Renaissance.* Ithaca, N.Y.: Cornell University Press, 1976.

Kaske, Carol. "Ficino's Shifting Attitude Towards Astrology in the 'De vita coelitus comparanda,' the Letter to Poliziano, and the 'Apologia' to the Cardinals." In *Marsilio Ficino e il ritorno di Platone: Studie e documenti,* edited by Gian Carlo Garfagnini, 2:371–81. Florence: L. S. Olschki, 1986.

Klibansky, R., E. Panofsky, and F. Saxl. *Saturn and Melancholy: Studies in the History of Natural Philosophy, Religion and Art.* New York: Basic Books, 1964.

Kristeller, P. O. *The Philosophy of Marsilio Ficino.* Translated by Virginia Conant. New York: Columbia University Press, 1943.

Merkel, Ingrid, and Allen G. Debus, eds. *Hermeticism and the Renaissance: Intellectual History and the Occult in Early Modern Europe.* Washington: Folger Shakespeare Library, 1988.

Michel, Paul-Henri. "Renaissance Cosmologies," *Diogenes* 18 (Summer 1957): 93–107.

Pico della Mirandola, Giovanni. *Oration on the Dignity of Man.* Translated by A. R. Caponigri. Chicago: Regnery Gateway, 1956.

Robb, Nesca A. *Neoplatonism of the Italian Renaissance.* 1935. Reprint. New York: Octagon Books, 1968.

Secret, François. *Les Kabbalistes chrétiens de la Renaissance.* Paris: Dunod, 1963.

Torre, Arnaldo della. *Storia dell'Accademia platonica di Firenze.* Florence: Tip. G. Carnesecchi e figli, 1902.

Trinkaus, Charles. *In Our Image and Likeness: Humanity and Divin-*

ity in Italian Humanist Thought. 2 vols. Chicago: University of Chicago Press, 1970.

Vickers, Brian, ed. *Occult and Scientific Mentalities in the Renaissance.* Cambridge: Cambridge University Press, 1984.

Walker, D. P. "Orpheus the Theologian and Renaissance Platonist." In *The Ancient Theology: Studies in Christian Platonism from the Fifteenth to the Eighteenth Century.* Ithaca, N.Y.: Cornell University Press, 1972.

————. "The *Prisca Theologia* in France." *Journal of the Warburg and Courtauld Institutes* 17 (1954): 204–59.

————. *Spiritual and Demonic Magic from Ficinio to Campanella.* 1958. Reprint. South Bend, Indiana: University of Notre Dame Press, 1975.

Warden, J. "Orpheus and Ficino." In *Orpheus: The Metamorphoses of a Myth,* edited by J. Warden, 85–110. Toronto: University of Toronto Press, 1982.

Wind, Edgar. *Pagan Mysteries in the Renaissance: An Exploration of Philosophical and Mystical Sources of Iconography in Renaissance Art.* 3d ed. Oxford: Oxford University Press, 1980.

Zambelli, Paola. "Platone, Ficino, e la magia." In *Studia Humanitatis: Ernesto Grassi zum 70. Geburtstag,* edited by E. Hora and E. Kessler, 121–42. Munich: W. Fink, 1973.

————. "Le problème de la magie naturelle à la Renaissance." In *Magia, astrologia e religione nel Rinascimento.* Wroclaw: Zaklad Narodowy im Ossolinskich, 1974.

Magic and Utopianism in the Sixteenth and Seventeenth Centuries

Ashmole, Elias. "Verses Belonging to an Emblematicall Scrowle: Supposed to be invented by Geo: Ripley." In *Theatrum Chemicum Britannicum Containing Severall Poeticall Pieces of our Famous English Philosophers, who have written the Hermetique Mysteries in their owne Ancient Language.* Compiled and edited by Elias Ashmole. London, 1652. Reprint. New York: Johnson Reprint Corporation, 1967.

Bruno, Giordano. *La Cena de le ceneri* (*The Ash Wednesday Supper*). Translated and edited by Edward A. Gosselin and Lawrence S. Lerner. Hamden, Conn.: Archon Books, 1977.

————. *Spaccio della bestia trionfante.* (*The expulsion of the triumphant beast*). Translated and edited by A. D. Imerti. New Brunswick, N.J.: Rutgers University Press, 1964.

Campanella, Tommaso. *La Città del Sole: Dialogo Poetico* (*The City of the Sun: A Poetical Dialogue*), translated by Daniel J. Donno. Berkeley: University of California Press, 1981.

Fludd, Robert. *Apologia compendiaria fraternitatem de Rosea Cruce suspicionis et infamiae maculis aspersam, veritatis quasi fluctibus abluens et abstergens.* Leiden: Godfrid Basson, 1616.

―――. *Robert Fludd and His Philosophicall Key: Being a Transcription of the Manuscript at Trinity College, Cambridge.* New York: Science History Publications, 1979.

―――. *Tractatus apologeticus integritatem societatis de Rosea Cruce defendens.* Leiden: Godfrid Basson, 1617.

―――. *Utriusque cosmi maioris scilicet et minoris metaphysica, physica atque technica historia.* Oppenhemii: AEre Johan-Theodori de Bry, 1617–[1624?].

Godwin, Joscelyn. *Robert Fludd: Hermetic Philosopher and Surveyor of Two Worlds.* Boulder, Colo.: Shambhala, 1979.

McKnight, Stephen A. "The Renaissance Magus and the Modern Messiah." *Religious Studies Review* 5 (1979): 81–89.

―――. *Sacralizing the Secular: The Renaissance Origins of Modernity.* Baton Rouge: Louisiana State University Press, 1989.

―――. "Understanding Modernity: A Reappraisal of the Gnostic Element." *Intercollegiate Review* 14 (1979): 107–17.

Mueller-Jahnke, W. D. "Von Ficino zu Agrippa, Der Magie-Begriff des renaissance-Humanismus im Ueberblick." In *Epochen der Natur mystik*, edited by A. Faivre and R. C. Zimmermann. Berlin: E. Schmidt, 1979.

Nauert, Charles G. *Agrippa and the Crisis of Renaissance Thought.* Urbana: University of Illinois Press, 1965.

Westman, Robert S., and J. E. McGuire, eds. *Hermeticism and the Scientific Revolution: Papers Read at a Clark Library Seminar, March 9, 1974.* Los Angeles: William Andrews Clark Memorial Library, University of California, 1977.

Yates, Frances. *Astraea: The Imperial Theme in the Sixteenth Century.* London: Routledge and Kegan Paul, 1975.

―――. *Giordano Bruno and the Hermetic Tradition.* Chicago: University of Chicago Press, 1964.

―――. "The Hermetic Tradition in Renaissance Science." In *Art, Science, and History in the Renaissance*, edited by C. S. Singleton. Baltimore: Johns Hopkins Press, 1967.

―――. "Hermeticism." In *Encyclopedia of Philosophy.* New York: Macmillan, 1967.

―――. *Lull and Bruno.* London: Routledge and Kegan Paul, 1982.

―――. *The Occult Philosophy in the Elizabethan Age.* London: Routledge and Kegan Paul, 1979.

―――. *The Rosicrucian Enlightenment.* London: Routledge and Kegan Paul, 1972.

―――. *The Valois Tapestries.* London: Warburg Institute, University of London, 1959.

Science and the Longing for Innerworldly Fulfillment

Science, Religion, and Utopianism in the Sixteenth and Seventeenth Centuries

Bacon, Francis. *The Philosophical Works of Francis Bacon.* Edited by James M. Robertson. 1905. Reprint. Freeport, N.Y.: Books for Libraries Press, 1970.

———. *Works.* 14 vols. Edited by James Spedding, R. L. Ellis, and D. D. Heath. 1857–1874. Reprint. Stuttgart: Friedrich Fromann, 1963.

Ball, Brian W. *A Great Expectation: Eschatological Thought in English Protestantism to 1660.* Leiden: Brill, 1975.

Bauckham, Richard, ed. *Tudor Apocalypse: Sixteenth Century Apocalypticism, Millennarianism and the English Reformation.* Oxford: Sutton Courtenay Press, 1978.

Böhme, Jakob. *Sämtliche Schriften.* Edited by Will-Erich Peuckert. 11 vols. Stuttgart: F. Frommanns Verlag, 1955–1961.

Christianson, Paul. *Reformers and Babylon: English Apocalyptic Visions from the Reformation to the Eve of the Civil War.* Toronto: University of Toronto Press, 1978.

Davis, J. C. *Utopia and the Ideal Society: A Study of English Utopian Writing, 1516–1700.* Cambridge: Cambridge University Press, 1981.

Dubos, Renée. *The Dreams of Reason: Science and Utopias.* New York: Columbia University Press, 1961.

Firth, Katharine R. *The Apocalyptic Tradition in Reformation Britain, 1530–1645.* Oxford: Oxford University Press, 1979.

Hill, Christopher. *The World Turned Upside Down: Radical Ideas During the English Revolution.* London: Temple Smith, 1972.

Jacob, J. R. "Restoration, Reformation and the Origins of the Royal Society." *History of Science* 13 (1975): 155–76.

Jacob, James and Margaret Jacob. "The Anglican Origins of Modern Science: The Metaphysical Foundations of the Whig Constitution." *Isis* 71 (1980): 251–67.

Jacob, Margaret C. *The Cultural Meaning of the Scientific Revolution.* Philadelphia: Temple University Press, 1988.

———. *The Newtonians and the English Revolution, 1689–1720.* Ithaca. N.Y.: Cornell University Press, 1976.

———. "Seventeenth-Century Science and Religion: The State of the Argument." *History of Science* 14 (1976): 200–201.

Jobe, Thomas H. "The Devil in Restoration Science: The Glanville-Webster Witchcraft Debate." *Isis* 72 (1981): 343–56.

Jones, Richard F. *Ancients and Moderns: A Study of the Rise of the Scientific Movement in Seventeenth-Century England.* 2d ed. St. Louis: Washington University, 1961.

Lemmi, Charles. *The Classic Deities in Bacon: A Study in Mythological Symbolism*. 1933. Reprint. New York: Octagon Books, 1971.

Linden, Stanton J. "Alchemy and Eschatology in Seventeenth-Century Poetry." *Ambix* 31 (1984): 102–24.

Kuhlmann, Quirinus. *Neubegeisterter Böhme: Begreiffend Hundertfünftzig Weissagungen*. . . . Leiden: Loth de Haes, 1674.

Merchant, Carolyn. *The Death of Nature: Women, Ecology, and the Scientific Revolution*. San Francisco: Harper and Row, 1980.

Morgan, John. "Puritanism and Science: A Reinterpretation." *Historical Journal* 22 (1979): 535–60.

Rattansi, P. M. "Paracelsus and the Puritan Revolution." *Ambix* 11 (1963): 24–32.

Rossi, Paolo. *Francis Bacon: From Magic to Science (Francesco Bacone: dalla magia alla scienza)*. Translated by Sacha Rabinovitch. Chicago: University of Chicago Press, 1968.

Rudrum, Alan. "Theology and Politics in Seventeenth-Century England." *The Clark Newsletter: Bulletin of the UCLA Center for Seventeenth and Eighteenth-Century Studies* (Fall 1988), 5–7.

Thomas, Keith. *Religion and the Decline of Magic: Studies in Popular Beliefs in Sixteenth- and Seventeenth-Century England*. 1971. Reprint. Harmondsworth: Penguin, 1973.

Walsh, David. "The Historical Dialectic of Spirit: Jacob Boehme's Influence on Hegel." In *History and System: Hegel's Philosophy of History*, edited by Robert Perkins. Albany: State University of New York Press, 1984.

———. *The Mysticism of Innerworldly Fulfillment: A Study of Jacob Boehme*. Gainesville, Fla.: University Presses of Florida, 1983.

Webster, Charles. *The Great Instauration: Science, Medicine and Reform, 1626–1660*. New York: Holmes and Meier Publishers, 1976.

Weinberger, Jerry. *Science, Faith and Politics: Francis Bacon and the Utopian Roots of the Modern Age*. Ithaca, N.Y.: Cornell University Press, 1985.

Whitney, Charles. *Francis Bacon and Modernity*. New Haven: Yale University Press, 1986.

Zilsel, Edgar. "The Genesis of the Concept of Scientific Progress." *Journal of the History of Ideas* 6 (1945): 325–49.

Science, Pseudo-Science, and Perfection in the Eighteenth and Nineteenth Centuries

Bengel, Johann Albrecht. *Sechzig erbauliche Reden*. Stuttgart: Christoph Erhardt, 1747.

Benz, Ernst. *Schellings theologische Geistesahnen*. Abhandlungen der

Adademie der Wissenschaften und der Literatur in Mainz, no. 3. 1955.

———. *Les Sources mystiques de la philosophie romantique allemande.* Paris: J. Vrin, 1968.

Comte, Auguste. *Cours de philosophie positive (1830–1842).* Edited by E. Littré. Paris: Bachelier, 1864.

Condorcet. *Esquisse d'un tableau historique des progrès de l'esprit humain: Entwurf einer historischen Dartsellung der Fortschritte des menschlichen Geistes.* Edited by Wilhelm Alff. Frankfurt: Europäisch Verlagsanstalt, 1963.

Gelbart, Nina Rattner. " 'Science' in Enlightenment Utopias: Power and Purpose in Eighteenth-Century French 'Voyages Imaginaires.' " Ph.D. diss., University of Chicago, 1973.

Hegel, Georg Wilhelm Friedrich. *Grundlinien der Philosophie des Rechts.* Edited by Georg Lasson. Leipzig: Felix Meiner,.1911.

———. *Phänomenologie des Geistes.* Edited by J. Hoffmeister. Hamburg: Felix Meiner, 1952. Translated as *Phenomenology of Spirit.* Oxford: Clarendon Press, 1977.

———. *Vorlesungen: Ausgewählte Nachschriften und Manusckripte,* Bd. 9, *Vorlesungen über die Geschichte der Philosophie,* Teil 4. Edited by Pierre Ganiron and Walter Jaeschke. Hamburg: Felix Meiner, 1986.

Marx, Karl, and Frederick Engels. *Collected Works.* Translated by Richard Dixon, et al. New York: International Publishers, 1975–.

———. *The Marx-Engels Reader.* Edited by Robert Tucker. New York: Norton, 1978.

Oetinger, Friedrich Christoph. "Die güldene Zeit." In *Abhandlungen von den letzten Dingen,* edited by Karl Chr. Eberhard Ehmann. Stuttgart: J. F. Steinkopf, 1864.

Olson, Theodore. *Millennialism, Utopianism and Progress.* Toronto: University of Toronto Press, 1982.

Reuther, Rosemary. *The Radical Kingdom: The Western Experience of Messianic Hope.* New York: Harper and Row, 1970.

Schelling, Friedrich Wilhelm Joseph. "Philosophie und Religion." In *Schellings Werke,* edited by Manfred Schröter, 4:1–60. Munich: C. H. Beck, 1927.

Sebba, Gregor. "History, Modernity and Gnosticism." In *The Philosophy of Order: Essays on History, Consciousness and Politics,* edited by Peter J. Opitz and Gregor Sebba. Stuttgart: Klett-Cotta, 1981.

Taubes, Jacob, ed. *Gnosis und Politik.* Munich: W. Fink, 1984.

Voegelin, Eric. *From Enlightenment to Revolution.* Edited by John Hallowell. Durham, N.C.: Duke University Press, 1975.

———. "On Hegel: A Study in Sorcery." *Studium Generale* 24 (1971): 335–68.

———. *Science, Politics and Gnosticism: Two Essays.* Chicago: H. Regnery, 1968.

Vondung, Klaus. *Die Apokalypse in Deutschland.* Munich: Deutscher Taschenbuch Verlag, 1988.

Walsh, David. "The Essential Ambiguity of Hegel's Political Thought." *Modern Age,* forthcoming.

Zubel, Hermann. "Verweltlichung Säkularisierung: Zur Geschichte einer Interpretations-Kategorie." Ph.D. diss., Münster, 1968.

NOTES ON CONTRIBUTORS

Wilbur Applebaum is Professor of the Humanities at the Illinois Institute of Technology. His research and publication center on seventeenth-century astronomy and the Scientific Revolution. He has contributed to major journals in intellectual history and the history of science, including the *Journal of the History of Ideas, Notes and Records of the Royal Society*, and the *Journal for the History of Astronomy*.

Allen G. Debus is Morris Fishbein Professor of the History of Science and Medicine at the University of Chicago. His writings on the Chemical Philosophy and related subjects have been translated into several languages including Chinese. His most recent book, *The French Paracelsians*, appeared in 1991.

B. J. T. Dobbs is Professor of History at the University of California, Davis. She has lectured extensively in the United States and Europe, and her seminal work, *The Foundations of Newton's Alchemy*, has been translated into French and Japanese. Her latest book is *The Janus Faces of Genius* (1992).

Stephen McKnight is Professor of History at the University of Florida. His books include *Sacralizing the Secular* (1989) and *The Modern Age and the Recovery of Ancient Wisdom* (1991).

Klaus Vondung is Professor of German Literature at the Universität Gesamthochschule, Siegen, Germany. He has published extensively in the fields of literature, philosophy, political science, and history. His most recent book is *Die Apokalypse in Deutschland* (1989).

David Walsh is Chair of the Political Science Department at the Catholic University of America. He has published two books and numerous articles on politics, philosophy, theology, and pseudo-science. His most recent book is *After Ideology* (1990).

INDEX

Adam, 4, 6, 17, 60, 72, 100, 102, 104, 105, 148, 155n26, 156
Agrippa, Heinrich Cornelius, 102–6, 113, 115
Alchemy, 16, 23, 25, 27, 29, 31, 38, 39, 46, 47, 48, 55–59, 62–64, 67, 69, 70, 71–73, 81, 83, 85–87, 132, 144, 182
Ancient Wisdom, 89, 93, 98, 99, 101–7, 113, 114, 116, 126. *See also* Prisca Theologia
Apocalypticism, 69, 87, 115, 118–20, 124–26, 158
Aristotle (Aristotelian), 3, 4, 20, 37, 38, 40, 42, 47, 50, 51, 63, 66, 93, 129, 175, 178, 181, 185, 186, 188
Asclepius, 94–99. *See also Corpus Hermeticum*
Astrology, 23, 103, 109, 150
Astronomy, 4, 6, 8, 10, 16, 20, 21, 26, 28, 35, 38, 39, 45, 54, 118, 123, 176
Augustine, 79, 92, 128

Bacon, Francis, 9, 10, 13, 18, 28, 37, 55, 89, 110–16, 143, 144, 146, 160, 173, 175, 178, 181nn23, 24, 181–83, 188, 191–93, 197, 200
Bengel, Johann Albrecht, 120, 121, 123
Böhme, Jakob, 120, 130, 152–56, 160, 161, 163
Bostocke, R., 3–7
Bruno, Giordano (Nolan), 25, 105–8, 110, 146, 149, 150
Butterfield, Herbert, 23, 24, 32, 34, 55, 173, 173n10, 174n11, 200

Cabala (Kaballah), 102, 104, 112, 114, 140, 143, 144, 148, 164n42
Campanella, Tomasso, 108–10, 130, 132, 149, 150
Chemical Philosophy, 38, 45, 47, 48, 51-54
Chemistry, 1, 3, 4, 6–8, 13, 16, 19, 22, 28, 38–40, 43, 45, 47, 49, 51, 118, 191
Christ, 62, 65–70, 72, 73, 79, 85, 87, 90, 104, 108, 132, 153, 154, 156, 156n24
Christianity (Christian), 4, 10, 23, 29, 45, 58, 67, 68, 81, 83, 84, 87, 89, 90, 92, 93, 100, 102, 104, 108, 110, 115, 116, 119, 121, 128, 129, 130–32, 139, 144, 145, 147, 150–52, 158, 160, 191
Church, 10, 11, 13, 30, 47, 72, 87, 102, 104, 106, 108, 119, 120, 128, 129, 150, 178, 192
Cohen, I. Bernard, 6n11, 19, 21, 22n33, 158n29
Comte, Auguste, 10, 11, 15, 125, 158, 165, 168
Copernicus, Nicholas (Copernican), 4, 20, 23, 30, 37, 45, 51, 53, 105, 106, 107, 172, 173, 176, 181, 192, 194, 200
Corpus Hermeticum, 4, 94, 95n15, 96n16, 101, 114, 127–33, 138, 139, 146
Cosmos, 2, 6, 7, 20, 45, 71, 97, 99, 102, 106, 111, 113, 123, 127, 132, 133, 134, 138, 147, 182, 184. *See also* Macrocosm
Creation, 17, 39, 42, 47, 49, 58, 60, 62, 69, 71, 72, 95, 99, 101, 105, 107, 133, 134, 136, 138, 139, 148, 149, 152, 153, 155, 156, 175–76, 192
Creator, 2, 39, 50, 96, 98, 101, 105, 140, 152, 163, 164, 175, 176

Debus, Allen, 1, 2n2, 4nn5, 6, 27n41, 37, 39n2, 40n6, 41n7, 45n12, 49nn20, 21, 51n24, 52n25, 53n27, 110n34
Descartes, René, 26, 30, 37, 46, 57, 126, 173, 182, 184, 186, 188, 191, 196
Dobbs, B. J. T., 27, 55, 55nn2, 3, 58n7, 59n10, 72n40
Draper, John William, 11–14, 18, 168
Duhem, Pierre, 14, 15, 20, 174

Enlightenment, 2, 6, 8n13, 9, 10, 13, 18, 26, 89, 91, 98, 107, 108, 110, 116, 150, 156–58, 168, 169
Erastus, Thomas, 4, 42, 52

Ficino, Marsilio, 93, 94, 98, 99, 102, 103, 108, 115, 128–30, 132, 133, 146, 147, 147n7, 175